Mixed or single-sex school?
Volume III: Attainment, attitudes and overview

Mixed or single-sex school?

Volume III
Attainment, attitudes and overview

R. R. Dale
formerly Reader in Education, University of Wales, Swansea

London   Routledge & Kegan Paul
New York   Humanities Press

First published in 1974
by Routledge & Kegan Paul Ltd
Broadway House, 68–74 Carter Lane,
London EC4V 5EL
Printed in Great Britain by
Butler & Tanner Ltd,
Frome and London
© R. R. Dale 1974
No part of this book may be reproduced in
any form without permission from the
publisher, except for the quotation of brief
passages in criticism

ISBN 0 7100 7744 1

Contents

Contents

Tables

Tables

MSS—A*

Appendix tables

Appendix tables

Figures

Preface

In the preface of the first volume of *Mixed or single-sex school?* it was stated that there were three volumes to follow. In practice two of these volumes have been compressed into one so that this third volume is the last of the series. In spite of the length of the work already published in the three volumes there is much that remains to be done, though this must perforce be left to others. In this future research the two following lines of approach appear to be the most likely to yield useful results. The first has been mentioned in previous volumes—the gathering of objective evidence about the emotional and social development of pupils in opposing types of school—for example the incidence of juvenile delinquency, truancy, school-girl pregnancies, homosexuality at school and later, prostitution and criminal sexual offences. Some of these are long shots and there are certainly difficulties such as amassing this type of evidence reliably and establishing a base-line of relevant total population against which to set the incidence of say adult homosexuality in relation to the type of school, but the results might determine how lasting are some effects of being educated in these very different communities—mixed or single-sex secondary schools. The results would, however, be suspect unless powerful variables such as social class and urban/rural background could be controlled or allowed for.

The second suggestion is less necessary in view of the evidence presented in this book, but it might remove some of the uncertainties which remain. It is that the comparative attainment of matched pairs of pupils from the two types of school should be tested by means of national sampling specially designed to contain large numbers of schools. Pupils would have to be matched on 'intelligence' (preferably from figures obtained at age 11 or a little later), on the occupational class of the father, and roughly on age. Schools themselves might even be matched for average intelligence level and occupational class of the father as these forces, if contrasted strongly, might have a powerful effect on the strength of the 'learning drive' within each school and hence affect the individual pupils over and beyond the influence of their own intelligence and occupational class levels. An eye would still need to be kept on a few other variables such as the qualification of the teachers, their length of stay, and pupils' dropping of weak subjects. Crucial to the success of such a scheme is that the matching should be done independently of the heads of schools from a list copied from the attendance register, and if any testing is carried out in schools the administrative arrangements should allow for a re-visit to the school to test any pupils absent or otherwise unavailable on the first occasion.

In view of recent comments on the work of university departments of education it should be noted that the first three chapters of this book are based almost entirely on research carried out by members of the staff and research students of the departments of education of the 'redbrick' universities. Most of it has been reposing unread on library shelves, and unpublished for want of money. Much of it was carried out without clerical assistance, and though finance from foundations, the Social Science Research Council and the Department of Education and Science has improved the position for established research workers there is still a need for some individual universities, including the writer's, to earmark a proportion of clerical staff for research purposes. Unless it is so earmarked it will be swallowed up by departmental administration. It is a waste of the country's resources for highly qualified men to spend much of their time licking stamps and addressing envelopes, and researchers in departments of education—and such other departments as economics—need clerical assistance in the same way as science departments need their technical staff.

Thanks are due to Tyson, King, Pidgeon, and Sutherland and to the Middlesex Education Committee and the Ministry of Education of N. Ireland, for permission to quote from their work, to the schools and colleges of education who took part in the field work, to my research assistants, Miss J. Macdonald succeeded by Mr G. Lyons and later my research officer, Dr Patrick Miller, for help with parts of the second section, to my colleagues Mr D. Sharp and Mr H. Rothera who so generously gave up some of their valuable time to read and comment on the manuscript, to Mrs M. A. Watkin who kindly gave some voluntary help with a rather onerous task, and to Mrs R. M. Lewis for her skilful help with the clerical and statistical aspects of the work. The registrars and staffs of the University Colleges of the University of Wales and especially Mr H. Smale of the University College of Swansea, the Welsh Joint Education Committee and the Director of Education and staff of the West Riding of Yorkshire all gave generous assistance to various projects. The research also owes something to the Leverhulme Trust for an award which freed the writer from university duties for nine months. A special word of thanks is due to Mr G. F. Peaker, CBE, for being instrumental through the Department of Education and Science in providing funds for my first clerical assistance and with unfailing generosity giving sound and encouraging advice. Without this breakthrough in assistance much of this research would never have been completed. Education is greatly indebted to Mr Peaker as the chief architect on the statistical side of the notable series of official reports on education in this country, and for additional important work at the international level. A further grant was made by the Department of Education and Science and later one by the Social Science Research Council. The Department of Education and Science from time to time has been most helpful to the project. The writer is also grateful to Dr Sutherland for her kindly and understanding reaction to my re-interpretation of one or two aspects of her valuable work.

Shortened versions of the chapters 1, 3 and 6 have previously appeared in *Educational Research*, chapter 12 in *Research Papers in Physical Education* (*No. 2*), chapters 7 and 15 and part of 16 in the *British Journal of Educational Psychology*, chapters 14 and part of 4 in *Educational Review*, part of chapter 4 in *Northern Teacher*, chapter 13 in *Swansea Collegiate Faculty Journal*, and chapter 5 in *New Education*.

The author is also grateful to the N. Ireland Council for Educational Research for permission to quote from its work.

Finally, these three volumes, together with two other books and many articles, have occupied most of the writer's leisure time for the last twenty-seven years, and without my wife's patient forbearance the work could not have been completed.

Introduction

This third and final volume of *Mixed or single-sex school?* endeavours to compare not merely the level of attainment in the two types of grammar schools but their relative merits as institutions of academic learning. These are two different concepts. Using the first we might compare a famous single-sex direct grant school with a rural co-educational maintained grammar school, bringing perhaps the finding that pupils in the former have the higher level of attainment, and arousing (or maintaining) the belief that a single-sex school is the better institution for pupils to learn in. Yet there is no evidence whatsoever that any school secures a better standard of learning because it is single-sex. The general public, and even many educationists, have tended to assume that the gaining of university open scholarships, which is the hall-mark of a direct grant school, is associated with especially good teaching, and because this occurs in a single-sex school this type of institution is therefore better than a co-educational school for the instruction of pupils. There is inadequate realization that as the direct grant schools cream the best high ability pupils from the maintained grammar schools, they would indeed be bad schools if their pupils did not gain open scholarships. This is no denigration of direct grant schools, but an objective appraisal of the situation. Comparison by the first concept tells us little, but comparison by the second, either by opposing schools of similar standing or by allowing for the variables that handicap principally the co-educational schools, should be much more informative. An extreme example has been deliberately chosen because it serves to illuminate the facile and misleading straight comparison that is often made between single-sex and co-educational secondary schools, as if calling them by the same name—e.g. grammar schools—makes them automatically equivalent in type of school and in type of staff. It is surprising how intelligent people can so naïvely argue that the attainment of the single-sex school is better (itself questionable), therefore single-sex education is better for academic learning, and how astonishingly unaware they are that the 'therefore' is unjustifiable, and that other factors such as an intake higher in intelligence and in social class could in itself explain any such differences between the two types of school.

Protagonists of single-sex education, especially women, used to continue the argument by saying that boys and girls would not work well in the same classroom because each sex would be distracted by the other. The reply divides naturally into two sections, one presenting a summary of the research findings about the attitudes of the pupils of both types of school towards work in the classroom, towards those of the opposite sex and towards sex itself; the other, more decisive, having recourse to the test mentioned above—the actual nature of the difference in the level of attainment in the two types of school if they are not too dissimilar in standard of pupil entry.

The book starts with this last test, and chapters 1, 2, 3 and 6 examine critically and minutely all the research done in this area, commencing about 1927 and continuing to the present day. Some of the research has been re-calculated from the raw data as a check, but in other cases only the final tables of results were available. Though the limitations of the raw data and the complexity of the problem make the work difficult, there does seem to emerge a clear answer to those who claim that single-sex schooling, because it is single-sex, provides the best academic training. As in the comparisons between the two types of schools published in the first two volumes, we are looking for a common pattern in the research. If this did not appear the conclusions would probably be of little importance, but here the findings are astonishing in their virtual unanimity. They are also important because they add to the research an appreciable amount of 'more objective' data.

Almost all the research analysed in this volume is concerned with the comparison between mixed and single-sex grammar schools, not through any wish to exclude other secondary schools, but because there is little reliable research concerned with these other types. There seems, however, to be no prima facie reason why co-education, if found to be beneficial in grammar schools, should not also be found helpful in comprehensive and secondary modern schools. Naturally no research claim is made that this is so, but failing any research directly on such schools the evidence presented here would appear to be more applicable than any other. The chief queries which arise in the generalization of the findings are first, the effect of the lower social class of the pupils in such schools, accompanied possibly by some changes in the relationship between the sexes, and second, the lower level of intelligence and academic ability in them which might reduce the pupils' interest in academic work (especially if, as is often the case, the curriculum and methods of teaching are too exclusively book-centred), and therefore make the pupils more easily distracted by the presence of the opposite sex. Neither of these seems a likely change but the possibility needs to be indicated.

The chapters following the section on attainment have a bearing on this theme but are not written as an integrated whole, being only a collection of articles on the comparative attitude of co-educated and single-sex educated pupils to academic work in general, and to a number of school subjects. It seemed fitting to include them here, in order to present in the three volumes virtually all the writer's research on co-education.

Part I

Attainment

General attainment I

Single-sex and co-educational grammar schools are often compared, but the comparison is usually characterized by a maximum of prejudice and a minimum of facts. In the two previous volumes of the series an attempt has been made to provide facts on some aspects of the effects of co-education, especially about the school life as seen by both teachers and pupils. This chapter attempts to provide evidence on a different part of the problem—that concerned with academic attainment; it presents not merely a summary of the available research findings but a critical and considered analysis of them. It is necessary to emphasize this because a statement of the original findings, without such critical analysis, might be misleading. An exhaustive study has been made of all important work done on this topic, much of it until now buried in the vaults of university libraries. The object is not to sustain a case for either side, but by marshalling research from a variety of fields and bringing it to bear on the point under discussion, sometimes after re-interpretation, to arrive at as near an approximation to the truth as present knowledge allows.

The analysis is prefaced by an acknowledgment that high academic attainment is not the most important aim of a school. We are all agreed that good character, right attitudes and healthy emotional development are of far more value. Here, however, we must limit ourselves to attainment, while realizing that the close interaction between intellectual ability and emotional attitudes, occasionally dramatic, normally quiet but pervasive, has a decisive effect not only on the academic attainment but also on the adjustment or maladjustment of the individual pupil. This and the following chapter will concentrate on a comparison of overall academic progress; two later ones will deal with some of the intriguing differences found between the two types of school in individual subjects.

In the Introduction mention was made of the loose thinking which is prevalent about the comparative standards of single-sex and co-educational grammar schools. To compare direct grant single-sex schools with the normal co-educational grammar schools and ascribe the possible superiority of the direct grant schools to the segregation of the boys or of the girls is untenable. Yet one can understand how the high prestige of the old established and semi-independent direct grant schools—and of the Public Schools—has fostered this impression.

It is clear then that if we are to decide whether educating boys and girls together or educating them apart provides the better setting for academic progress we must start with schools which are not too unequal in the ability of the pupils entering, and in their staffing. If equality in these and in other relevant factors is not practicable in its entirety, we must endeavour to have a sufficient knowledge of the differences and of their effect on attainment, and be able to make allowance for these in our final conclusions. It would be possible, of course, to set up a planned experiment with samples in which the relevant factors were given equality, but until recently this would have needed greater financial resources than were available. Researchers have therefore been compelled to make their surveys by utilizing institutions and examinations as they found them, and the most convenient tool has been those external examinations at School Certificate or Ordinary level which were taken largely by single-sex and co-educational grammar schools of a similar type, namely the day maintained grammar school. This is a ready-to-use measuring rod which is reasonably accurate for the comparison of large numbers of pupils. Though the two samples of these schools are in none of the surveys as equal or as pure as is desirable, yet we can be sufficiently confident that, provided we keep certain proved inequalities in mind, a valid result will be reached. That this can be done is due in part to the well-defined trend taken by the findings.

Before examining these a brief comment is perhaps needed about the strength of the various forces which affect the attainment of the pupil. Readers will appreciate that by far the strongest are (a) the academic aptitude of the pupil together with the strength of his motivation to learn, and (b) the skill, personality and knowledge of the teacher. The range of average marks gained in any one subject by pupils of schools of the *same* type—whether co-educational or single-sex—will therefore vary widely, and there will also be a considerable overlap in the average marks between schools of the two types. The social class of the pupil, acting through his motivation, through the richness or poverty of his cultural background and here and there through the educational guidance given by, or occasioned by, the parents, is probably less strong in its average effect than pupils' and teachers' abilities, but can be decisively strong for some individuals. The force which is being considered in this book—the changes in the academic *progress* of pupils in co-educational as compared with that of pupils in single-sex schools—would not be expected to be anything like as strong in any subject as that which can be exerted by the good or poor ability of the teacher. On the other hand if the existence of such a pervasive force is demonstrated

4

it should certainly be of interest to educationists. Each survey will now be examined, roughly in chronological order.

Readers may be surprised to see that the first research examined concerned a period as early as 1925 to 1926, but there are good reasons for its inclusion. Not only is this study by Tyson by reason of its size and comprehensiveness probably the most important of all, but its inclusion strengthens the present survey in other ways, first because the survey then covers all the research of sufficient size to be representative which has been made on this topic, whatever its outcome; second, because the survey also then demonstrates that the same broad picture emerges in almost all the studies made from that time until the present in spite of the changes which have occurred in the organization and curricula of schools and in society.

The Tyson survey

Tyson (1928), working in the Department of Education, University of Manchester, used the examination statistics of the Northern Universities Joint Matriculation Board, supplied by the secretary, J. M. Crofts. His samples were very large, the smallest one being 1,500 for boys in co-educational schools. The examination was taken mainly by maintained grammar schools in the north and midlands, and for this reason and also because there was an appreciable number of co-educational schools among the towns of Lancashire and the West Riding, the rival samples are more equal in character than they would have been under some other examining boards, though the sprinkling of direct grant schools with their more selective entry may give a slight start to the single-sex schools.[1] Fortunately the interpretation of the results is easier with this bias of the sample favouring the single-sex schools than would have been the case if it had been in the opposite direction. One would have been more satisfied, however, if there had been a more vigorous attempt to obtain evidence about the amount and nature of the differences between the two samples of schools, or to select matched pairs of schools. Yet in spite of these limitations—probably unavoidable because of the limited resources available—it is a valuable survey— (Table 1.1).

Tyson took as his criterion the difference between the percentages of candidates reaching credit standards in the three samples, i.e. boys', girls' and co-educational schools, in nine subjects in 1925 and 1926. Contrary to popular expectation he found that in almost all subjects

[1] The sample for 1926 included 30 girls' direct grant schools with 670 candidates, 17 boys' direct grant schools with 721 candidates and one co-educational direct grant school with 17 candidates. Two boys' schools of very high prestige, with 300 candidates, were included in the 17 direct grant schools.

TABLE I.I *Differences between the percentages of candidates from co-educational and single-sex schools reaching credit standard;*[1] *Tyson (1928, NUJMB). First external examination*

The group superior in attainment is indicated by a C (co-educational) or S (single-sex)

Subject		Boys		Rural boys		Girls		Rural girls	
English	1925	6·1	C			1·9*	S		
	1926	4·7	C	(1·3)	C	5·7	S	(0·0)	
History	1925	9·0	C			6·7	S		
	1926	7·7	C	(2·6)	S	11·4	S	15·9	S
Mathematics[2]	1925	7·3	C			7·2	C		
	1926	5·9	C	10·0	C	5·2	C	12·0	C
Physics[2]	1925	7·4	C			(3·5)	S		
	1926	8·0	C			11·3	S		
Chemistry[2]	1925	7·6	C			(3·1)	S		
	1926	9·9	C	16·1	C	3·9*	S	(2·4)	S
French	1925	9·2	S			2·9*	C		
	1926	6·8	S	3·8*	S	3·4	C	5·9	C
German	1923/5/6	12·6	C			(0·2)	C		
Latin[2]	1925	(2·7)	S			(1·2)	S		
	1926	6·8	C			3·3*	C		
Art[2]	1925	13·5	C			4·0	S		
	1926	11·9	C	14·9	C	7·4	S	12·6	S

[1] Differences which are not statistically significant are in brackets. One or two marked with an asterisk are significant at the 0·05 level and all others significant at or beyond the 0·01 level.

[2] The following footnotes indicate where the opposing samples diverge from rough equality in the percentage of their pupils sitting individual subjects.
Mathematics In the main sample 8 to 9 per cent more of the co-educated girls sat. In rural schools 3 per cent more.
Physics In 1925 17 per cent of co-educated girls sat and 4 per cent from girls' schools.
Chemistry In the main sample *at least* 5 per cent more of the co-educated girls sat in 1925 (may be considerable underestimate) and 14 per cent more in 1926. In rural schools 34 per cent more.
In rural schools the boys' schools had 9 per cent more candidates. Equal in main sample.
Latin 17 per cent fewer co-educated boys sat, and 5 per cent fewer co-educated girls.
Art Co-educated boys 60 per cent of candidates compared with 25 to 30. Co-educated girls 8 to 9 per cent more.

boys' work was better in his mixed schools than in his boys' schools. This difference is statistically significant in seven out of the nine subjects and for both years (all at 0·01 level and beyond). Boys in mixed schools also had a significant superiority in one year in Latin. Only in French was there a statistically significant difference in the opposite direction (for both years),[1] though in Latin there was a similar but small non-significant difference for one year. It should be emphasized that this result represents hundreds of schools and thousands of pupils, and its main features occur in two successive years.

The figures for the girls' samples were much closer together in most subjects, but with the girls' schools in the lead on eleven occasions and the girls from mixed schools on six. There is a statistically significant difference in favour of girls in girls' schools in history (two years), art (two years), English (two years), physics (one year) and chemistry (one year), with small non-significant differences in the same direction in physics (one year), chemistry (one year) and Latin (one year). The co-educated girls had a statistically significant superiority in mathematics (two years), French (two years), Latin (one year), and a negligible lead in German (average of three years).

But things are not always what they seem. Tyson himself points out that whereas the boys' samples are equal in average age, the girls in mixed schools are three months below the average age for *all girls* combined. There may therefore be four to five months' difference between the girls' samples, and the girls' schools might well be expected to do better on this count alone.

Another important variable indicated by Tyson is that co-educational schools are usually situated principally in sparsely populated districts, while single-sex schools predominate in the large towns and cities.[2] This is true even for the Northern Joint Board, though moderated somewhat as stated above. It will be demonstrated later that this should be of considerable benefit to the single-sex schools academically because of the nature of their intake.[3] Their staffs should also have been better qualified and more experienced as there was keener competition for posts in large town and city grammar schools than for those in remote rural areas. Tyson later endeavoured to counter this rural–urban effect by removing from his large samples all schools situated in places where the density of population was more than ten persons to the acre. He then worked out the differences in the percentages for the samples for six of

[1] This exception in French is intriguing. Stevens (1962) mentions the possible embarrassment in oral French of the boy whose voice is changing.

[2] Clark demonstrated this in a table, in which 64 per cent of the co-educational schools were in districts of less than 10,000 people (p. 181).

[3] Cf. Macpherson, J. (1958), *Eleven Year Olds Grow Up*, p. 151, table 78, Scottish Council for Research in Education, London.

the subjects, giving twelve new differences in the two years (Table 1.1). The co-educated boys increased their lead in three subjects and reduced their deficiency in French to almost below statistical significance (0·05), but English and history were discrepant as in the former the lead of the co-educated boys was reduced below the statistical threshold, and in the latter the boys from single-sex schools even gained a very small, though non-significant superiority. On the whole, however, the movement in all subjects combined is in the expected direction.

When we consider the girls in rural areas there is a similar result. In mathematics and French the lead of the co-educated girls is increased, in English their deficiency disappears, and in chemistry it almost disappears, but history is again discrepant, the girls from single-sex schools increasing their lead, and the same occurs in art.

To summarize, in rural schools the co-educated boys have a decided superiority in three subjects, a negligible lead in one, and a negligible deficiency in two, compared with boys from boys' schools. The rural sub-sample was of course limited to six subjects. The co-educated girls have a good lead in two subjects, a decided deficiency in two, a negligible deficiency in one and equality in the sixth, compared with girls in girls' schools. Tyson demonstrates, therefore, that this urban–rural factor handicaps the co-educational schools; it will also operate in the other researches (except perhaps in Middlesex) though it is not usually mentioned.

The picture changes yet again, though in the same direction, when another factor, not considered by Tyson, is taken into account. This is the percentage of rival samples which are entered for the examination in each subject. As the criterion of success is the percentage of candidates reaching credit standard, this criterion is seriously affected if a greater proportion of weak pupils in one sample than in another are withheld from the examination in any subject. The occurrence of this special selection has been shown by such research workers as King (1949), with regard to physics, but educationists with an intimate knowledge of the grammar schools knew that it was happening earlier, that it extended to other subjects,[1] and that the movement was gradually increasing. A little simple arithmetic will give us the necessary information from Tyson's figures. He does not provide any overall total of candidates for each sample, but we can obtain a reasonably reliable guide if we take as our denominator instead the number taking English, a subject then taken by almost all candidates for the School Certificate examination (cf. footnotes, Table 1.1).

A brief examination is now made of the percentage of pupils taking the examination in various subjects. The superiority of the co-educated girls in mathematics was not due to finer selection, as approximately

[1] Clark points out that this was occurring in NUJMB results in 1923.

96 per cent of the sample (rural) took the examination compared with 93 per cent of girls from rural girls' schools; in the large sample the same differences for the two years were increased to 8 per cent and 9 per cent in the same direction. In chemistry the non-significant 'superiority' (about 3 per cent of credits) in favour of girls from girls' schools could easily be explained by the restriction of their sample to the better candidates; whereas about half the co-educated in rural schools sat the examination, only 16 per cent did so from the rural girls' schools; in the large sample this difference in the percentage of pupils sitting was 5 per cent (*sic*—possibly an underestimate) in 1925 and 14 per cent in 1926. In physics the only available figures are those from the large sample in 1925, when 17·4 per cent of the co-educated girls sat the examination and only 4 per cent of the girls from girls' schools; this would be more than enough to account for the slight non-significant superiority (3·5 per cent of credits) of the latter. A similar argument would be applicable to the larger superiority of 1926, but precise figures for the number of candidates sitting are not available. The superiority in art of the girls from girls' schools (rural) over the co-educated girls might be explained in part, though not entirely, by finer selection, as only 54 per cent of them sat, while in co-educational schools the percentage was 62·5; in the larger sample the selection effect is much increased and could more than account for the small superiority of the girls from girls' schools.

In the case of the boys' sample the percentages of pupils taking the examination are closer together. This is so in English, history, mathematics and French. In chemistry, in rural schools, the co-educational lead of 16 per cent of credits could only partially be accounted for by the 9 per cent larger sample of candidates who sat from boys' schools. In the complete sample the percentages of candidates sent in from the two groups are similar, but the co-educational lead in credits is substantial. The superiority of the co-educated boys in physics could not be explained by the sending in of a sample of candidates which was only 2·5 per cent 'more refined', on average, than that from the boys' schools. On the other hand, the slight superiority of co-educated boys in Latin might be due to their more refined sample—they sent in 17 per cent fewer candidates out of their group. In art the decided lead of the co-educated boys occurred in spite of an entry of 60 per cent of candidates compared with the boys' schools' average over the two years of 27·5 per cent.

Other variables which almost certainly handicapped the co-educational schools but are not due to co-education are that they probably took in a higher proportion of the 11-plus age group than did the single-sex schools, and their pupils were also of rather lower social class. There would, however, be a greater percentage of premature leavers from the mixed schools and these would tend to be below average in academic ability. On balance the mixed schools would appear to be decidedly the more handicapped. These variables are, however, discussed more fully later in the chapter.

The Crofts-Clark survey

Clark, working in the Department of Education, University of Liverpool, was much later than Tyson but included in his thesis some statistics for earlier years provided by J. M. Crofts, then secretary to the Northern Universities Joint Matriculation Board. These concerned over 13,000 candidates from 142 boys', 180 girls' and 85 co-educational schools, taking the NUJMB examination in 1923. Clark was more occupied with the differences in attainment between boys and girls than with co-education, but some of his work is of interest here. In particular he presented a table of statistics sent by Crofts, which compared the percentages of successful candidates reaching matriculation standard in single-sex and co-educational schools. The figures are in Table 1.2.

TABLE 1.2   *Percentages of candidates matriculating (Crofts–Clark)*

Boys' schools	40·82
Boys in mixed schools	42·64
Girls' schools	38·27
Girls in mixed schools	37·32
Overall for mixed schools[1]	40·2
Overall for single-sex schools[1]	39·8

[1] These figures clearly depend on the proportion of boys and girls in each sample and are the true averages. Incidentally, between 1923 and 1927 the age of boy candidates averaged five months less than that of girls.

These results, like those from Tyson's survey, ought not to be taken merely at their face value; the co-educational schools suffered certain disadvantages which might have been expected to prevent them reaching equality with the single-sex schools. Clark identified most of the possible variables in his work on the differences in attainment between boys and girls, with the exception of social class which research showed to be important much later. The smallness of the raw differences is, however, the chief feature of this survey. It should also be noted that the criterion—matriculation—is not exactly the same as that of Tyson who was using the credit standard in individual subjects.

Gott's survey

Sir Benjamin Gott, then Director of Education for Middlesex, analysed the School Certificate results of 17 co-educational, 13 boys' and 10 girls' schools in his county, from 1921 to 1926. The information available is limited to a table published in B. A. Howard's *The Mixed School*, as the county authorities have unfortunately been unable to supply further details. These statistics are reprinted in Table 1.3, but to enable readers to obtain a quick overall appraisal the writer has summarized the table

TABLE 1.3 *Comparative academic attainment—Middlesex schools (School Certificate) 1921–6[1] (compiled by Sir B. Gott)*

(17 mixed schools, 13 boys' schools and 10 girls' schools)

Boys in boys' schools	Boys in mixed schools	Girls in girls' schools	Girls in mixed schools
Percentage passes at School Certificate standard[2]			
73·0	76·0	47·0	67·0
74·2	76·4	66·6	62·5
72·2	74·1	66·9	66·2
70·2	72·7	67·2	71·2
73·4	67·0	61·2	72·4
66·9	63·4	73·6	53·5
Percentage passes at credit standard			
59·0	52·0	29·0	40·0
54·0	60·2	34·6	41·5
45·5	52·8	27·2	33·3
44·7	54·6	34·8	46·5
38·0	49·3	26·5	33·5
35·2	39·1	25·2	32·5
Percentage at honours standard			
15·0	17·0	2·0	9·0
7·1	8·8	1·7	6·7
12·7	3·5	1·9	4·2
8·4	—	5·0	—
4·6	7·7	3·1	3·0
5·9	8·5	2·6	2·8

[1] Reprinted from B. A. Howard, *The Mixed School*, University of London Press, 1928.
[2] This appears to mean 'School Certificate standard and above', and similarly for credit. The table has been accepted as originally published.

by comparing the number of years in which co-educational or single-sex schools were superior. (Differences of less than 1 per cent are ignored.) This is a little crude mathematically as the extent of the superiority varies somewhat from year to year, but the information necessary for a more precise method is lacking.

Girls in girls' schools were more successful than those in co-educational schools at the pass standard (or better) in two years out of six, with one equal. There are, however, two wild fluctuations of the figures, in one year girls' schools being 20 per cent inferior and the other year 20 per cent superior; such changes rarely happen in practice and one wonders whether an error has occurred. At the credit standard one can be confident, however, as there is a consistent and marked trend. In all six years the co-educated girls have a decisive superiority. This includes a slight lead at the honours standard also, in three years out of six, with two equal. A similar clear pattern emerges in the case of the boys, the co-educated having the better pass rate in four years out of six, and a superiority in five years out of six at the credit standard. At the honours stage the co-educated boys had a better result in four years. Note that though the co-educational schools in Middlesex might have suffered from some of the disabilities mentioned earlier, such as younger girl candidates and less refined selection of candidates in individual subjects than in girls' schools, the force of the urban–rural factor would be very much diminished, if indeed it exerted any influence at all.

Gott himself, writing in Adams's book *Educational Movements and Methods* (1924), had this to say about the Middlesex schools:

> So far as examination tests are any guide it would seem, from our experience in Middlesex, that the system [i.e. co-education] tends to develop the capacities of both boys and girls to a higher degree than when they are educated separately. The results of the Matriculation and General Schools examination of London University show fairly uniformly, year after year, that girls do much better in mixed schools than they do in schools devoted entirely to their own sex, and that boys do equally well and often better in mixed schools.

Walton's survey

Gott's survey was renewed during 1929–33 by Walton, secretary to Middlesex Education Committee (see Table 1.4). In the case of the boys the previous result was confirmed, the co-educated boys having a minimal superiority at the pass level in four of the five years and being decisively superior in four out of the five years at the credit standard with the difference ranging from 5 to 12·5 per cent of credits. At the honours

TABLE 1.4   *General Schools Examination results in Middlesex secondary schools 1929–33 (Walton survey)*

	Total no. of candidates	Total passes	Total % of passes	% of passes Boys in:		% of passes Girls in:	
				Boys' schools	Mixed schools	Girls' schools	Mixed schools
1929	1,437						
General Schools		1,229	85·52	80·67	86·28	92·76	85·86
Honours		112	7·79	10·65	9·71	3·10	5·17
Matriculation		677	47·11	45·56	58·0	42·76	41·03
1930	1,525						
General Schools		1,261	82·7	81·0	84·4	85·5	81·5
Honours		124	8·13	8·6	9·07	6·87	7·1
Matriculation		652	42·75	42·3	47·1	45·04	39·3
1931	1,922						
General Schools		1,508	78·4	76·14	76·78	83·09	78·32
Honours		110	5·72	7·32	8·04	3·05	3·76
Matriculation		661	34·39	34·06	39·95	30·55	33·23
1932	1,980						
General Schools		1,697	85·71	85·71	86·32	84·92	86·04
Honours		135	7·0	5·45	10·98	6·35	4·84
Matriculation		790	40·0	38·29	44·4	39·09	38·46
1933	2,090						
General Schools		1,779	85·12	86·29	82·12	87·5	85·02
Honours		156	7·46	9·57	7·99	6·0	4·59
Matriculation		938	44·88	50·43	41·67	42·5	42·27

level there was again rough equality, with the co-educated boys having a slight advantage. The position of the girls' samples, however, was the reverse of that in Gott's survey. Girls from girls' schools were some-what superior at the pass level in four years out of five, the difference ranging from 7 per cent to 2 per cent of passes, and minimally superior at the credit level, the overall crude averages being 40 per cent of credits for girls' schools and 39 per cent for girls in mixed schools. In three years out of five, however, the co-educated girls were slightly superior at the honours level. These results, like the previous ones, should not be quoted without mention of the known forces which would in total be expected to handicap the co-educational schools but are not a necessary part of the single-sex or co-educational type of education.

Yet the two surveys do present a problem. Why did the girls' schools improve their position in Walton's day? One asks first of all whether the schools were selected on the same basis for both surveys, with Walton's merely adding newly built schools. As the second survey was obviously intended as a comparison with the first, one presumes that this was the case, but the evidence is lacking and unobtainable. The most likely explanation of the change is the effect on the girls' schools of the knowledge that they were slightly behind in the first survey; this would lead to a greater drive for examination success and maybe to an intensification in girls' schools of girls dropping their weaker subjects. In addition it was during these years that the heads of girls' schools wisely pioneered the inclusion of biology as a science in girls' schools —for which the girls showed greater aptitude and liking than for the previous alternatives of physics and chemistry.[1] The mixed schools were rather slower in adopting the same policy. The anomaly may, on the other hand, be due to some special feature of the Middlesex scene unknown to the author.[2]

In both surveys, as also in those of Tyson and Clark, when the results of boys and girls are combined the co-educational schools have an advantage.

Field's survey

This survey was limited to four boys', three girls' and three co-educational schools in the Birmingham area, and was concerned mainly with sex differences in attainment rather than with co-education. Because of the unreliability of results from such a small sample of schools her findings are not given here, but those who wish to look them up should note that

[1] It is not impossible that the abolition after 1929 of the Board of Education rule that whole forms must be entered for the examination assisted girls' schools more than mixed, e.g. by the non-entering by the girls' schools of those girls judged not ready to pass in sufficient subjects.

[2] Late information on this point is given in chapter 17. See also chapter 11.

Field did not allow for the appreciable age difference between the segregated and co-educated girls, nor did she pay any attention to the much greater incidence of the dropping of weak subjects in her girls' schools. This research, however, is one of the few to indicate differences between the various types of school in the amount of time devoted to individual subjects, and the first to point out that the attainment of a pupil in mathematics is probably raised if that pupil also includes physics and chemistry in his or her studies.

King's survey

King, working at the London University Institute of Education, analysed the results of the London General School Certificate examination for the year 1945, completing his work in 1949. Unfortunately he was unable to obtain separate data for the two sexes in mixed schools, which makes his survey less useful for our purpose than it might have been. In his summary he presents a table showing the level of achievement of the three types of school in fifteen subjects; elementary mathematics is counted as three. The data are derived from 70,246 boys in boys' schools, 70,626 girls in girls' schools and 33,298 *pupils* in co-educational schools.

TABLE 1.5 *Attainment in London General School Certificate 1945* (*King, 1949*)

School	No. of subjects taken per pupil	Failures per pupil	A Pass	B Credit	C Very Good	A + B + C Crude total
Boys'	9·2	2·3	2·0	3·5	1·4	6·9
Girls'	8·6	1·7	2·1	3·8	1·0	6·9
Mixed	9·3	2·1	2·1	3·7	1·3	7·1

Readers will note that the co-educated pupils obtained a pass or better in an average of 7·1 subjects per pupil, compared with 6·9 for both boys and girls in single-sex schools. As the failure rate of the co-educated pupils at 2·1 subjects per pupil is less than that for the boys in boys' schools (at 2·3) the former have clearly the better all-round performance. The comparison between co-educated pupils and girls in girls' schools is more complex because the former have a heavier subject load at 9·3 per pupil compared with 8·6. Thus although the co-educated pupils have a pass or better in more subjects per pupil, they also have more failures (2·1 subjects per pupil compared with the 1·7 of the girls' schools). Other things being equal a greater number of failures would be expected because the smaller subject load of the girls in girls' schools means that they must have dropped their weaker subjects—they would hardly be likely to drop their best—and would therefore be less likely to fail. The only safe verdict therefore is that the comparison between the girls' and co-educational schools is inconclusive, as far as the raw scores are concerned. On the other hand in view of the evidence presented no one can safely say, as has been said often in the past, that because girls' schools are single-sex the girls reach a higher level of attainment than they would in co-educational schools.

Analysing the results in another way King shows that the co-educated pupils had more passes than boys' schools in ten out of fifteen subjects, more credits in thirteen out of fifteen and were slightly better at the very good stage in eight subjects. In comparison with girls' schools, co-educated pupils had more passes[1] in seven (*sic* or six) subjects, more credits in only three subjects,[2] and more very goods in seven. At the fail level the co-educated had more fails in three out of fifteen subjects than boys' schools and more fails in eight subjects than girls' schools. King pointed out that in the girls' schools only the better girls tended to offer physics (3 per cent of the pupils); it should be added that this comment also applied to chemistry (7 per cent of the pupils) and to a lesser extent to mathematics. Any measured superiority of the girls' schools in any of these three subjects is therefore quite spurious.

As girls at the age of 16 or 17 tend to have a better performance in literary and language subjects while boys excel on the mathematical and physical science side we would expect the mixed schools to have more passes, credits and very goods combined than boys' schools in the literary subjects and more than girls' schools in mathematics and the physical sciences. In fact the mixed schools did better than the boys (on the above criterion) in English language, English literature, geography, Latin, French, algebra, geometry, physics, chemistry, general science and biology. The comparison with girls' schools conforms more closely to the basic differences between the sexes with the girls' schools better in English language, English literature, history, Latin, German, algebra, general science and art (the algebra only minimally and because of

[1] Passes here do not include credits or very goods.
[2] A fairer picture is given if we compare the percentages of those who did well in each subject by combining the credits and very goods; pupils from mixed schools were then better in 7 subjects out of 15 and equal in one, compared with girls' schools. The performance of the girls' schools at the credit level was artificially boosted by their much more restricted entry in arithmetic, algebra, geometry and chemistry (though it did not prevent them being inferior in physics); this, however, did not suffice to give them superiority at the very good level except in physics.

restricted entry). In this last case the mixed schools did better in geography, French, arithmetic, geometry, physics, chemistry and biology.

The general variables which have been mentioned in other researches apply probably more strongly in this one. Except in Middlesex a much greater proportion of the co-educational schools would be rural, whereas the London schools for example were at that time almost entirely single-sex. The metropolis, with its higher rate of pay and its high percentage of famous schools, would tend to attract the more highly qualified and experienced teachers and the single-sex schools in general would probably have a more finely selected entry of pupils. In Middlesex, again, there might be equality on these counts. Similarly they would almost certainly have a social class advantage. But the chief reason why one should hesitate to give this enquiry equal weight with the others is that it was made when large numbers of men teachers were serving in the forces. The girls' schools would be able to recruit staff much more easily than the boys' schools, with the co-educational coming somewhere in between. Moreover, there is the problem whether in say 1944 and 1945 the evacuation of schools would have affected the issue. These factors had little or no effect on King's main enquiry which was not primarily concerned with co-education.

Sutherland's survey

Sutherland made a valuable analysis of the attainment of single-sex and co-educational Protestant grammar schools in the Northern Ireland Senior Certificate examination in 1957, using as criteria both success in gaining the certificate, and the average mark in each principal subject. There were 9 boys', 17 girls' and 23 co-educational schools, and these were not so dissimilar in the type of pupils entry as to make the comparison hopelessly unreasonable from the start. There were, however, certain important differences which this writer believes should have been taken into account in the final reckoning, though Sutherland appears to dissent.

On the first criterion, the gaining of a certificate on the whole examination, Sutherland found the usual superiority of boys from co-educational schools over boys from boys' schools (not quite statistically significant) but an even greater difference in the opposite direction when the girls' groups were compared. Now previous research (cf. Tyson, Clark, Gott and Walton) had found a larger difference between the boys' than between the girls' groups, and the question is immediately posed as to why the Northern Ireland results should be an exception. If we examine the results closely we find that the discrepancy arises, at least in part, because the passing of the certificate examination as a whole is an artefact of the regulations. To obtain a certificate it was compulsory to pass in English language, and this is one of the three subjects in which these boys' schools have a superiority over the co-educational schools; this superiority in the compulsory subject reduces the effect of their greater deficiency in most other subjects. (In Tyson's survey the co-educational boys were superior also in English.) In the case of the girls' groups their lead in the one compulsory subject operates to increase an overall

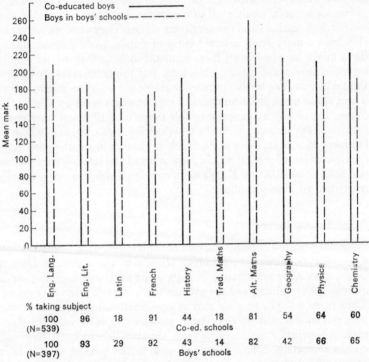

% taking subject									
100 (N=539)	96	18	91	44	18	81	54	64	60
				Co-ed. schools					
100 (N=397)	93	29	92	43	14	82	42	66	65
				Boys' schools					

NOTE: This visual interpretation of Table 1.6 shows the smallness of the average difference between the two types of school in each subject.

FIGURE I.I   *Academic performance, Senior Leaving Certificate (boys): N. Ireland (1957)*

superiority which is actually much smaller than that of the boys (in the opposite direction), when results in individual subjects are taken as the criterion. The co-educated girls in this examination obtain no compensating advantage for their lead in another key subject, mathematics, as this is not compulsory and the girls' schools are able to offer such subjects as biology and even domestic science as alternatives to mathematics.

A truer picture is therefore shown by the average marks obtained in each subject (Table 1.6), as Sutherland herself realized. As in all the other principal surveys except one, the co-educated boys did better than the boys in boys' schools, with statistically significant leads in seven out of ten subjects and a corresponding statistical inferiority in only English language. Now, as found in previous research, the differences between

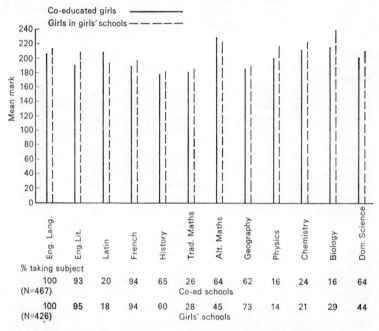

NOTE: This visual interpretation of Table 1.6 shows the smallness of the average difference between the two types of school in each subject.

FIGURE 1.2 *Academic performance, Senior Leaving Certificate (girls): N. Ireland (1957)*

the boys' groups are much larger than those between the girls' groups. While the lead of the co-educated boys exceeds 20 (maximum mark 400) in five of the subjects, the segregated girls have such a large lead over co-educated girls in only one subject—biology, which Sutherland indicates may not be representative as it is taken by only a few schools. In all, however, the segregated girls have a statistically significant advantage over the co-educated girls in five out of twelve subjects, a useful lead in physics and small leads of 1 to 2 per cent in two others, with the co-educated having the better score only in Latin and—once

TABLE 1.6 *Academic performance, Senior Leaving Certificate, co-educational and single-sex schools, N. Ireland (1957) (Sutherland)*[1]

Subjects	Boys in co-ed schools			Boys in boys' schools			Difference[2]
	N	Mean max 400	% of total candidates	N	Mean max 400	% of total candidates	Single-sex minus co-ed
English lang.	539	199·00	100	397	209·84	100	10·84*
English lit.	515	181·80	96	370	185·67	93	3·87
Latin	97	200·60	18	117	169·04	29	−31·56†
French	493	173·62	91	365	178·21	92	4·59
History	239	192·80	44	169	174·40	43	−18·40†
Trad. maths	95	198·14	18	57	168·26	14	−29·88*
Alt. maths	434	257·67	81	327	229·06	82	−28·61‡
Geography	293	213·05	54	168	190·14	42	−22·91‡
Physics	343	212·06	64	262	192·20	66	−19·86‡
Chemistry	326	219·32	60	260	191·65	65	−27·67‡
	Girls in co-ed schools			Girls in girls' schools			
English lang.	467	205·51	100	426	212·78	100	7·27†
English lit.	435	191·26	93	415	208·04	95	16·78‡
Latin	93	208·56	20	75	193·64	18	−14·92
French	441	189·79	94	402	199·30	94	9·51*
History	304	179·94	65	256	180·60	60	0·66
Trad. maths	121	180·67	26	121	185·82	28	5·15
Alt. maths	297	229·17	64	191	223·58	45	−5·59
Geography	291	186·38	62	310	189·78	73	3·40
Physics	74	200·43	16	59	217·10	14	16·67
Chemistry	113	212·68	24	90	222·27	21	9·59
Biology	74	213·84	16	123	239·90	29	26·06‡
Dom. science	300	200·74	64	188	210·39	44	9·65*

[1] Reprinted by permission of Sutherland and the *British Journal of Educational Psychology*. Percentages of candidates added by the present writer.
[2] Those marked * are statistically significant at 0·05 level; † at 0·01 level; ‡ at 0·001 level.

again—alternative mathematics (in spite of a much higher percentage entry).

As we have said before, things are not always what they seem and Sutherland herself perceptiently indicates several problems. One of these is that the number of boys' schools is rather small (9) and the score of their pupils might be unduly influenced by the existence of perhaps one large school which, for some special reason, was either very good or very bad. She therefore used a small sample technique of statistical analysis which used the school means as the unit and tested whether the variability between the various individual school averages in, say, English was so great as to throw doubt on the significance of any difference apparently due to co-education. This is a much more conservative test, and she reported that the only significant differences which remained were in four subjects in which co-educated boys were superior to boys from boys' schools. None of the differences in favour of the girls from girls' schools remained significant.

VARIABILITY AND RANGE OF MARKS

In a related study Sutherland demonstrated that a most interesting difference existed between (a) the comparison of the mean scores of the two groups of girls (where the girls in girls' schools tended to have a slight advantage in most subjects) and (b) the comparison of the percentage of pupils scoring over 300 (out of 400) in the two groups (Table A2.8).[1] In the latter the co-educated girls did better in six subjects and worse in four, though—and this should be emphasized—no difference either way was as large as 4 per cent. None the less, at the top end of the distributions there is some reversal of the previous verdict. At the bottom end of course the girls from girls' schools return to their advantage, having slightly fewer scoring less than 100 in seven subjects (with equality in English language and traditional mathematics and inferiority in chemistry).

In the case of the boys the advantage of the co-educational schools shows itself clearly with this criterion though not quite as markedly as in the comparison of mean scores. This co-educated group had more high scorers in six subjects, marginally fewer in three and virtual equality in one, by far the greatest difference being in alternative mathematics where they had 17 per cent more high fliers—rather more than one-third of their group. This general advantage is even clearer at the bottom ends where they had fewer low scores in nine subjects and equality in one, the largest differences being in traditional mathematics and chemistry (the large Latin lead is probably due to the co-educated lower percentage entry).

[1] A2 signifies Appendix 2.

INTERVENING VARIABLES

Sutherland attempted to compare the three groups for intelligence, but was unable to secure sufficient data to make definite conclusions. The incomplete evidence showed a rough equality between the groups and as there were only some 400 quotients missing out of 1,800 it is unlikely that any appreciable differences existed. It is to be regretted, however, that this information is not available.

Sutherland also found that, as in some of the previous surveys, the co-educated girls were younger than the girls from girls' schools, the average difference being three months, while there was no difference between the two groups of boys.

Though there is a large area of agreement between Sutherland and the present writer about the interpretation of her research there are two points of divergence: one is the influence of age and the other the influence of social class. As these are basic to the interpretation of all the surveys they have to be argued at some length. First we will deal with age; the discussion centres on the problem whether the younger average age of the co-educated girls represents a handicap which might appreciably affect the results or not.

AGE

The tenor of Sutherland's statement on the matter is that age difference was not such a handicap. She writes, 'We may note firstly that three months is a short period to give marked differences in attainment.' But we are not concerned with marked differences, as the overall difference between the girls' groups was only some 2 per cent. Neither did the three months' average difference operate as three months for each person, but more usually as a year for a smaller number of candidates. Calculating the percentages from data in Sutherland's article we find that between one-third and one-quarter (29·1 per cent) of the co-educated girls took the examination one year early, by taking a faster five-year (3 + 2 years) course rather than the usual six-year course (4 + 2 years), while only about one-eighth (12·2 per cent) of the girls in girls' schools took this shorter course. As the differences in subject averages are mostly of the order of 1 or 2 per cent it seems that if the extra 17 per cent of these younger and presumably better co-educated girls had pursued their studies for an additional year, putting them on an equal basis with their opposite numbers, they would have made an appreciable improvement and raised their group's average in all subjects, and this factor alone might have brought about equality (at least) with the girls' schools' averages.

Though Sutherland finds negligible (and even negative) correlation between age and attainment for her sample this does not mean that age is having no effect on attainment. Such low correlations are frequently produced in these situations by the bright children taking the examina- tion a year earlier than the rest, and even by some of the duller ones being held back a year before taking it. None the less it is incontestable that each individual, apart perhaps from an odd exception, is improving in standard during the year (cf. Lee, 1955).

Even if we construct a mark distribution table according to age and demonstrate, as Sutherland did, that the girls from girls' schools had rather better marks within most of the age groups this does not prove that the co-educated girls are not handicapped by their younger age, because this age distribution table is affected by at least two different hidden variables—social class, and the dropping of weak subjects—both of which are acting against the co-educated girls. (A calculation from Sutherland's data indicates that the girls from girls' schools took an average of about 6·23 subjects per pupil and the co-educated girls about 6·44. The difference between these subject loads may seem small but it means that one in five of the co-educated girls took an extra subject.)

It should be acknowledged that although Sutherland in discussing her results is resistant to the idea that the difference in average age between the co-educated girls and those from girls' schools might be causing the differences in attainment, in her summary of conclusions she writes: 'No direct association between greater age and higher attainment could be traced, though differences in school policies which affect age of presenta- tion for the examination may have affected level of attainment, and handicapped co-ed girls in comparison with segregated girls.'

SOCIAL CLASS

Now we come to the effect of social class on attainment in the grammar school, and in particular, in Sutherland's research. This is of con- siderable importance as Sutherland shows that the single-sex schools in her sample are of markedly higher social class;[1] this factor almost certainly also affects all the other surveys. Sutherland, however, main- tains that in her survey social class has little or no effect on attainment. The extent of the social class difference between the schools is shown by working out from Sutherland's figures the percentage belonging to the combined social classes one and two in the two types of school; in the girls' schools it is one-third and in the co-educational schools 19 per cent. The difference is roughly reversed at the bottom end, again handicapping the co-educational schools.

In examining the effects of social class Sutherland gives two tables in which the average marks for the opposing groups of pupils are given for the pupils belonging to each social class, for each subject (English,

[1] The occupational class distribution is in Appendix 2 (Table A2.9).

English literature, French, etc), according to the pattern shown in Table 1.7.

TABLE 1.7   *Social class and average marks (Sutherland)*

Girls	Max	Social class								
		A	B	C	D	E	F	G	Farmers	Un-classed
English										
Segreg.	400	219	213	223	213	220	214	210	204	204
Co-ed	400	210	217	213	216	204	201	214	192	202

From the figures in these tables, one for boys and one for girls, Sutherland deduces, first that social class has no (or an insignificant) effect on attainment, second that as the segregated girls have a higher average mark in most of these social class divisions, this shows that the superiority of the segregated girls is not due to social class advantages. Under the first heading she writes that other factors 'have reduced to insignificance differences which might otherwise result from the social level of the home'. Under the second she argues, 'The data do not indicate that a preponderance of any one or two social classes was the cause of raising the mean of co-ed boys or segregated girls in comparison with segregated boys and co-ed girls.'

The reply is that the data do not show this social class influence because the manner in which the tables are presented accidentally conceals it. This concealment is caused by the presence of other contaminating factors, such as age differences and finer subject selection, which have not been taken out of the table. This is best demonstrated by a concrete example. Examining the first pair of figures in the table we find that segregated girls whose parents belong to social class A are superior in English literature by an average of 9 marks out of 400, or roughly 2·5 per cent, to co-educated girls from class A. But the difference might well be caused by 17·5 per cent of the co-educated girls being one year younger than their rivals and having had one year's less schooling. The age factor affects the comparison of all the paired figures in the table, for all subjects; one cannot therefore examine any of these differences in relation only to the social class factor.

Finer subject selection is restricted to four subjects, but is pronounced in mathematics. The table purports to compare, say, the average mark in mathematics of segregated girls whose parents are in class D with the mark of the corresponding group of co-educated girls. What the table does not tell us, however, is that 89·5 per cent of the co-educated girls and only 73 per cent of segregated girls took the subject, giving the latter a distinct advantage as they would have fewer weaklings to lower their group's average.

Sutherland also writes, 'The segregated schools do have more fathers in the higher occupational levels; but this trend is the same for both boys and girls. If lower attainment were to be expected from those with fathers in the lower occupational groups, this factor should lower the results of co-ed boys as well as of co-ed girls.' The reply is that social class factors probably do lower the marks of co-educated boys, but these boys are superior *in spite of* this handicap, and because of other forces. Their attainment may, for example, be more favourably affected by co-education than that of the girls.

A close analysis of the social class tables also reveals that in spite of the other factors present, the figures are actually in agreement with the findings of research, i.e. that children of high social class tend to do better in the grammar school than children of low social class. The rankings of the social class groups, calculated from the averages of the total marks, are as in Table 1.8. One would not expect to find a perfect

TABLE 1.8   *Social class ranking by average mark (Sutherland)*

	Social class							
	A	B	C	D	E	F	G	Farmers
Girls' schools	2	3	1	8	4	7	6	5
Co-educated girls	1	3	4	2	8	6	5	7

progression from A to G; the main concern is with the contrast between say the top two groups and the bottom two, where the effect should be most powerful, and where the social class differences between the schools are greatest. Combining the two types of school the average placing of social classes A and B is 2·25 compared with an average placing of 6 in classes F and G.[1]

This matter of the age tables and social class tables may be better understood if we imagine that the segregated and the co-educated girls

[1] Correlation between the theoretical 'exact matching' of attainment and social class and the order of ranking for girls' schools (omitting the ambiguous 'farmers') yielded a coefficient of 0·63 and 0·75 for co-educational schools. Both approach statistical significance.

are going to have a running competition in which comparison will be based on average speed of running. Suppose we know that the older girls and those with red hair run the quickest, and we know that the co-educated girls are younger and have fewer red-haired girls. We suspect that co-education itself may have some effect. If in order to test this hypothesis we prepare a table, comparing the co-educated with the single-sex educated girls at each age, but neglecting to allow for red hair, the comparative speeds for each age will not allow for the hidden incidence of red hair. If on the other hand we draw up a similar table for each school type, confined to red-haired girls but neglecting to allow for age, our table will remove the influence of red hair on the comparison but conceal differences of speed due to age. When there is a third hidden variable, in this case fineness of subject selection, the situation is worse.

An even simpler illustration would be a chemical experiment in which one is asked to separate out pure water from a mixture of water, oil and ipecacuanha. When the oil is separated out there is left water contaminated with ipecacuanha; if the oil is then poured back and the ipecacuanha is separated out we are left with water contaminated with oil!

Finally, other research has shown conclusively the effect of social class on attainment in the grammar school. In Table 7 of the Ministry's Early Leaving Report, for example, we find that whereas 54 per cent of the sons of the professional and only 11 per cent of those of the unskilled class were placed in the highest academic group in the grammar school, only 6 per cent of the sons of the professional and 24 per cent of those of the unskilled were placed in the lowest category—those who had completed a five-year course without obtaining School Certificate or as many as three passes at Ordinary level. This finding is supported by a number of other researchers. Floud and Halsey (1951) state that:

> In the English grammar school . . . changes in the rank order of
> entrants are systematically related to their social class origin, to
> such effect that the proportion of children in the top one-third of
> the performance hierarchy who are drawn from working class
> homes falls steadily from about two-thirds at the beginning to
> around one-third at the end of the seven year course.

Campbell (1952) made a case study of overachievers and underachievers compared with control groups and found that those pupils who made better progress had better home backgrounds with regard to culture and the attitude of the parents towards education. Three of the writer's own research students, Stephen Griffith (1958),[1] H. G. Evans (1961) and Vernon Jones (1962), have found the same trend in various grammar

[1] Cf. also Dale, R. R. and Griffith, S., *Downstream*, London 1965.

schools in Wales. In view of this weight of evidence there appears to be no doubt whatever that the co-educational grammar schools are seriously handicapped in academic attainment by their social class composition, as compared with single-sex schools. This is true in England and Wales as well as in Northern Ireland.

To conclude this section, although a small part of Sutherland's findings have been modified here, the writer wishes to acknowledge the appreciable contribution her research has made towards a solution of the problem now before us.

Northern Ireland check (1959)

In spite of the disagreement with Sutherland over interpretation, even her survey maintains the common pattern of these researches, i.e. that the co-educational schools, though handicapped by factors such as lower social class pupils and a lower standard of entry, produce a better academic standard among their boys in almost all subjects and only a slightly less high standard for their girls in a smaller number of subjects (in spite of their younger age and dropping fewer weak subjects) than do the single-sex schools, as tested by the Ordinary level results.

Up to this point, then, the researches, with minor discrepancies, support each other, but the writer, tempting providence, made a check on the Northern Ireland results by processing the 1959 Senior Certificate figures. This was not meant to be a full survey as no attempt was made to gather information on relevant variables, but the results must be reported as they were discrepant (Table 1.9).

Taking the *raw scores* we see that for the only time in these researches the boys' schools did rather better than the boys in co-educational schools. The former had a lead in six subjects, while the latter was in front in four, with one virtually equal. The leads of the boys' schools were statistically significant in four subjects; those of the co-educated boys in two. Curiously, even in this reversal the co-educational schools retained their superiority in mathematics—their strongest subject throughout. (This in spite of the boys' schools having the better qualified teachers.)

Again confining ourselves to raw scores the table shows that the girls in girls' schools did rather better than those in co-educational schools in eight subjects while the latter did better in two, with two virtually equal. Four of the differences in favour of the girls' schools were statistically significant but neither of those in favour of the co-educated girls. Here also mathematics was one of the best subjects for the co-educated girls, in spite of a 90 per cent entry compared with the 81 per cent of girls in girls' schools. (Amalgamating the scores in alternative

TABLE 1.9 *Academic performance, Senior Leaving Certificate, co-educational and single-sex schools, N. Ireland (1959) (Dale check)*

Subjects	Boys in co-ed schools			Boys in boys' schools			Difference[1] Boys' schools minus co-ed	Direction
	N	% sitting	Mean (Max. 400)	N	% sitting	Mean (Max. 400)		
English lang.	685	100	198·88	550	100	207·98	9·10	B
English lit.	630	92	176·07	458	83·3	178·03	1·96	(B)
Latin	85	12·4	215·76	163	29·6	203·61	−12·15	C
French	620	90·5	177·11	514	93·5	193·11	16·00*	B
History	258	37·7	166·19	279	50·7	189·30	23·11*	B
Alt. maths	602	87·9	240·80	511	92·9	224·37	−16·43*	C
Geography	329	48·0	199·96	222	40·4	188·35	−11·61*	C
Physics	408	59·6	206·20	320	58·2	212·24	6·04	B
Chemistry	370	54·0	218·86	312	56·7	229·06	10·20*	B
Biology	69	10·1	208·94	43	7·8	236·11	27·17*	B
Art	55	8·0	176·56	29	5·3	158·96	−17·60	C

Subjects	Girls in co-ed schools			Girls in girls' schools			Girls' schools minus co-ed	Direction
English lang.	549	100	203·79	473	100	209·63	5·84	G
English lit.	492	89·6	183·18	443	93·7	204·66	21·48	G
Latin	141	25·7	229·51	73	15·4	229·67	0·16	Equal
French	500	91·1	198·84	404	85·4	200·84	2·00	(G)
History	303	55·2	172·53	273	57·7	179·25	6·72	G
Trad. maths	85	15·5	175·43	66	14·0	213·25	37·82*	G
Alt. maths	407	74·1	224·23	316	66·8	219·04	−5·17	C
Geography	328	59·7	193·85	301	63·6	188·28	−5·57	C
Physics	93	16·9	202·84	82	17·3	221·09	18·25*	G
Chemistry	120	21·9	209·50	97	20·5	244·85	35·35*	G
Biology	68	12·4	205·60	119	25·2	213·88	8·28	G
Art	103	18·8	176·21	146	30·9	195·28	19·07*	G

[1] Those marked * are statistically significant.

and traditional mathematics produces a slight lead for the girls' schools, which is far from being statistically significant and might well be due to their lower percentage entry mentioned above.)

As there is little change from the previous occasion in the difference between the two groups of girls, and the handicaps of the co-educational schools are presumably still applicable, comment will be confined to the reversal in the case of the boys. Perhaps the most obvious point is that the knowledge of the results of the previous survey may have stimulated the nine boys' schools—most of them of high prestige—to do something to improve their performance, such as 'demoting' teachers whose pupils had poor marks—or warning them that if there was no improvement changes would have to be made. We have already seen such a change-round in the case of the Middlesex girls from Gott's survey to that of Walton, though there is no proof that the foregoing reason is the correct or indeed the only one.

The main factor in the situation, however, would seem to be that eight of the nine boys' schools (and a majority of the girls' schools) are 'voluntary schools', whereas some two-thirds of the co-educational schools are 'maintained' in status. For reasons of history and school independence the voluntary schools have a higher prestige than the maintained schools. In reply to a query a director of education in Northern Ireland wrote, 'Of the 9 boys' schools, 8 are fairly old foundations with long traditions of fathers sending their sons.' The head of one of these wrote, 'A high proportion of the parents are professional men', and added that the staff:student ratio was 'extremely favourable'. A number of these boys' schools are also boarding and collect their high social class entry from a wide area. In short the contrast in type of entry and in staffing was on this occasion too great a handicap for the co-educational schools to overcome. In a survey of the qualifications of teachers of mathematics in Northern Ireland Protestant schools the boys' schools proved to have by far the best qualified teachers (see chapter 4).

Northern Ireland Council for Educational Research

Finally, in February 1969 the Review Procedure Panel of the above body published a valuable report which among other things compared the attainment of *qualified* pupils in co-educational and single-sex grammar schools (Protestant and Catholic) in Northern Ireland by following up a complete form of pupils in each school from 1963 to the O-level examinations in 1968. This is a larger survey than Sutherland's or the writer's 'check' and from that point of view is more dependable, the number of schools being increased to 19 boys', and 34 girls', with 21 co-educational. On the other hand the Catholic grammar schools are single-sex and are reputed to have a rather lower social class entry; this, however, may be held roughly to counter the higher social class entry of the Protestant single-sex schools. The Council's thorough statistical analysis increases the survey's importance.

The result is a reversal of the writer's raw 'check' findings, and a confirmation of the general trend of the series of researches from 1925 to 1969 (Table 1.10).

In the words of the report, 'in the Qualified category pupils in voluntary co-ed schools did better than . . . pupils in single-sex voluntary schools'. Also in general, 'Qualified pupils at co-ed schools show a

TABLE 1.10 *Academic performance at O-level, N. Ireland (1968)* *(summary of Table A2.10)*

	Qualified pupils						
	Boys			Girls			
	Co-educational schools		Single-sex schools	Co-educational schools		Single-sex schools	
	Vol.	County	Vol.	Vol.	County	Vol.	County
Average no. of subjects attempted by examinees	8·46	8·25	8·22	8·33	8·07	8·02	8·14
Proportion of subjects passed to subjects attempted	81·64	80·04	78·95	81·48	81·10	82·31	81·74
Average no. of passes per examinee	6·91	6·60	6·49	6·79	6·55	6·61	6·65
% of entry who left school early	2·2	4·5	5·1	2·7	6·4	6·4	4·0
Exam. not taken[1] though still at school	2·7	3·2	2·4	0·9	1·1	4·5	1·7
Transfers to secondary tech. or 'modern'[2]	2·3		4·0	4·8		5·7	
Unknown, e.g. possible transfers or early leavers	1·3		3·9	3·1	1·8	1·6	0·9
Total[3] at start of follow-up (1963)	428	343	1285	355	394	1098	333

[1] Transferred pupils are excluded from both 'early leavers' and the percentage basis.
[2] As percentage of gross total followed up.
[3] Includes a few who transferred to other grammar schools or died, and are not given under section headings.
NOTE: Adapted from Table A2.10, from report of the Review Procedure Panel, Feb. 1969.

significantly superior performance to Qualified pupils in single-sex schools.' Another factor of importance is that the co-ed pupils dropped fewer weak subjects: 'Qualified pupils attending co-ed schools attempted significantly more subjects than Qualified pupils attending single-sex schools.'

If we analyse the data in Table 1.10[1] in additional ways by comparing the number of subjects passed with the number failed for each type of school (e.g. voluntary co-educational or voluntary girls') we find that the boys from the co-educational schools have a highly significant better ratio of subjects passed to subjects failed than boys from the boys' schools, in spite of taking a slightly higher number of subjects per individual (8·37 to 8·22). This better performance was due almost entirely to the Protestant voluntary co-educational schools; on the other hand *all* the boys' schools were voluntary, though some were Catholic and some Protestant. There was little difference between co-educational and boys' schools in the incidence of early leaving, or of boys not having taken the examination, but rather more boys from boys' schools had left 'for unknown reasons' and this would include 'early leavers' as well as possible transferees. Similarly slightly more of the boys' schools' pupils transferred to technical and 'secondary modern' schools.

The difference between girls in co-educational and girls in girls' schools in percentage of subjects passed to subjects taken was smaller than in the case of the boys' groups and minimally in favour of the girls' schools, but it was far from statistical significance, and this is what was found to be the general trend. However, if the data are analysed as to the average number of subjects passed per examinee the co-educated girls now have a minimal advantage (6·67 compared with 6·62—which is virtual equality). As in previous research the co-educated girls took a greater number of subjects per individual than did the girls in girls' schools (8·2 compared with 8·05), and the latter held back rather more pupils from the examination (3·5 per cent compared with 0·95 per cent) though these would include in both types of school those who were too ill to take the examination. The two groups had nearly the same proportion of 'early leavers' and of those transferring to technical and 'secondary modern' schools.

An overall appraisal of this analysis is that the co-educated boys are slightly superior to those in boys' schools in spite of the several handicaps shown by the table, and girls in girls' schools are approximately equal to the co-educated girls, with again the latter handicapped as above. Unfortunately there is no evidence about the respective intelligence and social class levels of the opposing groups. This summing up must, therefore, conclude by emphasizing that we lack important facts, the group differences are small, and the variations from school to school *within* each group are much larger, as one would expect from the varying degree of efficiency of individual teachers. None the less the outcome fits into the general pattern established over a period of some forty-five years, with very large numbers of schools and of pupils, and in many and different parts of the country.

[1] By chi-square.

General consideration of other variables

PERCENTAGE OF ENTRY

It is well known that the percentage of the 11-plus age group of children who entered grammar schools during the period of the surveys analysed in this chapter varied from one district to another; the range of fluctuation was from the region of 50 per cent entry to about 10 so that although all had the name 'grammar school' some were very different institutions from others. It is not so widely realized that it is mostly schools with rural catchment areas that admitted a large percentage of the age group, while city and large town schools admitted only a low percentage. Now the co-educational grammar schools happened, for economic reasons, to be mainly in rural catchment areas while city and large town areas had predominantly single-sex schools. It follows that quite certainly the single-sex schools would have an appreciably more intelligent (and higher social class) intake of pupils than the co-educational ones. (The general position was exacerbated, if not caused, by the movement of population from rural areas to the large towns and cities.) This point has been inadequately stressed by most of the researchers, though it might not have been so applicable in the Middlesex surveys.

That the single-sex schools tended to have a higher social class intake was shown by Sutherland for Northern Ireland schools; this is demonstrated in the writer's survey described in the next chapter where the somewhat higher intelligence level of the pupils from single-sex schools is also to be seen (see Tables 2.2 and 2.3).

'PREMATURE' LEAVING

Those pupils who left the grammar schools before either completing a five-year course or obtaining a School Certificate may be termed 'premature leavers'. These are, on the average, less able academically than those pupils who stay at school. If a greater proportion of such pupils left prematurely from say the co-educational than from the single-sex schools this would cause the average mark of the remaining co-educational pupils to be greater than it otherwise would be, and it might be argued that this would give them an undue advantage over their rivals. On the other hand it might equally well be argued that such extra premature leavers would only reduce the social class and selective entry advantages of the single-sex schools and could scarcely operate on such a scale as to overcome them. Unfortunately there appear to be only a few shreds of evidence to help us to discover the truth.

In Sutherland's survey we do not know whether there was any appreciable difference between the two types of school in the incidence of premature leaving, but fortunately we do know that even if this did occur it left the single-sex schools with a decided advantage in social class composition. It would be reasonable, therefore, to discount this factor as one which might invalidate our conclusions when assessing the outcome of Sutherland's research. One further piece of evidence is available. The invaluable Early Leaving Report gives figures for the premature leaving from grammar schools of pupils belonging to the 1946 intake (Table 4, p. 76). In the boys' schools 14·6 per cent of the pupils were 'premature leavers' (academic category F), whereas the figure for boys in co-educational schools was 23·4. The gap of 8·8 per cent is too great to be dismissed lightly but it is doubtful whether this would be sufficient to compensate the co-educational schools for their lower standard of entry, especially as we know that the percentage of good pupils among premature leavers is very low for single-sex direct grant schools and is probably higher for the co-educational schools than for all boys' grammar schools combined. Yet we must bear this factor in mind when assessing the evidence of the findings. The figures for the girls are 20·2 per cent (girls' schools) and 23·9 per cent, and in view of the difference between the two types of school in the percentage of entry the gap can be discounted.

Unfortunately these scanty data give us little if any information about the schools during the period of the earlier surveys. All we can do is set this variable off against those which handicap the co-educational schools in any comparison of raw scores, and the odds are strongly against the 'premature leaving' variable outweighing the others. One would be happier, however, if the statistics were available.

STAFFING

Here again precise evidence is lacking. It appears to be generally agreed that there is a tendency for co-educational grammar schools, because they are often in rural places and because they are newer foundations, to be not quite so well staffed as single-sex schools, which are more frequently in the cities and large towns (Middlesex may be a notable exception). This point is not stressed because the evidence is vague, but it seems unlikely that the single-sex schools as a whole would be handicapped in this respect, though possibly girls' schools might be less well-off for teachers of mathematics and physical science in recent years, a deficiency which would almost certainly be compensated for on the literary side and maybe in biology.

In order to obtain a little firm evidence on this point the writer made large-scale surveys in four contrasted regions about the qualifications of teachers of mathematics in the three types of grammar school. The operative date was pushed back as far as practicable in order to relate it to the Sutherland research, i.e. to January 1962. The survey is described more fully in the chapter on mathematics, but is summarized here. Boys' schools were easily the best staffed, as judged by any of several criteria used, and this is probably true of all the surveys. In terms of well-qualified teacher per pupil the co-educational schools came next, but if the criterion had some regard to the number of pupils taking mathematics (a) at Ordinary level and (b) Advanced level, the girls' schools would come nearer to the co-educational because far fewer pupils took the subject in the girls' schools than in the co-educational. These are admittedly rough statistics but more precise information is not available. The staffing position for physics and chemistry may be fairly similar to that in mathematics. In the twenties and thirties (the period of the early surveys) girls' schools were probably better off for such teachers than they are now, though even at the present time the scene is changing with the appointment of more and more men teachers of mathematics and sciences to girls' schools. We must also remember that the basis of the survey was the *academic attainment* of the teacher, and the correlation between this and *teaching efficiency* (it is the latter with which we are concerned) is only of the order of 0·2 or 0·3 (see chapter 4), so that any difference between the schools in the academic attainment of the teachers would be much reduced if we could use the criterion of teaching efficiency instead.

THE EXAMINATION CRITERION

In none of these researches is there any explicit realization that the direction and amount of the differences between the various groups of pupils is in part an artefact of the regulations which control the examination and of the particular standard of attainment which is adopted as a criterion. An example of this occurred in the Northern Ireland results. It is best illustrated by the more obvious examples of sex differences in attainment. As girls at the age of sixteen tend to be better than boys in English, they have a big advantage if this subject is compulsory, especially if it is the only compulsory subject. In the case of mathematics the boys would have a similar (and probably larger) advantage. If a pass (or credit) in a physical science is demanded the boys again are given a considerable start. If, however, the demand is only for 'a science', the girls gain equality by offering biology at which they are good or domestic science (if allowed) where they establish their own pass rate. Further, any comparison between the attainment of the sexes must be profoundly affected by the number of literary subjects as opposed to the number of mathematical subjects which are used, as up to the age of 16 plus girls tend to be better in the former and boys in the latter.

In the comparison between co-educational and single-sex schools effects similar to those above are not so clearly discernible, but they are to be found if we look sufficiently deeply. Two examples must suffice. There is a strong tendency for co-educated girls to be better in mathematics than girls from girls' schools. If a pass (or credit) is obligatory in mathematics the co-educated girls therefore have an advantage. On the other hand the girls' schools stole a march over the co-educated schools in the thirties in the development of biology courses, since girls proved to be much better in the non-mathematical biology than in physics or chemistry, and a pass (or credit) in biology satisfied the examination requirements in group III (science). Here the comparison is obviously affected not only by the examination regulations but also by the nature of the educational guidance. Similarly, educational guidance determines whether a girl will drop her weak mathematics, physics or chemistry, and as this occurs much more often in girls' schools than in co-educational schools, this factor has an important effect on any comparison in attainment. We are not here concerned with the principles of education which underlie this policy or with the needs of the nation in relation to it.

The nature of the comparison is also affected by the particular standard of attainment which is used as the criterion. If a pass mark is adopted this favours the girls as against boys since their marks have a greater tendency to group round the mean. This is well demonstrated, in King's thesis and by Crofts and Jones (1928). If, on the other hand, the criterion is a high credit mark (or even very good), this favours the boys as their marks have a greater spread. We have insufficient evidence of the effect of co-education on the variability of the marks either of boys or girls to be able to say whether this factor would have any effect on the comparison with single-sex schools. Here and there, however, the evidence suggests tentatively that the gap between the sexes, for most subjects, is less in co-educational schools than it is between schools of different sex. This difficulty of criterion is largely circumvented if the average mark is used, as in the Sutherland survey.

Conclusions

Throughout the analysis of the evidence one fact stands out with remarkable clarity. This is the superiority in attainment, at the Ordinary level stage, of boys from co-educational maintained grammar schools over boys from boys' maintained grammar schools. (In most of the surveys the single-sex school sample included direct grant schools.) The writer has endeavoured to find some reason for this other than a superiority due to co-education, and has failed. The boys are of the same average age, but those from single-sex schools tend to be of higher social class and higher intelligence, to be very slightly more selective in choice of subject, and probably to have a rather more highly qualified

35

and experienced staff. The higher rate of premature leaving from co-educational schools might be set off against the higher percentage entry to these schools, though the pupils in the single-sex schools would still be of rather higher social class than their rivals.

The principal reasons for the co-educational superiority may well be as follows. Psychologists agree that girls tend to be more conscientious than boys, and this may influence the co-educated boys, particularly in their homework.[1] There is also evidence of a friendly rivalry between the two sexes in co-educational schools which should help to raise the attainment standard (cf. vol. I, pp. 36–50). In addition, the different approach made to problems by the male and female mind, both in staff and pupils, might contribute to a broader understanding. Teachers and ex-pupils who have attended both types of school maintain that discipline is better and more natural in a mixed school than a boys' school (cf. Dale, 1969, chs 4 and 9).

It should be emphasized very strongly that there is a considerable difference between individual schools in attainment, and many a boys' school will be better than many a mixed one, and many teachers in boys' schools will be teaching better than many teachers in mixed schools. *It can no longer be said, however, that a mixed school is bad for boys because the presence of girls distracts them from their work.* If indeed there is an occasional stray glance this must be more than offset by factors working in the opposite direction.

For girls the trend is by no means clear. In Gott's survey the co-educated girls showed a definite superiority. In the remaining surveys they were, superficially, slightly inferior, though the difference between the two girls' groups was not as great as in the case of the boys. There is no doubt that the key word in the preceding sentence is 'superficial', for the following reasons. The co-educated girls were handicapped by being younger, dropping fewer weak subjects, and being, on the average, of lower social class and probably of lower intelligence; they might also have been taught by a less highly qualified staff, though one cannot say this definitely, and the position with regard to science and mathematics teachers may be different now from that of the period of most of the surveys. In view of the handicaps of the co-educated girls and the smallness of the difference between the raw scores of the two groups it can be said with confidence that the evidence affords no ground whatever for anyone to state—as so often has been stated in the past—that single-sex education for girls produces, because it is single-sex, a higher attainment than co-educational schooling. On the other hand let no one

[1] Mathews (1925) demonstrates that the girls' greater conscientiousness is still to be seen in a co-educational school, where 68 per cent of the girls achieved the median of the boys in term work but only 47 per cent reached this level in examinations. Yet the girls' example may still be exerting an influence.

think that this chapter is even slightly critical of the dedicated work of headmistresses and the staffs of girls' schools. Finally, when the evidence about the attainment of boys and girls is combined the advantage in survey after survey lies with the co-educational school.[1]

[1] The findings of Douglas and Ross in *All Our Future* (1968), though not wholly opposed to this finding, differ in details which seem to the writer to be questionable and are excluded from this chapter, but the reasons for the statement are given in Appendix 3.

2

General attainment II:
a special study

Not long after the start of these researches a plan was constructed to compare the academic progress of co-educational and single-sex educated pupils by administering 'intelligence' tests to them in a number of schools in one area, obtaining their ages and the social class of the fathers and relating these to the usual criterion—performance in the Ordinary level examination.[1] A year's illness halted this work, and later the consequent delegation of half the testing caused the intelligence scores of three schools to be invalidated. Though the study is therefore appreciably smaller than was designed it is not without interest.

Apart from these three schools, a sample of 30 pupils[2] was tested in each of four girls' and four boys' schools and 30 boys and 30 girls in each of four mixed schools in 1949 and the procedure was repeated in six girls', eight boys' and nine mixed schools in 1950. The verbal test of 'intelligence' was supplemented by a non-verbal one in both years, but as the Ravens Matrices 1938 test was found to be too easy it was replaced by the 1947 test for the 1950 testing. A major difficulty which arose was that the girls' schools did not adhere sufficiently strictly to the sampling procedure set out, whereas the co-educational schools did, and we therefore need to approach the girls' results with caution. This bias in sampling did not occur with the boys. As the interpretation of the girls' results is more complex than that of the boys the girls' results are taken first.

The girls

THE SAMPLE

The sampling procedure was designed to obtain a representative cross section of all pupils in each school who were taking the Ordinary level examination. When the departures from the set procedure were discovered it was necessary to assess the extent and direction of the effects. This was done by comparing the examination results of the pupils in the sample with the results of those excluded from it, in each subject in each

[1] Acknowledgment is made to the administrative officials and the schools for their co-operation in this work.
[2] The full 30 pupils were not available in some instances.

38

TABLE 2.1 *Tested groups compared with excluded pupils, School Certificate: girls, 1949 (Dale)*

Average marks (maximum 100)
(Figures in brackets indicate numbers of pupils)

	English	Eng. lit.	History	Geog.	French	Arith.	Algebra	Geom.	Biol.	Physics	Chem.
Co-ed schools											
School 1, excluded	47·3 (4)	51·8 (4)	54·5 (4)	46·0 (4)	53·7 (1)	40·5 (4)	52·0 (1)	48·0 (1)	38·0 (3)	41·0 (1)	75·0 (1)
tested	44·7 (28)	44·7 (28)	41·3 (22)	41·5 (26)	42·9 (11)	36·5 (28)	43·3 (16)	45·5 (16)	43·3 (17)	18·0 (1)	25·3 (7)
School 2, excluded	47·9 (14)	50·3 (14)	42·3 (12)	38·1 (8)	42·9 (5)	39·6 (14)	51·5 (6)	33·3 (6)	55·2 (13)		31·7 (3)
tested	46·1 (25)	45·9 (25)	29·5 (23)	28·2 (22)	43·3 (14)	35·4 (25)	39·3 (12)	27·5 (12)	44·7 (25)		24·1 (11)
School 3, excluded	48·8 (27)	54·7 (27)	43·5 (27)	51·2 (23)	56·4 (9)	32·9 (27)	36·2 (12)	29·2 (12)	56·0 (27)		47·3 (3)
tested	49·4 (30)	52·7 (30)	39·2 (27)	49·7 (19)	44·3 (19)	36·4 (30)	45·1 (13)	38·6 (13)	51·6 (30)		42·6 (9)
School 4, excluded	60·6 (5)	66·2 (5)	48·0 (4)	40·0 (2)	56·2 (4)	40·0 (5)	36·8 (5)	35·6 (5)	58·0 (2)	67·0 (1)	
tested	52·7 (20)	54·1 (20)	48·0 (20)	48·2 (11)	47·5 (15)	52·5 (20)	54·9 (20)	52·8 (20)	46·0 (14)	19·0 (2)	
Girls' schools										*Gen. sci.*	
School 5, excluded	39·5 (2)	35·5 (2)	43·4 (2)	46·0 (1)	18·3 (1)	41·0 (1)	49·0 (1)	46·0 (1)	46·5 (2)		
tested	53·7 (16)	47·2 (16)	49·8 (13)	47·8 (11)	40·9 (13)	55·4 (12)	49·7 (12)	47·1 (12)	43·8 (10)		
School 6, excluded	57·0 (4)	51·8 (4)	44·0 (4)	54·0 (4)	62·5 (2)	38·3 (4)	27·5 (2)	23·5 (2)	54·8 (4)		
tested	49·1 (31)	53·4 (31)	43·6 (22)	51·4 (31)	57·3 (17)	39·5 (30)	39·6 (7)	32·0 (7)	50·4 (31)		
School 7, excluded	53·1 (9)	53·0 (9)	51·0 (9)	38·3 (3)	48·1 (9)	50·2 (9)	52·0 (8)	49·3 (8)	45·2 (5)	47·8 (4)	
tested	54·2 (30)	55·0 (30)	48·8 (30)	45·0 (20)	50·7 (30)	43·5 (24)	54·3 (19)	48·8 (19)	61·8 (12)	55·5 (18)	
School 8, excluded	56·5 (8)	52·1 (8)	39·6 (8)	49·6 (8)	57·8 (7)	59·8 (6)	58·0 (6)	49·8 (6)		51·0 (6)	
tested	59·0 (30)	53·9 (30)	44·5 (29)	52·8 (29)	64·9 (24)	62·7 (24)	61·5 (24)	58·0 (24)		48·2 (17)	

Note: For Schools 7 and 8 the figures shown in the Physics column are for Gen. sci.

Attainment

school (omitting those who sat fewer than five subjects). The compari- . sons for the year 1949 are given in Table 2.1; unfortunately the calculation was not possible for 1950 as the examining board's relevant documents had been destroyed by flood.

If in Table 2.1 we compare the mean scores of girls in the sample with those left out of it, we see that for girls' schools those left out have appreciably worse results than those who are in; of 37 possible comparisons, taking subject by subject in each of the girls' schools, those in the sample had the higher average mark in 27 cases, the lower in 7 and the same in 3. Of 41 possible comparisons in the co-educational schools those in the sample had the higher average mark in only 8 cases, a lower average mark in 30 and the same in 3.[1] In this comparison a difference of less than 1 per cent is counted as equality, French as one subject only and arithmetic, algebra and geometry as one each. Though it is admittedly a rough comparison the difference revealed is so widespread that there is no doubt about its existence and there seemed to be no point in making any more precise calculation. We can say without hesitation that the 1949 sample from girls' schools is biased in favour of them and the opposing sample of girls from co-educational schools is biased against the co-educational schools. This position was arrived at in spite of the writer's deliberate attempt to avoid it, and at one time it seemed that because of this bias all the work might have to be jettisoned. After consideration, however, it was decided to continue the analysis and report it because, first, the comparison of the boys' groups had no such one-sided bias, yet could scarcely be published without the comparison of the girls' groups; second, that a way was found of making the girls' comparison fairer—though there was not sufficient data available with which to reduce the opposing samples to complete equality of ability and assiduity.

With this important point established, other aspects of the samples are examined. Most of the girls' schools are urban, with an intake from children aged 11 appreciably less in proportion than that of the opposing co-educational schools, which are mainly rural or 'small urban'. Hence the sample of girls from girls' schools is, as expected, of higher verbal and non-verbal 'intelligence' level and appreciably of higher social class, than that from the co-educational schools (Tables 2.2 and 2.3). In the present case the difference between the two groups might of course be partly due to the bias in the samples. In 1949 the girls in girls' schools

[1] To secure a comprehensive objective result all subject comparisons are included; however, even if we omit all comparisons in which the excluded pupils number only one or two the overall result is only modified, the figures being as follows: the sample in girls' schools had the higher mean in 17 cases, the lower in 6 and the same in 2; the co-educated sample had the higher means in 7 cases, lower in 23 and the same in 3.

TABLE 2.2 *Mean 'intelligence' scores of samples of pupils taking School Certificate (Dale)*

Type of test	Co-educational schools			Single-sex schools			
	No. of schools	No. of pupils	Mean score	No. of schools	No. of pupils	Mean score	
Boys							
1949 Verbal	4	92	116·8	4	95	125·3	2·990†
Non-verbal[1]	4	97	42·3	4	99	44·6	2·842†
1950 Verbal	9	133	113·7	8	108	118·2	1·904
Non-verbal	8	124	23·2	8	121	24·8	2·259*
Girls							
1949 Verbal	4	99	115·4	4	106	127·7	4·801‡
Non-verbal	4	103	41·5	4	107	44·5	2·953†
1950 Verbal	9	134	110·9	5	87	122·0	4·533‡
Non-verbal	9	150	23·8	6	115	25·4	3·738†

* indicates $P < 0.05$; † $P < 0.01$; ‡ $P < 0.001$.
[1] In 1949 Raven matrices 1938 version; in 1950 Raven matrices 1947 version (a stiffer test).

TABLE 2.3 *Parental occupational class of samples of pupils taking School Certificate (Dale)*

	Occupational classes[1]													
	1		2		3		4		5		6[2]		Total	
	N	%	N	%	N	%	N	%	N	%	N	%	N	%
Boys in co-ed schools														
1949	9	7·3	8	6·5	50	40·7	32	26·0	3	2·4	20	16·3	123[3]	100
1950	4	2·6	13	8·6	71	47·1	40	26·5	8	5·3	15	9·9	151	100
Boys in boys' schools														
1949	12	12·1	23	23·2	44	44·5	9	9·1	8	8·1	3	3·0	99	100
1950	11	8·9	14	11·3	70	56·4	13	10·4	8	6·5	8	6·5	124	100
Girls in co-ed schools														
1949	8	6·4	13	10·4	38	30·4	43	34·4	4	3·2	19	15·2	125	100
1950	16	9·4	9	5·3	80	47·0	30	17·7	15	8·8	18	10·6	170[3]	100
Girls in girls' schools														
1949	11	10·3	13	12·1	53	49·6	18	16·9	4	3·7	7	6·5	107[3]	100
1950	12	10·4	23	20·0	62	53·9	11	9·6	4	3·5	3	2·6	115	100

[1] The occupational class categories were those used by Peaker in the Early Leaving Report. Class 1 includes professional, administrative, managerial and teachers; class 2 clerical workers; class 3 skilled manual workers; class 4 semi-skilled, and class 5 unskilled.
[2] Unemployed, deceased, etc.
[3] Includes a few unclassifiable.
In 1949 there were 5 co-educational schools, 4 boys' schools and 4 girls' schools. In 1950 the corresponding numbers were 10, 8 and 6.

were also seven months older than their opposite numbers, though in 1950, probably because of a change in minimum age regulations, the two groups were the same age. The age difference for 1949 is in line with that found in previous surveys, commencing with that of Tyson in the 1920s.

To remove the gross inequalities each girl from the girls' schools was matched with one from the co-educational schools who was her equal

TABLE 2.4 *Mean 'intelligence' scores of samples of pupils taking School Certificate (Dale)*

Matched pairs sample

		Co-educational schools			Single-sex schools		
		No. of[1] schools	No. of pupils	Mean score	No. of schools	No. of pupils	Mean score
Boys							
1949	Verbal	4	49	122·7	4	50	122·1
	Non-verbal (1938 version)	4	51	44·2	4	51	44·2
1950	Verbal	9	84	115·7	8	79	114·5
	Non-verbal (1947 version)	8	84	24·1	8	89	24·2
Girls							
1949	Verbal	4	41	120·6	4	42	120·9
	Non-verbal	4	42	43·5	4	42	43·6
1950	Verbal	9	79	115·5	5	66	119·2
	Non-verbal	9	88	24·9	6	88	25·0

[1] Within each of the matched samples numbers on each side in this table are not equal because scores for some pupils were available only for one of the tests. This applies also to the schools.

in verbal 'intelligence', social class and age. The process was continued until no more suitable matchings could be found.[1] The above matching would reduce the effect of bias in the selection of the samples, though it would not remove it, as those chosen because of their high attainment, for the girls' schools sample, are probably working reasonably close to the level of their intelligence, while those from the co-educational schools with whom they are now matched merely on high intelligence

[1] This process admittedly might not entirely discount the effect of the 'majority ethos' in the school.

might not work to the expected level. However, the reduction of the inequalities was considerable and the best that could be effected under the circumstances. This new sample will be referred to as the 'matched pairs sample'. Its remaining inequalities in 'intelligence' are brought about mainly because matching on verbal 'intelligence' while ignoring non-verbal intelligence caused a negligibly higher average for the latter to occur for girls' schools in 1950, but partly because the pupils of one school and a few individuals had to be matched on their non-verbal scores, producing the only appreciable difference in verbal intelligence

TABLE 2.5   *Social class distribution (Dale's survey)*

Matched pairs sample

		Social classes						
		1	2	3	4	5	6[1]	Total
Boys								
1949	Co-educated	4	4	27	12	1	3	51
	In boys' schools	5	3	29	7	5	2	51
1950	Co-educated	2	11	51	22	2	1	89
	In boys' schools	4	8	57	12	7	1	89
Girls								
1949	Co-educated	4	5	17	13	1	2	42
	In girls' schools	5	3	24	8	2	0	42
1950	Co-educated	13	6	52	12	3	2	88
	In girls' schools	8	13	53	11	3	0	88

[1] Class—unemployed or deceased.

scores—that in favour of girls' schools in 1950 (119.2 to 115.5). For this matched sample there was equality in age for both years.

The social class matching was strict for a large central core, but the need to secure a sufficient number of pairs for reliability caused the rules to be relaxed later by a process of 'compensatory balancing' between adjacent classes.

The result of the matching and balancing is shown in Tables 2.4 and 2.5.

Comment on the comparative intelligence levels of the two groups of girls has already been made. The girls' social class distributions are also fairly close together, with a slight over-weighting of the co-educated girls at the lower end of the distribution, from which the academic failures are most likely to come.

Attainment

COMPARATIVE ATTAINMENT

If the average Ordinary level (i.e. School Certificate) examination marks of *all* the co-educated girls in the schools tested were compared with those of *all* the girls in the girls' schools, without any allowance for the substantial higher intelligence and higher social class of the latter, the girls in the girls' schools would have the better results; the imbalance in ability is in this instance too great for us to expect otherwise. However, such a comparison serves no useful purpose. We are not interested in which type of school has the higher attainment but rather in which type

TABLE 2.6   *Mean subject differences of girls in co-educational and girls' schools (Dale)*

Matched pairs sample (maximum mark 100)

	1949			1950		
	N pairs	Mean difference	t value	N pairs	Mean difference	t value[1]
English	42	1·76	1·06	88	−1·40	1·37
English lit.	42	0·38	0·15	87	−0·03	0·02
History	34	2·74	0·80	57	1·89	0·68
Geography	24	4·46	1·28	51	3·63	1·65
French	21	4·88	1·17	42	−3·17	0·85
Maths						
(Arith.)	34	5·26	1·58	73	2·77	0·86
(Algebra)	14	4·00	0·69	43	−1·28	0·31
(Geometry)	14	−1·14	0·19	43	8·07	1·70
Biology	16	4·06	0·80	40	4·25	1·60
Chemistry				8	10·25	2·02*

NOTE: Subject samples less than 8 pairs are omitted as unreliable. Minus difference means advantage to co-educational schools.
[1] * indicates P < 0·05.

secures the better progress from its pupils, given equality of ability, social class, age, etc. What then happens when the comparison is made through the present matched sample, remembering the sample's small bias in intelligence and social class in favour of the girls in girls' schools, and that the original bias in the same direction in the choice of students for the sample cannot have been removed entirely by the matching? The results are presented in Table 2.6.

From Table 2.6 we see that in the first year of the survey the girls in girls' schools did better than the co-educated girls in eight subjects and worse in only one. However, the differences were small, none of them were statistically significant, and there were only four schools on each side and only 42 matched pairs.

In the second year, with six girls' and nine co-educational schools, and more than twice the number of matched pairs (88), the opposing groups were much nearer together, the girls' schools being better in six subjects and worse in four. The only difference which was statistically significant was in chemistry in favour of the girls in girls' schools, but here the opposing samples were only eight matched pairs.[1] If allowance is made for the slight lead of the girls from girls' schools in verbal intelligence (119 compared with 115) and for the other handicaps of the co-educated girls there can be very little difference between the two groups.

A further factor which needs to be taken into consideration is the incidence of the dropping of weak subjects among the opposite groups. In Table 2.7 the data reveal that the co-educated girls in 1949 took an average of 7·79 subjects each out of 12 subjects for which the marks had been made available, while those in girls' schools took only 7·45 each, which means that in 12 of the 42 pairs the co-educated girl took an extra —and usually weak—subject. This greater refinement of the subject-entry among girls' schools has again been a factor present in many previous researches. In mathematics and the sciences these weak candidates often produce very low scores and have a pronounced effect on the average mark. In 1950 the difference in the average number of subjects taken was still in the same direction but a little smaller—7·83 (co-educated girls) compared with 7·70 (girls in girls' schools). The effect of this dropping of weak subjects is not removed by the matching process, as any student in the matched sample who drops a subject is simply excluded from the sample (*with his pair*) for that particular subject.

Throughout this discussion an important assumption has been made —that the standard of the teaching was at least as good in the girls' as in the co-educational schools. For financial reasons and to maintain harmonious relations with the schools it was impossible to send a cohort of specialists into each of the schools to assess the standard of the teaching. Better than nothing would have been a census of the academic qualifications of the teachers, and this was attempted; but for various understandable reasons, such as a few key schools being rather sensitive about 'league tables', the census could not be completed. The matter is also far from as simple as it appears. For example, though girls' schools are thought to be better staffed than co-educational schools on the arts side, they may be worse staffed in mathematics (see chapter 4), probably

---

[1] The fact that the co-educated matched girls were drawn from schools where 32 per cent of the girls took chemistry, as opposed to 19 per cent for girls from girls' schools, would account for at least part of the lead of the girls' schools.

in physics and possibly in chemistry; it could be argued, however, that co-educational schools *need* to be better staffed in these subjects because a far greater percentage of *pupils* (i.e. boys and girls) in these schools take mathematics and the physical sciences at both Ordinary and Advanced level, and indeed after the age of 13 or 14 in general. Approaching the topic from another angle we do know that girls in girls' schools complain of the pressure of work more than those in co-educational

TABLE 2.7   *Average number of subjects taken (girls) (Dale)*

Matched pairs sample

| No. and % taking | 1949 | | | | 1950 | | | |
| | Co-ed schools | | Girls' schools | | Co-ed schools | | Girls' schools | |
subject	N	%	N	%	N	%	N	%
English	42	100	42	100	88	100	88	100
English lit.	42	100	42	100	88	100	88	100
History	37	88·1	39	92·9	70	79·5	72	81·8
Geography	29	69·1	35	83·3	73	83·0	65	73·9
French	29	69·1	34	81·0	55	62·5	63	71·6
Arithmetic	42	100	34	81·0	83	94·3	78	88·6
Algebra	27	64·3	23	54·8	64	72·7	58	65·9
Geometry	27	64·3	23	54·8	64	72·7	58	65·9
Biology	33	78·6	21	50·0	56	63·6	60	68·2
General science			15	35·7	11	12·5	27	30·7
Physics	3	7·1	2	4·8	9	10·2	4	4·5
Chemistry	16	38·1	3	7·1	28	31·8	17	19·3
Average no. of subjects taken	7·79		7·45		7·83		7·70	

schools do (chapter 9). Whether this pressure is desirable is debatable but one would think that it would raise the level of attainment in girls' schools.

From these results it would be unwise to come to any firm conclusions. Protagonists of co-education could certainly not claim that the survey proves that co-educated girls make better progress, but in view of the demonstration given here of the various factors which handicapped the co-educated girls in the matched pairs sample and because of the narrowness of the difference in attainment in any one subject and the smallness of the overall advantage of the girls' schools in the much larger second-year sample, it would also be unwise of the protagonists of girls' schools to use these results to support any claim that girls make better academic progress in girls' schools than in co-educational schools. The verdict is inconclusive. If things had gone as planned it might have been otherwise. Yet in spite of the disappointments the labour has not been wasted, as will be seen when these girls' results are considered in relation to those of the boys.

SOME INDIVIDUAL SUBJECTS

At first sight the results seem to indicate that the usual advantage of the co-educated girls in mathematics has vanished, but note first that the only advantage of the co-educated girls in the first year was in a mathematical subject—geometry; second, that whereas all the co-educated girls took arithmetic this was dropped by almost one-fifth of the girls in girls' schools and the difference in selectivity was maintained in algebra and geometry. The matching of the girls for intelligence and social class removes some of this selectivity effect but not all of it because it is possible for a quite intelligent girl from the girls' schools to be poor in mathematics; if she therefore drops all three branches of the subject there are two effects which concern the interpretation—first, the girls' schools average is not reduced by her poor performance, and is higher than it 'should be', second, the co-educated girl with whom she is matched is also quite intelligent and might be good at mathematics, yet she is removed from the sample by the absence of her pair. The greater subject selectivity of the girls' schools therefore gives them a spurious advantage. Overall this also happens slightly in science subjects (1949) but in the present sample the process is reversed in French.

The boys

THE SAMPLE

For the boys the background of the schools and the nature of their intake resembled closely those of the girls. The boys' schools were usually in urban areas while the co-educational were mainly in rural areas or small towns, the intake of the boys' schools being appreciably more selective than that of the co-educational schools. The difference shows up in the higher verbal intelligence and social class of the boys from the boys' schools in the sample (see Tables 2.2 and 2.3).

In order to ascertain whether there was any bias in the sampling the same procedure was used as with the girls, that is, the average mark obtained by the pupils in the sample in the Ordinary level examination was compared in each subject with the average mark of the pupils left out. In 1949, owing to the imposition of a minimum age, together with the method of determining the sample, the marks of the pupils in the sample tended to be lower than the marks of the pupils left out, but this is so for both boys' groups, and though the difference in the amount for the two groups would penalize the co-educated boys in the comparison of attainment more than it would their rivals this proves in the end to be immaterial because if the difference had any effect at all it would reinforce the findings. In this instance the excluded co-educated boys were better than those in the sample in 28 subject comparisons, worse in 9 and the same in 5; the excluded boys from boys' schools were better than those in the sample in 21 instances, worse in 11 and the same in 7.

The inequalities between the schools in the nature of the intake were largely neutralized by use of the same matched pairs procedure as was used for the girls. The resulting intelligence and social class distributions in these two *matched* samples are given in Tables 2.4 and 2.5. It will be seen that in the matching the boys' schools retained a minimal overall advantage in social class in 1949 which increased to a small advantage in 1950, but in view of the results this bias is in the safe or conservative direction. In verbal intelligence the co-educated boys had a negligible lead in 1949 and a small lead of about 1 per cent in 1950 (115·68 to 114·45), and the boys in boys' schools had a very small lead in non-verbal intelligence in 1950. In other words the two groups are virtually equal for our purposes. They were also of the same average age, and took approximately the same subject load in the examination—8·24 (co-educated) to 8·71 in 1949 and 8·53 to 8·35 in 1950 with the larger sample.

COMPARATIVE ATTAINMENT

Because of this degree of similarity in the two samples we can proceed immediately to the comparison of attainment in the two types of school (Table 2.8).

The data in Table 2.8 show that in the first year of testing the co-educated boys did better in six subjects—and worse in four; the differences in English literature and in history[1] were statistically significant in favour of the co-educated boys, and in French (interestingly so as we shall see later) the difference was in favour of the boys' schools. In the much larger sample of the second year the co-educated boys did better in nine subjects and the boys in boys' schools had the advantage in one, though it is again of some interest in view of both previous and later findings that the boys in boys' schools also had an advantage in one of the three examinations in French—the oral part.

[1] But only 37 of the 51 co-educated boys took history compared with 46 from the boys' school sample. The co-educated advantage, however, was large and statistically very highly significant.

Three of the differences in favour of the co-educated boys were statistically significant, well beyond the 0·05 level—in English language, English literature and biology—all subjects in which they might be held to benefit from the interest and ability of the girls. The boys in boys' schools had a statistically significant superiority in algebra (inexplicably so) though they were slightly lower than the co-educated boys in the other two mathematical subjects. A superiority of the boys in boys'

TABLE 2.8 *Mean subject differences of boys in co-educational and boys' schools (Dale)*

Matched pairs sample (maximum mark 100)

	1949			1950		
	N pairs	Mean difference	t value[1]	N pairs	Mean difference	t value[1]
English	51	2·49	1·48	89	−2·85	2·79†
English lit.	51	−4·12	1·98*	89	−4·49	2·71†
History	33	−10·03	3·03‡	47	−1·96	0·66
Geography	15	−0·73	0·15	47	−3·34	1·57
French	22	12·29	2·81†	27	−0·83	0·17
Maths						
(Arith.)	51	−2·08	0·76	85	−1·40	0·49
(Algebra)	46	1·04	0·24	80	7·11	2·31*
(Geometry)	46	−2·26	0·66	80	−0·41	0·13
Physics	14	−3·86	0·73	27	−6·00	1·32
Chemistry	34	0·29	0·08	34	−1·26	0·29
Biology				9	−13·22	2·89†

NOTE: Subject samples of less than 8 pairs are omitted as unreliable. Minus difference means advantage to co-educational schools.
[1] * $P < 0·05$; † $P < 0·01$; ‡ $P < 0·001$.

schools in oral French in spite of their less selective entry,[1] conforms to the findings later in the book about the extra polarization of the expressed interest of co-educated boys away from French and the rather greater reluctance to 'speak out in class'. On the other hand the co-educated boys did perform better than the boys in boys' schools this second year in the written papers, maybe because of the less selective entry of the boys' schools. This greater polarization of interest in the sciences amongst co-educated boys, demonstrated later in chapter 9, seems to be reflected in a better performance by them even though their entry for these subjects is in this instance much less selective than that of the boys' schools.

[1] Not shown in the table, where three French marks are amalgamated.

From the 89 boys in boys' schools there were 111 candidate entries for physics, chemistry and biology combined while from the 89 co-educated boys there were 151 entries.

These attainment results for the boys are completely in line with research after research since the 1920s, in which the boys from co-educational schools almost invariably fare better than those from boys' schools in spite of the better intake of the boys' schools and almost certainly their better staff. (In this enquiry of course some inequalities of intake are neutralized.) Though the differences between the results from boys in the two types of school are nothing like as great as differences caused by good and bad teaching they are persistent enough to show that this is no temporary or spasmodic phenomenon. Its most likely cause would seem to be friendly rivalry with the girls in co-educational schools, and the influence of the girls' greater assiduity and conscientiousness. It may be, too, that the feminine outlook in class gives an additional dimension or greater breadth of interest to subjects like English literature and history.

Overall (boys and girls)

What of the overall picture? If we adopt the crude process of adding the number of subject superiorities for co-educated pupils and similarly for pupils from single-sex schools the co-educated have the slightest of advantages—a superiority over the two years in 20 subjects compared with 19 for the single-sex schools. However, 13 of the 20 co-educational superiorities were from the larger second-year sample and only 7 of the 19 of the single-sex schools. If we look at it another way the co-educated advantage was statistically significant in five instances compared with only two for the single-sex schools, of which one was from a small sample of eight matched pairs.

It is important to reiterate that this summation makes no allowance for the bias against the co-educated girls which is in the matched pairs sample and which has been explained previously. The difference in favour of the co-educational schools would naturally have been greater if these factors had been taken into account.

3

Attainment in mathematics

An overall comparison having been made between the attainment of pupils in single-sex and co-educational maintained grammar schools, we now turn to a critical examination of research into the differences between the same groups in two individual subjects. By far the most intriguing of these differences is that in mathematics.

Cameron's research

The first, and one of the most important studies on this topic, was made by Cameron at the University of London in 1923. It differed from most other research in its use of special tests designed to assess various mathematical abilities and it thereby achieved some analysis in depth. The most interesting difference which emerged was that the girls in the co-educational schools did better than those in girls' schools. When discussing the reasons for this Cameron first compared girls with boys, pointing out that her Test I required powers of synthesis which are probably related to the ability to view objects and situations as a whole, a faculty which is encouraged by the training of the boy as compared with the girl. She then noted that girls in co-educational schools had apparently developed these powers and attributed this either to the presence of boys in the class or to the sex of the teacher. More than half of these girls had been taught by a master during the whole of their time at the grammar school (i.e. up to the time of the test), and nearly all of them for at least two-thirds of the time. They had all been taught in the same classes as boys. Cameron put forward the hypothesis that continual contact with the masculine outlook had broadened the co-educated girls' minds, thereby developing these powers of synthesis required for success in Test I. She pointed out that this improvement appeared to be confined to one or two factors of mathematical ability. The finding of Piret (1965) that females solve problems better when in a group of both sexes links up with this, though further confirmation would be desirable.

The co-educated boys were superior to the boys in boys' schools in eight out of nine tests, and Cameron comments that the presence of girls in the classroom had evidently had no detrimental effect on the attainment of the boys.

This is a sound and discerning research except for certain faults in sampling, which need to be assessed in order to estimate the value of the results. The sample consisted of 500 grammar school pupils. This was a satisfactory total, but there were only six girls', five boys' and three co-educational schools. The small number of schools, therefore, makes the findings unreliable, except when used in conjunction with other research. Again, although the single-sex school pupils were largely taken from matched pairs of single-sex schools scattered about England and Wales the co-educated schools were in Middlesex only. Though a vague effort was made to equalize the opposing groups for social class, no scientific evidence was presented about this. The question of superior and inferior school streams also arises. Cameron gives no total figures, but it is possible to calculate them from her data. Ignoring those groups where all pupils of the relevant school year were included, we find that in boys' schools 66 pupils were in the 'A' stream and 25 in the 'B' stream; in girls' schools 53 were in the 'A' stream and 16 in the 'B' stream. These proportions are not very different from each other but in the co-educational schools 50 boys were in the 'A' stream and 43 in the 'B', while the figures for girls were 42 in 'A' and 38 in 'B'. Within the co-educational schools the streams are again fairly well balanced, but the comparison between pupils in single-sex schools and co-educated pupils shows that the latter, other things being equal, are an inferior sample, and therefore ought not to achieve as good a standard as the opposing group.

The age of the pupils is another factor affecting the sampling. Although Cameron omits the overall averages, these can be calculated from her data. They are 15 years 2 months for girls in girls' schools, 14 years 6 months for boys in boys' schools, and 14 years $3\frac{1}{2}$ months for pupils in co-educational schools. It was not possible to calculate separate averages for boys and girls in the last group. The discrepancy in age partly arose because Cameron took for her sample those pupils who were in their eighth term of algebra and, as far as possible, 'their eighth term of geometry'. The groups were, therefore, equal in length of tuition in algebra and geometry but not in maturity, the co-educated group being younger. In addition, the co-educated girls had one year less tuition in arithmetic than the girls in girls' schools. The only differences in time per week were in two cases where girls' schools had one period per week more than the corresponding boys' school, in one instance for one year and in the other for two. Though this research appears to put co-educational schools in a very favourable light with regard to the standard of attainment in mathematics, it is possible for the results to have occurred owing to the choice of three co-educational schools where the teaching of mathematics might have been extraordinarily good, though we do not know this. It is therefore necessary to turn to the results of other investigations.

Tyson's survey

We have already seen that in Tyson's large-scale survey among schools taking the School Certificate examination of the Northern Universities' Joint Matriculation Board, the girls in co-educational grammar schools were slightly younger, of lower social class, and gained a slightly lower percentage of credits[1] in a number of subjects than girls in girls' schools, but an important exception was mathematics where the superiority was reversed. The differences in favour of the co-educated girls were all statistically significant, being 7·2 per cent of credits in 1925, 5·2 per cent in 1926, and 12·0 per cent when only rural schools were considered. The co-educated girls reached a higher standard, even though a rather greater proportion of them took the examination than was the case of girls in girls' schools.[2]

The co-educated boys were approximately as superior to the boys in boys' schools as the co-educated girls were to the girls in girls' schools. This was so in both years and also when rural schools were taken separately. Almost all the boys in both types of school were candidates in mathematics. When we look at the results more closely we find that the difference between the sexes was almost the same within the co-educational schools as it was between the single-sex schools; it was consistently about 20 per cent of credits in favour of the boys, even though virtually all the boys were candidates. We should keep in mind, however, that whereas some 11 to 14 per cent of the girls from girls' schools dropped mathematics, only some 3 to 5 per cent of the co-educated girls dropped the subject. If the latter proportions were raised to the level of those of the girls in girls' schools the percentage of credits gained by the co-educated girls would be improved and the gap between them and the co-educated boys would be thereby reduced. The gap would be further narrowed if the co-educated girls were raised to the same age level as the girls in girls' schools. Hence, it would appear at first sight that co-education, in some way or other, possibly narrows slightly the gap between the sexes in mathematical attainment. This hypothesis is supported by Cameron (1923) who found a statistical difference in favour of boys in boys' schools as against girls in girls' schools, but no statistical difference between the sexes in co-educational schools. She was, of course, testing ability rather than attainment, and her numbers were so very much smaller than Tyson's that it would be more difficult for her differences to reach statistical significance. None

[1] Using as base the number of candidates sitting each subject.
[2] Calculating from Tyson's data, the differences in these proportions appear to be about 8 to 9 per cent in 1925–6 but only 3 per cent in rural schools. The co-educated girls were at least four months younger than the girls from girls' schools.

the less, the two studies show the same tendency, as does that of the National Foundation for Educational Research (Pidgeon, 1967), where it was reported that 'in co-educational schools the superiority of the boys to the girls was much less than in segregated schools'. The report suggested that girls do better when taught in an atmosphere where traditional feminine suspicion of mathematics is less noticeable and where perhaps teachers are less inclined to doubt their abilities in the subject. It was also found that the difference between the sexes in attitude towards mathematics was greater between the segregated sexes than between those in co-educational schools.

The same trend was observed by Field (1935) who found that co-educated girls performed better in mathematics than in any other subject as compared with girls in girls' schools, in spite of more of the weak co-educated girls taking the subject. Although her sample of schools was far too small for some purposes, it is rather more reliable for the comparison just mentioned. A narrowing of the differences between the sexes in average attainment in individual subjects among co-educated pupils has been found by a number of researchers. Burt as early as 1921, in a section on academic ability in general, wrote, 'In mixed schools, where the boys and girls have been educated side by side, such differences are by no means easy to demonstrate', though he does mention a few exceptions.

In mathematics, however, regard must be paid to an important variable—the distribution of well-qualified teachers of mathematics in co-educational, boys' and girls' schools. New data on this topic, given in a later chapter, shows an imbalance in the distribution which could contribute towards the lead of the co-educated girls over those in girls' schools and also to the narrowing of the gap between the sexes when pupils are co-educated.

King's survey

King based his survey on the results of the London General Schools Examination in 1945. Unfortunately, this was a period when many male teachers were in the armed forces, and the boys' schools in particular were handicapped. Unfortunately, also, King was unable to secure for the co-educational schools separation of the boys' results from those of the girls. When we compute from his data the percentage of pupils with passes plus those with credits and very goods, in the individual subjects, the pupils of the mixed schools are slightly superior to the boys' schools in two out of the three mathematical subjects and have a similar advantage over girls' schools. Incidentally this slight superiority over boys' and girls' schools in mathematics extends to all principal science subjects, except general science (where the question of the relative proportion of candidates in the rival groups arises) but the joint averages of the co-educated boys and girls are inferior to those of the girls' schools in literary subjects. As indicated above, these results have a question mark against them when used for the general comparison of attainment in different types of school, but within that setting it is probably valid to note that the mixed schools do best in mathematics and mathematical-type subjects. Another relevant fact is that whereas almost 98 per cent of boys in boys' schools take mathematics, and 96 per cent of the co-educated pupils, the percentage drops to only 81 in girls' schools. The true standard of attainment in the girls' schools is, therefore, hidden because so many weak pupils do not take the examination.

Dale's survey (1949–50)

At first sight it appears that in this survey the co-educated girls do worse than the girls from girls' schools in mathematics, but the impression is misleading (Table 2.6) as the sample from girls' schools is appreciably more finely selected (Table 2.7). For example in 1949 whereas all the co-educated girls took arithmetic it was dropped by 19 per cent of the girls from girls' schools. In mathematical-type subjects the inclusion of these weaker girls would have caused a considerable drop in the average mark of the girls' schools sample. (Incidentally a study of the mark sheets showed clearly that there is no doubt at all that almost all these girls are the weaker ones.) It should be noted that the co-educated girls had slightly the better result in geometry in 1949 in spite of entering a higher percentage of candidates, and this was the only subject in which the co-educated girls were better in a straight comparison without considering other variables.

The comparison of the boys' samples in mathematics is broadly in line with the results from other surveys, though by no means emphatically so (Table 2.8). Combining the 1949 and 1950 results the co-educated boys were better in four out of six subject results, but in one of the remaining subjects (algebra in 1950) the boys from boys' schools had a statistically significant lead. No explanation has been found for this unusual result in algebra and it may well arise from the comparatively small number of schools in the sample—eight on each side; this could cause one of the two sets of mathematics teachers to be much worse or much better than usual, and this might even occur in relation to algebra only. Summing up, the present survey is in agreement with the findings of the other surveys as far as arithmetic and geometry are concerned, but not for algebra.

Sutherland's survey

Sutherland compared the performance of co-educational schools with single-sex schools in the Northern Ireland Senior Certificate examination. If one combines her results for traditional mathematics with those for her alternative mathematics the co-educated girls have a slight superiority. With the theoretical maximum 400, girls in girls' schools averaged 208·93 and the co-educated girls 215·13. But whereas only 73 per cent of the segregated girls took mathematics, 90 per cent of the co-educated girls took the subject. As a pupil will be reluctant to drop a subject in which he or she is good, but be very ready to drop a weak one, it follows that the average mark of the segregated girls would be considerably reduced if an extra 17 per cent or so of the girls who had dropped mathematics had taken it instead. Similarly, we have already seen that there is an age difference working in the same direction, the co-educated girls being on the average three months younger than the girls from girls' schools. This difference was produced by some 29 per cent of the co-educated girls taking the faster five-year course, whereas rather less than one-eighth of the girls from girls' schools took this shorter course.

The co-educated girls were also of lower social class. Whereas in the single-sex schools almost one-third of the pupils who could be classified belonged to the two top social classes, less than 19 per cent of the co-educated pupils were in these categories. This social class difference would, according to the results of other research, depress the attainment of the co-educated pupils.

In the case of the boys the co-educated group had a statistically significant superiority, both in traditional and alternative mathematics, when each individual's score in a subject was taken as the unit; this became statistically not significant when each school's mean for the subject was used instead. The trend, however, was naturally in the same direction.

Northern Ireland check (1959)

In the 'check' made by the writer on the Senior Certificate results of the Protestant schools in Northern Ireland this same trend continues. In the chief mathematics paper (alternative mathematics) the co-educated girls had a lead which, though not significant statistically, was in direct contrast to the lead of the girls from girls' schools in other subjects. It is true that if traditional mathematics (taken only by a sixth of the pupils) is included the girls' schools have a minimal superiority of 0·5 per cent but they entered only 80 per cent of their girls for mathematics whereas the co-educated schools sent in 90 per cent.

Readers will recollect from the previous chapter that this 'check' was
the one survey in which boys from boys' schools had the better results,
but here again alternative mathematics was one of only two subjects in
which the co-educated boys had a statistically significant lead—in spite
of all their handicaps, including being taught by less highly qualified
teachers, as demonstrated in the next chapter.

Northern Ireland 1969 Report

This survey did not report on results in individual subjects.

Report of the NFER (1967)

This report resulted from the participation of England in the International Project for the Evaluation of Educational Achievement. A
national sample was taken of pupils at various ages through the school
population, beginning at 13 and ending at A-level. Though it was found
that in all six stages the boys' schools had a higher average in the
mathematics test than the co-educated boys, and girls' schools were
similarly superior to the co-educated girls, Pidgeon (the editor) wisely
refrained from suggesting that the difference might be due to co-
education, writing, 'Proportionately, more secondary modern schools
are co-educational than are grammar schools, and comprehensive
schools tend to be co-educational. These basic organizational facts may
explain the differences observed between segregated schools and co-
educational schools.' He thereby implied, and did so correctly, that
when his sample was divided in this way it produced two grossly unequal sub-samples, i.e. the co-educational sample would be lower in
intelligence and in social class. Even if the grammar and secondary
modern schools were taken separately a similar—though smaller—
difference would be found. The technical reasons for this are stated in
Appendix 3[1] but briefly it is because co-educational grammar schools,
situated mostly in less populated areas, tend to admit a much larger
percentage of the child population than the single-sex grammar schools,
often situated in large towns and cities. This—and other factors—results
in the average intelligence level of the co-educational grammar school
being lower than that of the single-sex schools, and similarly for its
social class level. This also causes the intelligence and social class levels
of the neighbouring co-educational secondary modern school to be
lower than those of the city secondary modern. If to this we add the
creaming of comprehensive schools (mostly co-educational) by the
neighbouring single-sex grammar school, we can see that the scales are
weighted now heavily against the co-educational schools in any straight

[1] The Douglas national sample—the problems are similar.

comparison made through a national sample. It is all the more surprising that in three large-scale regional studies (where these inequalities are reduced but not removed) the co-educational grammar schools produce the better results.

Douglas and Ross

Much of the work done by Douglas and Ross with their national sample of children is of considerable value, but in view of the publicity given to their work it seems necessary here to state that, for the reasons given in the preceding section and elaborated in Appendix 3, a minor offshoot of this work goes beyond the evidence and gives a misleading impression to the readers when attributing pupils' rate of academic progress to their attendance at a co-educational or single-sex secondary school. As it would serve no useful purpose to give their findings here, and only confuse the reader, they are omitted.

Other researches

Here and there in the research literature are additional pointers to the difference in attainment between co-educated and single-sex educated pupils being greatest in mathematics. Lillis (1965), using a sample of over a thousand pupils, compared academic attainment in single-sex and co-educational Catholic schools in five subjects. Three subjects showed no significant differences, and while in the tenth grade the segregated schools had a statistically significant superiority in Latin, the co-educated boys had a similar superiority in algebra. It would seem that, as in most of such studies, social class factors, as well as school type, are influencing the results, the co-educated pupils usually, for historical reasons and because of the urban–rural variable, being on the average of rather lower social class. Similarly Wawrzyniak (1959) in Bavaria, using a sample of 800 pupils, found that both boys and girls in co-educational schools were better in mathematical and technical thinking, though inferior in verbal ability, compared with pupils of the same sex in segregated schools. An old study by Oksanen (1919) in Finland, which took no account of the handicaps of the co-educational schools as to type of entry, rural position etc, found that although the boys in co-educational schools had in general lower standards than boys in boys' schools they had the highest standard of all groups in mathematics. The most likely explanation for such a result would seem, as mentioned before, to be that the pupils in the co-educational schools were of lower social class and though handicapped in literary subjects they excelled in the subject (mathematics) in which this factor would have least effect. It should not be inferred from this statement that social class is the only force at work.

Discussion

A number of points have been discussed already in the sections on individual researches, but we must now see whether any general pattern emerges and, if this does occur, attempt an overall interpretation. There is no difficulty about the former. Throughout the researches there is a clear superiority of co-educated boys over boys in boys' schools, in spite of the former being handicapped by being of lower social class status and probably of lower intelligence. No adequate compensating factor in favour of the segregated boys' schools has been found. Similar superiority may exist for the co-educated girls over the girls in girls' schools, though in preceding researches its amount is sometimes hidden by the operation of other forces. As we have seen previously, these are that the co-educated girls are younger, they are from a lower social class, and they have a less marked tendency to drop weak subjects. Nor can we ignore the fact that those co-educational schools which are in rural areas admit an appreciably higher percentage of the 11-plus population than do their opposite numbers in the large towns and cities.

The influence of age on attainment is well demonstrated in the work of Lee (1955), quoted already in the chapter on attainment in general, but re-quoted here because it deals specifically with mathematics. After giving tests of attainment to the first five-year levels of a co-educational grammar school she proved that 'the influence of age was strongest amongst the attainment tests at the fourth and fifth-year levels'. The average age difference of three months or more between the co-educated and segregated groups of girls, in most, if not all these researches, cannot therefore be dismissed lightly.

We cannot, however, be certain about the co-educational 'milieu' being responsible for the better progress of the girls, as there are additional factors about which we have insufficient evidence. One is the relative ability of teachers of mathematics in girls' schools compared with mixed schools and the influence of this on comparative achievement. At present there is a distinct shortage of good teachers of mathematics in all grammar schools, and the data in the next chapter provide new though inadequate evidence. On the other hand, the surveys of Cameron, Tyson and Field, from 1923 to 1933, were made before the present shortage of women teachers of mathematics was seriously felt. Indeed, the superior prestige of the older-established girls' schools and their geographical locations would have tended to give them better women teachers in most subjects though perhaps not in mathematics and physical science. If, also, the argument is put that men tend to become better qualified in mathematics than women, and possibly are also better teachers, and this would give co-educated girls an advantage, the reply, justly, is that this is one of the advantages of having co-educational schools.[1] It should be noted here that it is certain that the superiority of the co-educated boys is not due to co-educational schools attracting better teachers; for reasons already stated the boys' schools have an advantage in this respect (see also chapter 4).

A second doubtful factor is the amount of time devoted to mathematics in the two types of school. There is a little tentative evidence that this may be slightly less in both the day and homework timetables of girls' schools, though Cameron's study, *relating to 1923*, does not suggest this. It should also be remembered that the time indicated on a homework timetable does not necessarily represent the actual time spent. We would not be justified, however, in discounting this factor entirely. Nor must we ignore the support which the study of physics and (to a lesser degree) chemistry gives to those who are also studying mathematics; this occurs rather more frequently among girls in co-educational schools than among girls in girls' schools. This second factor, the time spent on mathematics, is the only one which remains to be set against the three forces handicapping the co-educated girls, namely, lower social class, younger age, and the taking of a greater number of weak subjects, and all three are known to be powerful factors. A fourth handicap—lower average intelligence level—has been inferred and also demonstrated for one region.

Though the balance of the argument appears to tip in favour of co-education as a factor in improving girls' attainment in mathematics we cannot say this with complete certainty. If there is such a force at work we do not know precisely how it operates; it may be that the men teachers are more fully qualified, it may be through a pupil variable in that girls learn mathematical reasoning from the boys, or that they acquire a better attitude to the subject, or that their standard improves through friendly rivalry with the opposite sex.

One of the writer's research students (Booth, 1967) investigated another explanation—the possible existence of a sex difference in the ability to teach mathematics, using a sample of over 1,100 boys, 750 girls, 58 male and 30 female teachers. The survey did not produce enough evidence to sustain a theory of sex difference in teaching ability in mathematics in general, but there was an indication that women might teach geometry better than men, because, combining all pupils and comparing the marks obtained by two sets of teachers, there was a statistically significant difference in favour of the women in geometry but not in arithmetic and algebra, though the trends were in the same direction. As, however, the IQ scores of a majority of the pupils were

[1] But see Booth, J. W., 'An examination of the hypothesis that the sex of the teacher is a source of variance in the "O"-level NUJMB mathematics results of pupils in certain co-educational grammar schools', MA thesis, University College of Swansea, 1967.

unavailable the general trends must be regarded with caution, and the result in geometry, though interesting, would need confirmation by other studies.

It is astonishing that so little work has been done to answer some of these questions. The writer also suggests that the social class handicap of the co-educated girls may be felt less in mathematics than in literary subjects, this influence not showing itself so clearly in physics and chemistry because of the low percentage of girls in girls' schools who take these subjects, and because even in these subjects language ability has an influence in examinations.

Finally, there is the general appraisal. When we consider boys and girls together we can say that co-education in some way or other appears to exert a beneficial influence on attainment in mathematics, as measured by external examinations and tests at the age of 16 plus. Though this cannot be said to be proved in a scientific sense there is considerable evidence in support, especially on the boys' side, while there is none whatever for any claim that sex segregation *per se* improves attainment in mathematics.

This conclusion should not be taken as a criticism of any group of teachers or any type of school. It is merely an attempt to establish facts in an area of study where facts have been sadly lacking. Its findings represent only a very small part of the criteria by which a school may be judged. They also relate only to the 'average' school, and this phrase covers a wide range of variation. There will be some single-sex schools where the teaching of mathematics is more efficient than in some co-educational schools.

4

Qualifications and distribution of teachers of mathematics

The survey given here is not based on a national sample but on the relevant population of three contrasted regions, of which two were included because the information was needed to connect up with other research, and the third was added partly as a contrast to the others. The work is an attempt to provide additional evidence bearing on the problem of the discrepancy between the attainment of girls' schools in mathematics, and their attainment in most other subjects, when compared with the attainment of girls in mixed schools, as measured by the first external examination. We have seen that girls in mixed schools, maybe because they took the examination some three months younger and were of rather lower social class, did slightly less well than girls in girls' schools, with mathematics a notable exception. Also relevant to the theme of the chapter is that boys in mixed schools did better than boys in boys' schools in most if not all subjects, including mathematics, in spite of a social class handicap.

Why should girls in mixed schools tend to reach a superior standard in mathematics? Recent research has failed to discover any evidence of a difference between men and women in the ability to teach mathematics as a whole[1] (though such a finding does not *prove* that they are, on the average, equal in this ability). Do the co-educated girls make better progress because they acquire from the boys in the class a more effective approach, or a deeper insight? Is it because they acquire a better attitude to the subject from the boys? Or might the discrepancy be due, in part or wholly, to a difference in the quality of the teachers which the two types of school are able to recruit? This chapter examines the last of these variables.

Academic attainment and teaching ability

The task, then, was to secure some measurement of the ability of the teachers of mathematics in the two types of school. A possible method would have been to send an assessor to see each teacher take a lesson, but this would have been extremely expensive and the necessary

[1] J. W. Booth (1967) in chapter 3. But he found that women may be better teachers of geometry than men.

resources were not available. In addition such an artificial situation might set up a systematic bias in that the two sexes of teachers might respond differently, whether they were forewarned or not. A more practicable method, though admittedly not perfect, was to discover and collate the academic qualifications of the relevant teachers. We know that a teacher with a high degree is not necessarily a good teacher, and a teacher with a poor degree, or no degree, may be a very good teacher indeed. On the other hand, many teachers with a poor degree might be unable to cope efficiently with the intricacies of Advanced level mathematics, and this weakness might conceivably operate at the Ordinary level, though probably only with a small proportion of teachers and only in a few portions of the syllabus. A tenable argument, however, is that the brilliant mathematician might be handicapped in teaching at the Ordinary level because he might be unable to see the difficulties only too apparent to lesser mortals. Rather than depend on such hypotheses, we are on a sounder basis if we rely on the known tendency, proved by research, for there to be a positive association between academic qualifications and classroom teaching ability.

The strength of this association is so central to the argument that it needs to be considered at some length. In this country Lawton (1939), using training college students, found a correlation of 0·45 to 0·48 between academic examination grades and teaching assessment. Vernon (1939), in a factorial analysis of the performance of 560 training college students, reported that teaching skill and marks in various subjects correlated from 0·43 in speech training to 0·17 in arithmetic. Research in America finds a similar association, correlations being usually in the range 0·3 to 0·4. For example Shannon (1941) found that the top third of graduates in scholarship were noticeably better in teaching skills than both the 'average' and the failing thirds.

In order to get more up-to-date evidence the writer found the correlations between the practical teaching marks and the degree class of all graduates studying for the Diploma in Education in the University College of Swansea for three years. The resulting correlations were as follows. In 1961–2, for 90 students 0·25, in 1962–3 for 102 students 0·302, but in 1963–4 only 0·085 for 124 students. When these three figures were combined[1] the mean *r* for the 316 students was 0·203 (±0·054). The low figure for 1963–4 requires comment. In that year the pressure of applicants on places increased and whereas most students with honours degrees were accepted on their academic performance, students with pass degrees were able to gain entry only if they had really good personalities for teaching or if their degree subject was in short supply. Pass students, therefore, being more finely selected on personality grounds, would tend to have a higher average teaching mark

[1] Using Fisher's *z* transformation.

than would a truly representative sample of pass students, thereby reducing the correlation. This factor would probably be operating also in the two previous years, though to a lesser extent. Many pass degree students who failed to gain entry, together with some first-class degree students, would enter the profession without training. The students within the department would therefore be more homogeneous than would the teachers in the schools and this factor would keep the correlation low for the department students. Finally an examination was made of the relationship between the degree class of the mathematics students for all three years and their final teaching marks. This yielded a correlation of 0·24. Though there were only 26 cases, and the figure is therefore not statistically significant, it is given general support by the trend of research findings in this field.[1]

Although this agreement is too low for us to be able to say with confidence that a man with a good honours degree will be a good teacher, it is high enough to enable us to predict with certainty that any very large group of highly qualified grammar school teachers will on the average be better practical teachers than a similar group of lowly-qualified teachers of the same subject, teaching at the same level. We should note that if the original gap between the two groups is according to academic qualification, the corresponding difference in the level of teaching ability will be much reduced, unless the standard of the subject matter taught becomes too difficult for easy comprehension by the less qualified teachers. When the subject matter is very simple there is little or no relationship between academic achievement and success in practical teaching, cf. Fuller (1946) with nursery school teachers. When the subject matter becomes more complicated the relationship becomes closer, cf. Knight (1922), who found that the correlation between intelligence tests and assessments of teaching efficiency was 0·446 for high school teachers but only 0·17 for elementary teachers. As the range of academic ability among the teachers of this survey is very wide, and as the level at which they are required to teach is fairly high, it seems reasonable to estimate that the correlation between their academic qualifications and their teaching ability would probably be somewhere between 0·3 and 0·4.

The samples and criteria

As already explained, the samples are not necessarily representative of the whole of England and Northern Ireland. They appear, however, to be reasonably representative of three areas, namely Northern Ireland,

[1] The correlation would again be kept low by the academic homogeneity of the sample, 18 out of the 26 students having pass degrees.

the West and North Ridings, and Hertfordshire; of these the two Ridings are combined in order to shorten the chapter. Returns were received from 222 schools out of 276, or 80·4 per cent. Of the replies 211 were usable, six of the 222 being excluded because they were comprehensive schools. In all there were 1,036 teachers. We have only one check on whether the non-replying schools had a similar, better, or worse qualified staff of mathematics' teachers than had the schools who replied, and that is that the schools who failed to reply until they received a gentle reminder were very similar to the others in the qualifications of their staffs.

As a check against possible pitfalls, three criteria of comparison were adopted:

1 The average number of pupils per first class honours degree in mathematics, and the average number per first and second class honours in mathematics.

2 The percentage of teachers of mathematics who had first or second class degrees, as above.

3 The degrees (in mathematics) of the highest and the second highest qualified teacher of mathematics in each school.

The figures are now summarized for each region, using the three criteria mentioned.

Northern Ireland

Table 4.1 shows that the boys' schools were appreciably better supplied with honours class I mathematicians than either the girls' or the mixed schools, judged by the number of pupils per class I graduate and by the proportion of such graduates to the other teachers of mathematics in the school. A long way behind come the mixed schools, with the girls' schools third but with not quite such a big gap. When class II are added to the class I graduates the boys' schools remain well in front, with the mixed schools an improved second and the girls' schools still a long way behind. Things, however, are not always what they seem to be, and another factor must be brought into consideration. A much smaller proportion of girls in girls' schools take mathematics, especially in external school examinations, than do pupils in mixed and boys' schools. Girls' schools do not therefore need quite so high a proportion of mathematics teachers per pupil in school. (We are not concerned here with the possibility that a better quality staff might improve the percentage taking mathematics.) It could be argued also, though not with the same cogency, that as girls' schools often have a smaller percentage of examination pupils than have mixed or boys' schools, much of the work is with junior and middle forms, hence the proportion of class I and class II graduates can justifiably be lower. However, girls' schools may rightly retort that the mathematics of any grammar school is probably impoverished if it has no honours graduate of class II or better. The data was therefore analysed in two additional ways: first, by comparing the three types of school according to the degrees of the highest and second highest qualified teachers, second, by comparing them on the basis of the number of candidates entered for the O-level examination (Tables 4.2 and 4.3).

TABLE 4.1   *Teachers of mathematics in N. Ireland grammar schools*[1]

		Pupils per teacher			Teachers' degrees			
	No. of schools	Hons class I	Pupils per class I	Hons I and hons II	Pupils per classes I and II	No. teaching maths	% with class I	% with class I and II
Boys'[2] schools	9	6	804	21	230	50	12	42
Girls' schools	13	3	1581	9	527	56	5·4	16·1
Mixed schools	20	8	1249	33	303	108	7·4	30·6

[1] Pass degrees in mathematics and another subject are classed as 'pass': degrees in other subjects (whatever class) are classed as 'others', together with qualifications like the Teacher's Certificate; a few class I teachers had general degrees including mathematics.
[2] The differences in degree distribution (class I, class II, and the others) between the boys' schools and the girls' schools are significant, by the chi-square test, beyond the 0·025 level, but those between the boys' and mixed schools, and between the mixed and girls' schools, are not statistically significant. As, however, the figures include almost the entire relevant population, we are not therefore concerned with a sample of the region, and there can be little fluctuation in the region itself. The trends are also similar in the other regions. In order to relate the survey as closely as possible to Sutherland's work the date was pushed back to 1962.

Table 4.2 shows that of the nine boys' schools, four had a first class honours graduate as their best qualified mathematics master, and four had a second class honours graduate. Of the twenty mixed schools six had a first class honours teacher as best qualified and eight a second class honours. The figures for the thirteen girls' schools were three first and four second class. At the lower end of the table we see that in only one of the nine boys' schools was a teacher in charge who had a lower qualification than class II (11 per cent). In the twenty mixed schools there were six schools in the same or worse plight (30 per cent), while in the thirteen girls' schools there were six similar cases, i.e. 45 per cent. Incidentally the voluntary schools had better qualified teachers of mathematics than the maintained schools had; the attractions of Belfast may be a partial explanation. (Belfast had eleven firsts in fourteen

TABLE 4.2   *N. Ireland: distribution of highest and second highest qualified teacher of mathematics (in each school) according to type of school*[1]

	Degree qualifications in mathematics				
	Honours				
	I	II	III	Pass	Lower
Boys' schools (9)					
Highest	4	4	0	1	0
Second	1	5	1	2	0
Girls' maintained (5)					
Highest	1	1	1	2	0
Second	0	0	0	4	1
Girls' voluntary (8)					
Highest	2	3	2	0	1
Second	0	1	2	4	1
Mixed maintained (12)					
Highest	2	5	2	2	1
Second	0	3	2	5	2
Mixed voluntary (8)					
Highest	4	3	0	1	0
Second	2	4	0	1	1

[1] If there were two teachers with first class degrees in the same school, one was classed as 'the highest qualified teacher' and the other as the second; similarly with other 'ties'.

schools while there were only five firsts in the twenty-seven schools of the rest of Northern Ireland, and Belfast had fewer pupils.)

To summarize, this table, like the previous one, shows the much better staffing of the boys' schools with first class honours graduates. Both mixed and girls' schools are a long way behind, but the mixed schools are the better staffed of the two.

If, however, the number of examination candidates is used as a basis of comparison, the problem is put into a different perspective

(Table 4.3). Though not a perfect criterion it can be used as a corrective against the faults of other criteria such as the number of pupils in the school. Clearly if an appreciable number of pupils are not taking mathematics—at O-level or before—they do not need teachers of mathematics.

TABLE 4.3   *Teachers of mathematics in N. Ireland grammar schools in relation to examination candidates (1962)*

	No. of schools	Candi- dates in maths O-level	Teachers Hons I in maths	Candi- dates per Hons I	Teachers Hons I and II in maths	Candi- dates per Hons I and II
Boys' schools	9	827	6	138	21	39
Girls' schools	13	580	3	193	9	64
Mixed schools	20	1665	8	208	33	50·5

In this table, though the boys' schools remain clearly the best staffed, the girls' schools have improved their standing. In the number of candidates per class I teacher they are rather better staffed than the co-educational schools, though not in the number per class I and class II teacher combined; the difference, however, has decreased markedly. This situation arises mostly because of the contrast in the percentage of pupils taking mathematics at O-level in the three types of school. If the number of pupils offering the compulsory subject English language be taken as a reasonable basis, the percentage of boys in boys' schools taking mathematics in 1962 was 98 per cent, that in co-educational schools[1] 92 per cent, and that of girls in girls' schools 78 per cent.

A further complication is that the classes in the science sixth of girls' schools are much smaller than those in boys' and co-educational schools (especially the former), and the apparent disadvantage of the girls' schools in staffing would be reduced and might even be removed if this were taken into account. This, however, is in the realm of intangibles.

[1] Boys 92 per cent and girls 91 per cent (to nearest whole number). The percentage of boys in boys' schools is slightly swollen by the inclusion of a number of boys who were re-sitting after a year in the sixth.

We now turn to the next region which is Yorkshire (except the East Riding).

Yorkshire

The boys' schools are appreciably better staffed than the others, particularly when the criterion is the number of pupils per honours graduate as in Table 4.4. In second place, but appreciably behind, are the mixed schools, while in this instance the girls' schools appear only a little less well staffed than the mixed.

TABLE 4.4 *Teachers of mathematics in Yorkshire (except East Riding)* *(Jan. 1962)*[1]

		Pupils per teacher			Teachers' degrees			
No. of schools		Hons class I	Pupils per class I	Hons I and hons II	Pupils per classes I and II	No. teach-ing maths	% with class I	% with classes I and II
Boys' schools	44	28	847	79	300	242	11·6	32·6
Girls' schools	40	11	1957	44	489	179	6·1	24·8
Mixed schools	36	14	1566	54	429	187	7·5	28·9

[1] Teachers with pass degrees in mathematics and another subject are classed as 'pass'; degree in another subject (whatever class) is classed as 'others', together with qualifications like a Teacher's Certificate; a few class I teachers had general degrees including mathematics.

In Table 4.5 the criterion of the qualifications of the best and second best qualified teacher in each school is used.

In this table, although the boys' schools come out best at the top end, they seem to be rather weaker than the mixed schools at the bottom end. Slightly less than a quarter of the girls' schools have a first class graduate as their best qualified teacher of mathematics, whereas the corresponding figure for mixed schools is one-third and for boys' schools rather more than a third. No less than a quarter of the girls' schools had a teacher with a pass degree or lower qualification as their best qualified teacher, whereas only one-eighteenth of the mixed schools and about a fifteenth of the boys' schools are so placed. An overall consideration of all three criteria places the boys' schools clearly in front, with mixed schools second and the girls' schools third.

TABLE 4.5 *Yorkshire (except East Riding): distribution of highest and second highest qualified teacher of mathematics in each school*

| | Degree qualifications in mathematics | | | | |
| | Honours | | | | |
	I	II	III	Pass	Lower
Boys' schools					
Maintained (32)					
Highest	12	12	5	3	0
Second highest	4	12	2	10	4
Independent and direct grant (12)					
Highest	4	8	0	0	0
Second highest	2	3	0	5	2
Totals (44)					
Highest	16	20	5	3	0
Second highest	6	15	2	15	6
Girls' schools					
Maintained (32)					
Highest	7	17	3	2	3
Second highest	0	10	4	11	6
Independent and direct grant (8)					
Highest	2	1	0	1	4
Second highest	1	1	0	2	3
Totals (40)					
Highest	9	18	3	3	7
Second highest	1	11	4	13	9
Mixed schools					
Maintained (36)[1]					
Highest	12	19	3	2	0
Second highest	1	13	11	7	3

[1] Includes one class II hons from one independent school.

Three rows do not add up to the number of schools because a few schools were not large enough to have a second teacher taking mathematics.

We now turn to the third region, Hertfordshire.

Hertfordshire

TABLE 4.6   *Teachers of mathematics in Hertfordshire (Jan. 1962)*

No. of schools		Pupils per teacher				Teachers' degrees		
		Hons class I	Pupils per class I	Hons I and hons II	Pupils per classes I and II	No. teaching maths	% with class I	% with classes I and II
Boys' schools	11	10	544	22	247	63	15·9	34·9
Girls' schools	24	8	1142	31	295	86	9·3	36·0
Mixed schools	14	6	1266	31	246	65	9·2	47·7

Here the position is not quite the same as in the other regions. Although the boys' schools have a very big lead in the proportion of teachers with first class degrees the mixed schools draw level with them in the number of pupils to teachers with class I and class II degrees, and even pass them when teachers with such degrees are reckoned as a proportion of the total mathematics teaching staff. Though the girls' schools are distinctly inferior to the boys' in their proportion of teachers with first class degrees, they come close to the mixed schools. With class II degrees included, however, they fall a little behind the mixed schools; on the other hand, while they are still appreciably behind the boys' schools in the number of pupils to teachers with class I and class II degrees, they even slightly pass them in the percentage of their mathematics staff who have such degrees. A general appraisal of the position is difficult but the boys' schools seem to have a slight lead, with the mixed and girls' schools also very close together. The analysis according to the degrees of the highest and second highest qualified teacher sheds some fresh light on the picture (Table 4.7).

We see that just over half of the boys' schools have a first class honours graduate as their highest qualified teacher, but only one-third of the mixed schools and one-fifth of the girls' schools. Whereas no boys' school has a teacher in charge of mathematics who has a degree lower than class II, there is one mixed school (out of 14) so placed, and almost one-third of the girls' schools. This method of analysis shows more clearly the weak points in the staffing of the girls' schools and places them again third.

TABLE 4.7 *Hertfordshire: distribution of highest and second highest qualified teacher of mathematics in each school*

	Degree qualifications in mathematics				
	Honours				
	I	II	III	Pass	Lower
Boys' schools					
Maintained (4)					
Highest	2	2	0	0	0
Second highest	0	1	1	2	0
Independent and direct grant (7)					
Highest	4	3	0	0	0
Second highest	3	2	0	0	1
Totals (11)					
Highest	6	5	0	0	0
Second highest	3	3	1	2	1
Girls' schools					
Maintained (8)					
Highest	2	6	0	0	0
Second highest	1	2	2	3	0
Independent (16)					
Highest	3	6	2	2	3
Second highest	1	4	1	3	3
Totals (24)					
Highest	5	12	2	2	3
Second highest	2	6	3	6	3
Mixed schools					
Maintained (11)					
Highest	3	8	0	0	0
Second highest	1	7	0	2	1
Independent (3)					
Highest	2	0	1	0	0
Second highest	0	0	1	0	1
Totals (14)					
Highest	5	8	1	0	0
Second highest	1	7	1	2	2

Comment

When the data for the three regions are tentatively combined the following picture emerges:

TABLE 4.8 *Northern Ireland, Yorkshire (except East Riding) and Hertfordshire: distribution of teachers of mathematics*

	Pupils per hons I	Pupils per hons I and II	% teachers hons I	% teachers hons I and II
Maintained schools				
Boys'	21,114	1,005	352	10·1	28·8
Girls'	24,189	2,199	432	5·2	26·3
Mixed	32,785	1,639	353	6·7	31·1
Voluntary, Independent, and direct grant schools				
Boys'	12,863	559	207	15·6	42·2
Girls'	11,224	1,020	401	10·2	25·9
Mixed	6,737	842	269	13·1	41·0

The table shows that, whichever criterion is used, the boys' schools, both maintained and non-maintained, are better provided with mathematicians who have first class honours degrees than are the girls' and mixed grammar schools. In second place, a long way behind, are the mixed schools, and the girls' schools bring up the rear; the gap between the boys' and mixed schools is a little larger than that between the mixed and girls' schools. When class I and class II graduates in mathematics are combined, the mixed schools draw level with the boys'. (Within this criterion, of course, the boys' schools still retain their superiority in the proportion of class I degrees.) Using the same criterion, the girls' schools draw up much closer to the other schools (with the above reservation) except in the non-maintained sector. *When assessing this position, however, we must again remember that the girls' schools in comparison with the others have a much smaller proportion of pupils taking mathematics, and in particular a much smaller proportion of pupils taking mathematics for the first and second external examinations.* Unfortunately this is a rather vague factor, for which it is difficult to

73

allow, but we have seen something of its effect in Northern Ireland, and examination statistics show us that the pattern is general.

The one certain fact which emerges is that the boys' schools are better staffed than either the mixed or girls' schools, whatever criterion is used. The apparent difference between the girls' and mixed schools is reduced when regard is paid to the argument set out in the previous paragraph.

Evidence from a later survey conducted by the National Foundation of Educational Research and published in the book *Achievement in Mathematics*,[1] is appropriate here. The data which relate to this chapter were obtained in 1964 from a national sample of 106 grammar and 97 direct grant and independent secondary schools. (Comprehensive schools were in the survey, but for this aspect the figures are said by the editor to be not as reliable as he would wish.) The number of schools is small when divided into girls', boys' and co-educational, but the sample has the advantage of being randomly selected from stratified categories.

It was found that the boys' schools had an average of 5·92 mathematics teachers for grammar schools, the girls' schools 4·73 and the co-educational 5·63. As the categories of schools were similar in size the smaller provision in girls' schools is rightly attributed to less need for mathematics teachers, girls' O-level classes and sixth form science classes being smaller than those of boys' and co-educational schools. Similarly in the direct grant and independent categories of school the boys' schools had an average of 6·34 teachers of mathematics and the girls' only 3·75; the low figure of 2·60 for co-educational schools is accounted for—at least in part—by their lack of the direct grant category.

More illuminating is the provision of mathematics teachers with specialist training. The average for boys' grammar schools was 3·86, for girls' 3·46 and for co-educational 3·22. For direct grant and independent categories the boys' schools have the highest average for specialists, the girls' schools come next and the co-educational last. Expressed as percentages of specialists to the whole mathematics staff the girls' grammar schools come out best at 73·2, the boys' schools next with 65·2 and the co-educational last with 57·2. Surprisingly the same order was obtained, again at a lower level, in the direct grant and independent category.

Combining the two surveys, i.e. the writer's and that of the NFER, an overall appraisal leads on the boys' side to the indubitable fact that in the years 1962–4 the boys' schools were easily the best staffed. The position for girls' schools is not so clear, especially when one endeavours to allow for the reduced demand for and maybe reduced load on teachers of mathematics in these schools, particularly in the science sixth.

[1] Acknowledgments are due to the NFER, the editor Dr Pidgeon and the contributors J. Hall, G. Peaker and N. Postlethwaite.

Tentatively it looks as if the co-educational schools might be slightly the better staffed—though the results from the small sample of schools in the NFER survey do not support this judgment.

Though these results are for the early sixties many of the principal factors contributing to them have been in action for most of the century. Co-educational grammar schools have always been predominantly in rural areas while single-sex schools have been sited more often in cities and large towns. Co-educational schools in this country are in general much newer foundations than single-sex schools, and direct grant status, with all the prestige that this implies, is almost confined to the latter. Again, good women teachers of mathematics have been in short supply for a long time, though the supply for girls' schools may have been better in the 1920s and 1930s when there seemed to be an abundance of teachers chasing too few jobs. It would have been easier and more satisfactory if the relevant statistics on the teaching staffs of co-educational and single-sex grammar schools had been available throughout the years since 1925, but in default of these the evidence provided here is not without value.

To conclude this aspect it should be emphasized that this data compares the *attainment* of groups of teachers; the differences between them in *teaching efficiency* will probably be less wide than are those in attainment.

What effect does this distribution of mathematics teachers have on the findings of past research on the comparative attainment of boys', girls' and co-educational schools in mathematics at the level of the first external examination? In the case of Northern Ireland it shows that the distribution was probably a hidden variable slightly handicapping the girls' schools; to what extent we do not know. If we use this argument, however, it is also applicable to the co-educational schools *vis-à-vis* the boys' schools, and as the boys in co-educational schools reached a rather higher standard than their counterparts in the boys' schools in Sutherland's enquiry (1961) this must have been in spite of their having less highly qualified teachers, a fact which has not been reported previously. Indeed there seems to be little doubt that for many years the boys' grammar schools in Britain have been appreciably better staffed in mathematics than the co-educational schools, and it is legitimate to ask why the co-educated boys, in survey after survey, reach a higher standard than boys in boys' schools. With the girls' groups the finding cannot be as clear-cut, but it would seem to be unlikely that the one variable which may be favouring the co-educated girls, i.e. the possibly slightly better qualified staff, when set against all those favouring the girls' schools —an intake higher in intelligence and social class, more drop-outs in mathematics, older age of candidates etc—could account for the steady superiority of the co-educated girls in mathematical attainment.

Addendum

In this addendum the main theme of comparison between single-sex and co-educational schools is put on one side in order to present some comments from heads which illustrate the scarcity of well-qualified teachers of mathematics.

First, the comments from girls' schools:

'Our best maths teacher went to New Zealand last year. I had *one* application, fortunately a fairly good one.'

'An honours graduate in physics, when appointed, had to teach all advanced mathematics because nobody else on the staff then was able to do it.'

'This school last had a teacher qualified to be head of department in maths in July 1952.'

'Failed degree in maths but is excellent teacher.'

'A pass graduate is in charge of the mathematics department. No honours graduate applied for the post in spite of the PSR allowance.'

'I had to fill in with an unqualified teacher as I had appointed her before she sat for finals (and failed one paper). She had enough for the Ministry to sanction appointment unqualified.'

Then the co-educational schools:

'For five years we were without head of department. No. 2, offered it, declined post not wanting responsibility. We usually have to ask our physics and chemistry teachers to do either four periods of advanced senior work per week or one junior form for the year.'

'I had no applications for a new maths–physics post needed owing to increased numbers.'

'Owing to increased numbers I needed a third full-time teacher and received one application from a third class honours holder.'

'There is no main honours specialist in mathematics in the school. The last effort to advertise for one produced only a graduate in engineering. The best pupils are not receiving the broad fundamental approach to Advanced level study in mathematics, so necessary for groundwork in the faculties of science and applied science at universities.'

Although this survey was made a few years ago there appears to be no evidence of any change for the better.

Educationists have been wondering why there are vacant places in the faculties of pure science and in engineering at the universities. Here appears to be at least part of the answer. Mathematics is not only an important subject in its own right, it is also an indispensable tool for good work in physics and in chemistry and in many other subjects. If the teaching in mathematics is poor it is not only the attainment which suffers; pupils become discouraged and turn to other subjects. This is a process which may have its beginnings even in the junior forms and act throughout the school. It may be that this is happening in many of the nation's schools.

5

Teaching of mathematics:
a new theory

The standard of mathematics teaching in schools and the shortfall in the supply of candidates for admission to university science departments are matters of national concern. Mathematics is so fundamental to success in the sciences that the two trends are probably connected. There is little likelihood of the difficulty being met by any immediate increase in the proportion of well-qualified teachers of mathematics, but the problem can be approached from another direction. During the discussion readers may wonder what relevance there is for the subject of the book, but that will appear later.

Good motivation in the pupils is fundamental to good attainment and fundamental to the desire among pupils to continue with the subject. From some research in which the writer has recently been engaged it appears possible that with the co-operation of the teachers this motivation might be markedly improved. The research has been dealing, among other things, with the popularity and unpopularity of teachers (anonymously) as viewed by some thousands of their ex-pupils, drawn from all over the country. In free responses on this topic the respondents gave reasons for the popularity estimates they made, naming teachers of mathematics far more frequently than teachers of other subjects as having a bad effect on them; the comments often added that this had caused them to hate mathematics. There was no need for these ex-pupils to mention any subject teacher as such, and indeed some subjects were not named at all and others only a few times. All the respondents were intending teachers, who would therefore not be the least able of the grammar school pupils and would be expected to have a favourable attitude to academic subjects in general.

Examples of these remarks are:

'Fear of some masters, i.e. maths, inhibited progress and likewise throughout life.'

'Maths teacher continually picked on me.'

'A sarcastic mathematics teacher [had a distinctly bad influence on my personality].'

'Frightened to participate in maths—teacher had temper if wrong answer given.'

'He nurtured in me an aversion for mathematics by always shouting and being sarcastic.'

'This teacher had a frightening temper and I have missed the chance of basic knowledge of maths. Also I now hate a subject which all my family are brilliant in, and I feel I should have been.'

'He gave me an inferiority complex where maths was concerned, which effect I felt for years.'

'The maths teacher put me off maths once and for all. I never had her as she only took the 4th and 5th years and she left in my 3rd year, but the fear of having her terrified me and this feeling was transferred to the subject.'

'In junior part of school—not very good at maths—frightened into doing it because I did not want to be a failure. *She was nice enough in other subjects.*'

'Sarcastic maths teacher very quick with nasty remarks—had various favourites. Made me sarcastic.'

'My first maths mistress had a definitely bad influence on my personality. She had bright red fingernails and shouted when I went wrong.'

In passing, the influence of this attitude on science teaching, where the subject matter is partly similar, is illustrated by:

'The master who taught science had such an antagonism towards those who could not understand the work that I still have a dislike (almost fear) of things scientific.'

As the research was not specifically comparing the popularity or unpopularity of the various subjects and of their teachers, many complaints did not specify the subject, but showed the influence of the same attitude, e.g.:

'Being weak in a certain subject the aggressiveness of the teacher undoubtedly caused nervousness and reticence', and, 'He came down on me for not being able to do the work—made the class laugh at me.'

It would be absurd to suggest that teachers of mathematics are as a group less pleasant than their colleagues, unless being dragooned into teaching a subject in which one is not properly qualified has this effect. Another explanation seems more likely, namely that the precise nature of the subject matter, with the oral work which is involved, either causes the teachers to be more impatient with pupils' incorrect answers or causes pupils to react more strongly when they have made a mistake and receive a scathing comment from the teacher. Answers are usually either right or wrong—sometimes blatantly wrong—and to be publicly shamed in front of classmates is something which many pupils feel deeply. Allied to this may be the relationship between the intellectual effort and attention needed for mental calculation and the interference with this process caused by emotional stress. Most of us have experienced these extreme examples when we have been pounced upon and required to give an immediate answer, only to find that we were unable to think at all. As Robert Bridges said, though with a different meaning, 'There are moments when all thought fled, scared from me, in my bewilderment.'

Emotional tenseness

Other elements in the situation would tend to add fuel to the flames. The public working out of mathematical processes produces the atmosphere of a test, and an emotional tenseness, and often anxiety, which would usually be absent in the teaching of subjects such as English (apart from grammar), history and geography. (A similar tenseness probably occurs in the teaching of certain aspects of other subjects where the subject matter demands a somewhat similar type of reasoning and gives rise to a 'test situation', as in French, Latin and the physical sciences, but as only parts of the lesson, and here the discussion will be limited to mathematics, as logically this seems to be the subject most affected.) This tenseness may even be shared to a minor degree by the teacher, who also has to work out the computation and try to avoid error. In an atmosphere of this kind it may not be quite as easy for the teacher to preserve an encouraging attitude as it is for those who are using literary material; from the pupil's viewpoint a scathing remark while in the stress of a test situation might well have a reinforced effect. Somehow the narrative and discussion of a lesson in history or in English literature would appear to produce an atmosphere in which an impatient retort to a pupil's mistake is less likely to arise. The writer can find no mention in any work on the teaching of mathematics of the effect on pupil–teacher relationships of this continual test situation.

We cannot suddenly alter the temperaments of teachers of mathematics, but if the publicity given to these findings can persuade enough of those teachers who habitually allow their impatience to get the better of themselves to modify their attitudes in the direction of encouragement, we might have a surprising—and in the event an apparently inexplicable—increase in the number of pupils who wish to continue with mathematics. In the training of teachers of mathematics this is a point which needs considerable emphasis. The argument is particularly applicable to girl pupils, who are less confident than boys and have a greater inner need of encouragement; at the secondary stage they tend to be somewhat afraid of the subject, and if fear of the teacher is added the only motivation the girl has is to avoid the subject at all costs.

The relevance of all this to co-education is that the two previous volumes of this series[1] have demonstrated that both boys and girls, particularly the latter, are happier in co-educational schools, and prefer their atmosphere to that of single-sex schools. (It is imperative to remember that we are speaking of averages as there is a wide range within each type of school.) Especially pertinent is the finding that the relationship between pupils and staff is friendlier in co-educational schools. This being so it is by no means impossible that there is less emotional tension in the mathematics lessons of co-educational schools than in those of single-sex schools, and the pupils, being more relaxed, enjoy the lessons more, or, in some cases—let's be realistic—hate it appreciably less. A possible sign of this is that in the researches described there has been a strong and persistent tendency for a greater proportion of girls from co-educational schools to take mathematics at Ordinary level than of those from girls' schools. Such a pleasanter atmosphere might also account for the tendency for co-educated girls, in spite of their handicaps, to have a higher standard of attainment in this subject than girls from girls' schools.

But the world is not a simple place and there are so many forces bearing on the academic attainment of pupils, some pulling in different directions, that it is difficult to strike a balance. However, the proof of the pudding is in the eating, and there is no gainsaying that girls in co-educational schools do reach a higher attainment level in mathematics than girls in girls' schools, and that this is pre-eminently the subject in which they do best when all subjects are compared. This does not mean that other factors cannot be put forward to explain the findings, e.g. that the social class handicap of the co-educated girls is likely to operate less in mathematics than in any other subject, or that the probably better qualified mathematics teachers of co-educational schools would in themselves ensure a high attainment level for their pupils. To this last argument two points may be made in reply. First, that in the previous chapter we have seen that as a much smaller percentage of girls in girls' schools take mathematics than do *girls and boys combined* in co-educational schools, they do not need the same proportion of qualified mathematics teachers *per pupil on register* as do co-educational schools. Second, that as the boys' schools have by far the best qualified mathematics staff how do we explain the astonishing steadiness of their inferiority to boys in

[1] Dale, R. R., *Mixed or single-sex school?* vols I and II, Routledge & Kegan Paul, 1969 and 1971.

co-educational schools in mathematics attainment at Ordinary level—and in spite of their superiority in social class and almost certain superiority in intelligence level—a combination which should ensure them a considerably better performance than their rivals?

For the boys the better atmosphere in the co-educational classroom seems to be the only remaining variable powerful enough to provide the explanation, though it is not claimed that this is proved. It may well be, however, that to raise the standard in mathematics in the junior and middle forms a somewhat unexpected solution would be to make all schools co-educational!

The problem is pursued below in chapter 10, 'Attitudes to arithmetic and mathematics'.

6

Attainment in English

This chapter compares attainment in single-sex and co-educational grammar schools in the most important subject in the curriculum. In the studies analysed here attainment in English is measured by the performance of pupils taking the external examinations at the School Certificate or Ordinary level; except for the special case of the 'matched samples' survey all are on a large scale, the smallest group being some 400 pupils. Unfortunately, however, there is not as much research material available as for the previous studies.

Tyson's survey

Tyson analysed the School Certificate examination results in English[1] of the Northern Universities Joint Matriculation Board—hundreds of schools and thousands of pupils. He compared the percentage of credits gained by candidates of four types—boys in boys' schools, boys in co-educational schools, girls in girls' schools and girls in co-educational schools. (It is important to observe the exact nature of the criterion in each of these surveys.) The 'raw findings' were as follows. Co-educated boys had a statistically significant greater percentage of credits in both 1925 (6·1 per cent) and 1926 (4·7 per cent), over boys in boys' schools. Segregated girls had a non-significant superiority of 1·9 per cent in 1925 and a significant superiority of 5·7 per cent in 1926.

Though the differences in 'raw scores' are small, they conform to the general pattern, i.e. that the difference between the boys' groups is in favour of the co-educational schools, and that between the girls' groups is smaller but in favour of girls' schools.

As a much greater proportion of co-educational than of single-sex grammar schools are situated in rural rather than urban areas, Tyson removed this variable by calculating the results for 1926 separately for rural schools. The hypothesis is that this sample of co-educational schools would be less handicapped in staffing and type of pupil when compared with similar types of single-sex schools. In seven out of ten instances, taking all academic subjects for which details are available, the results conformed to the hypothesis. The attainment of the girls in

[1] This included literature.

English changed as anticipated, the co-educated girls improving their position relative to the segregated girls, so that there was no difference in actual scores between the two groups. We would expect this improvement to be stronger in English than in other subjects, as attainment in English is probably more affected by the social class differences produced in part by the rural–urban factor. Rather strangely the marks of the boys in English did not conform to the pattern found in other subjects and that found with the girls in English, the superiority of the co-educated boys being reduced to a statistically non-significant advantage of 1·3 per cent of credits. Such a deviation from the expected pattern led the writer to make a very careful re-examination of the evidence. Though this revealed no obvious arithmetical slip it gives rise to the suggestion that the findings for rural boys in attainment in English be treated with some reservation, unless the result is confirmed by recalculation from the original raw data, or by another study.

We must now ask ourselves whether these samples of candidates from the four groups can validly be compared. On this occasion the subject was virtually compulsory; no group was made more finely selected than any other by candidates dropping a weak subject. The percentage of candidates taking English literature in 1925 was 99·5. There is, however, an appreciable age difference between the girls' groups, the co-educated girls being at least four months younger than the segregated girls. When both rural and urban schools are included in the sample, the pupils in the co-educated schools will almost certainly be handicapped by being of lower social class. This is because of the urban–rural differences, and also because the greater age of many of the single-sex schools gives them a higher prestige, and attracts pupils from higher class homes. The same reasons should help the single-sex schools to recruit a better qualified staff. We have noted before that the sample contains an appreciable number of direct grant schools, and only one of these is mixed. In this study, therefore, the co-educated pupils appear to do slightly better than the single-sex schools when the results of the two sexes are combined, in spite of the handicaps mentioned. The evidence must, however, be considered in the light of other research. This is especially important, as we lack a detailed picture of the 'clinical' situation in the schools, and know from experience that this can sometimes reveal the existence of a variable which surprises the researcher.

King's survey

King investigated the examination results at the *School Certificate*[1] level of the University of London Examination Board in 1945. As

[1] The O-level pass was designed to be equivalent to 'credit' in the School Certificate examination.

explained previously, King's results are not as valid for our purpose as we would like, as many men teachers were still serving in the armed forces at the time, and this might well have penalized boys' schools and to some extent mixed schools, compared with girls' schools. The figures are therefore presented tentatively, and before considering those variables which are extraneous to the co-education versus segregation controversy.

In English language the percentage of candidates who reached the pass standard or above was 85·1 for boys' schools, 86·1 for mixed and 91·0 for girls' schools. In English literature the percentages were 79·7 for boys' schools, 84·4 for mixed schools and 88·6 for girls' schools. Unfortunately, King could not obtain separate figures for boys and girls in mixed schools. Taking only the difference due to sex, we would expect the mixed schools to be approximately half-way between the boys' and girls' schools. In fact the mixed schools are well below this point in language, though still in between the others, while in literature they are slightly above it. If we take as the criterion the percentage of candidates obtaining either a 'credit' or a 'very good' the lead of the girls' schools is increased, the figures being: boys' schools 54·7 per cent; mixed schools 55 per cent; and girls' schools 62·8 per cent.

The question again arises whether the samples are sufficiently equal in nature as to make the comparison reasonably valid. This is more dubious than with Tyson's northern samples, partly because the co-educational schools are even more confined to the less populated areas, with the exception of those in Middlesex. This factor, together with the greater prestige of the longer established and sometimes independent or direct grant single-sex schools, is likely to increase the social class and staff differences, thereby handicapping the co-educational schools. In London itself, for example, there were in 1945 only two or three co-educational grammar schools, but a plethora of single-sex schools, many of them direct grant or independent. Many of these direct grant and independent schools would have a more highly selected entry than the average mixed school. On the other hand, only a proportion of the independent schools would take the London General Schools examination.

Another weighty factor is the average age of the samples. In all the other studies, the average age of the two groups of boys has been the same and the co-educated girls have been at least three months younger than the segregated girls, but in King's study the average age of the samples is not similarly investigated.

In view of the strength of the factors which cannot be assessed, especially the absence of men teachers in the armed forces, no definite conclusion can be made.

Sutherland's survey

Sutherland used the Ordinary level marks of pupils who sat the Northern Ireland Senior Certificate examinations in Protestant schools in 1957. There were 23 co-educational schools, 17 girls' schools, and 9 boys' schools. The last sample was unfortunately small if the school is taken as the unit, but the boys' schools tend to be large and sent in almost 400 candidates. Most of the nine are also of rather higher status than most of the co-educational schools, and if the staffing in mathematics is a fair criterion they are also better staffed. English language and English literature were taken as separate subjects, and a pass in the former was essential for the gaining of a certificate. A large majority of candidates attempted to gain the certificate at one sitting, though they were allowed two.

If we first look at the raw scores, without considering other factors, we find that the single-sex schools obtain slightly better scores in both subjects. The segregated girls have an average mark in English language which is 1·9 per cent higher than that of the co-educated girls, a lead statistically significant though small. In English literature the difference is 4·2 per cent and statistically highly significant. The difference is less between the boys' groups, the segregated boys averaging 2·7 per cent higher (significant at 0·05 level) in English language and almost 1 per cent higher in English literature.[1] Though this last difference lacks statistical significance, and may have occurred by chance, it is supported by the general trend of the results. On the other hand, the only difference which is of appreciable practical significance is that between the girls' groups in English literature, and new light will be thrown on it by an enquiry made by the writer which is described in the next section.

Sutherland wisely recognized that differences between schools within any one of the four groups (e.g. boys' schools) are of importance, particularly with small numbers of schools; she therefore carried out a more conservative small sample test of significance, in which the average mark gained by each school is used as the unit, instead of the marks of individuals. None of the differences between the segregated and co-educational schools in the two subjects remained statistically significant. This result indicates that the variation of the average mark gained by schools within each group is more important than the relatively small differences between the co-educated and segregated groups.

However, the pattern of slight superiority of score of the segregated

---

[1] The figures are Sutherland's. The writer, checking from the individual marks, confirms the averages for English language (boys) and English literature (co-educated girls), but his average for girls' schools is 207·0 instead of Sutherland's 208·0, but the alteration is quite minor. (Checks in other subjects confirm the accuracy of Sutherland's averages.)

schools was not entirely obliterated, and we must look for influences which might have produced this superiority. In the first chapter we saw for example that the co-educated girls were three months younger, on the average, than the segregated girls, because 29 per cent of the co-educated girls took the shorter five-year course, whereas this was taken by only some 12 per cent of the segregated girls. When pupils take the examination at a young age through being put in a quicker stream, this is usually because they are more able; such pupils would normally improve their mark appreciably after an extra year and this would have improved the average mark of the co-educated girls, though the extent of the improvement cannot be ascertained. In the case of the boys' groups the average ages are the same.

Further, we have seen that one-third of the pupils in the girls' schools are from the first two social classes, whereas only 19 per cent of the co-educated girls belong to these classes. The difference is roughly reversed at the bottom end. This factor might well be sufficient in itself to produce the small differences in the standard of attainment.[1] The position of the boys' groups is similar to that of the girls', and the same argument applies.

Dale's check

Because of the inadequacy of our knowledge in this field, the writer made a detailed analysis of the marks gained in English language and literature in the Ordinary level examination for the Northern Ireland Senior Certificate in 1959. The population consists of all those pupils from Protestant schools who had not already obtained passes in three or more of the compulsory subjects. This was the same type of candidate as in the Sutherland enquiry. This check—it makes no claim to be a complete survey—was made partly to confirm Sutherland's work, to see if similar differences were to be found in another year, but a more important aim was to see if a detailed study of the marks would give us more insight into the problem. Fortunately both aims were achieved. The results are closely similar to those of Sutherland, but an unsuspected factor was found.

We will begin with the 'raw scores' and later examine their meaning. The 'raw average' of the girls' schools in English language is 209·6 (*maximum 400*), and that of the co-educated girls 203·8, giving the former a small lead of 1·5 per cent (Sutherland in 1957, 1·9 per cent). In English literature, however, the girls in girls' schools had a more substantial lead, averaging 204·7 while the co-educated girls averaged 183·2, the difference being 5·4 per cent (Sutherland in 1957, 4·2 per cent). Passing on to the boys, the average mark of the boys from boys' schools was 208·0 and that of the co-educated boys 198·7, the difference

[1] Readers are referred to the discussion of this point in the first chapter.

being 2·3 per cent (Sutherland in 1957, 2·5 per cent). In English literature the difference was smaller, the boys from boys' schools averaging 178·0 and the co-educated boys 176·1, a difference of only 0·5 per cent (Sutherland in 1957, almost 1 per cent).

In three cases, the 1957 lead of the single-sex schools has been reduced; in the fourth—girls taking English literature—it has increased. A second apparently discrepant statistic is that the segregated girls have a greater lead in literature than in language, while the segregated boys reverse these positions. These factors, together with several other 'pointers', caused the writer to undertake a detailed examination of the mark sheets, particularly in English literature.

Before giving the results of this section of the work, it is necessary to mention that the forces affecting the marks in the Sutherland enquiry were almost certainly still at work in 1959. In brief, the co-educated girls will probably be handicapped in age, by the shorter five-year course, by being of lower social class,[1] and by having, on the average, less highly qualified teachers. Let us now return to the intriguing result in English literature. Here the mark sheets showed 'a reversal of expectancy'. Normally when a pupil 'drops' a subject it is because he or she is less good in that than in other subjects; frequently a subject is dropped because the pupil would be a certain failure. In this subject, however, other factors produced a reverse effect, so that the pupils who did not present themselves in English literature at Ordinary level were appreciably better than those who did present themselves, *as judged by their average mark in English language.*[2] The statement should be qualified by the consideration that some pupils who did not take English literature may have been able to devote more time to English language than pupils who took both subjects; this may especially have been the case for the pupils of the two boys' schools which appeared to adopt a policy of not entering boys for English literature—and these pupils formed the great majority of such cases in the group of boys' schools.

Apart from the time factor just mentioned, three main reasons for this reversal of expectancy could be distinguished, though there may be others. The first is, that almost a seventh of the candidates who *did not* take English literature at Ordinary level took it at Advanced level (*one third in the case of co-educated girls*). These were clearly good candidates and do not appear in the Ordinary level statistics, thereby reducing the

[1] The writer attempted to get information about the social class of each pupil so that this factor could have been held constant, but the responsible authorities rightly considered that the information would be too difficult to get retrospectively.

[2] Correlation between English language and English literature is of course far from perfect. For segregated girls the coefficient was 0·57 (by Sheppard's Method of Unlike Signs). For co-educated boys the corresponding figure is 0·47 (Tetrachoric correlation).

potential average mark of the co-educated girls. This illustrates how a hidden factor may change the interpretation given to differences in raw scores even when a number of unwanted factors have been taken into consideration. The second reason refers back to the two boys' schools of the previous paragraph. One of these had easily the highest average of all boys' schools in English language, yet only two of the 50 candidates took English literature. The second had the fourth highest average in English language, yet only 10 out of 42 took English literature. The

TABLE 6.1 *Performance in English language of pupils who also took English literature and those who did not: Northern Ireland Senior Certificate (Ordinary level), 1959 (Dale check)*

	Boys in:				Girls in:			
	Co-ed schools		Boys' schools		Co-ed schools		Girls' schools	
	N	Mean (Maximum 400)	N	Mean	N	Mean	N	Mean
English language	685	198·7	550	208·0	549	203·8	473	209·6
Did not take literature (Mark in language)	56	205·5	93	222·0	57	229·0	29	214·3
Took literature	629	198·1	457	205·3	492	200·9	444	209·2
Took A-level literature	10 of the 56		6 of the 93		18 of the 57		2 of the 29	

combined weight of these schools automatically produced the 'reversal of expectancy' for the boys. Yet there is probably a third factor, namely that English literature is not as important a career subject as French and Latin for those better pupils who wish to go on to the university, and these subjects are in the same examination group, as also are history and several other languages; English literature is therefore dropped.

What impact has all this on the comparison of attainment between the single-sex and co-educational schools? Many readers will see this more clearly in the following table, but the gist of it is as follows. The 8 per cent of co-educated boys who did not take English literature at the Ordinary level did not score sufficiently highly in English language to give us any confidence that they would have effected more than a small improvement in the co-educated boys' English literature mark if they had taken the subject, whereas the 17 per cent of segregated boys who did not take English literature at Ordinary level scored highly in English language, and might have brought about an appreciable improvement in the marks of segregated boys if they had taken the subject. With the girls the reverse might well have happened. The 10 per cent of co-educated girls who did not take Ordinary level English literature scored far higher in English language than those who *did* take English literature, and would probably have produced an improvement in the co-educated girls' average, whereas the 6 per cent of segregated girls who did not take English literature (O-level) scored only a little better in English language than those who did, and could have had little effect on the segregated girls' average. To sum up, the above factor probably 'artificially' increased the superiority of the segregated girls in 'raw score' and reduced that of the segregated boys. As was the case in Sutherland's research with regard to English language and literature the differences in the average attainment of schools within the co-educational group, and similar differences within the two segregated groups, are more important in practice (and statistically) than the amount of the difference between the co-educational schools on the one hand and the single-sex schools on the other. If, for example, we take the school as the unit, as Sutherland did, differences between single-sex and co-educated pupils, for both boys and girls, lack statistical significance, i.e. they may have occurred by chance. This does not mean, of course, that we have proved that there is no difference, and the fact that both researches find differences which are very similar in amount and direction should not be overlooked. Here, however, we are primarily concerned with demonstrating the amount of the difference in attainment between schools of the same type. This principle is of cardinal importance in all these comparisons.

If we examine the school averages for the girls, in English language, we find that the co-educational schools range from 237·1 (maximum 400) to 180·7, a difference of 56·4, i.e. 14·1 per cent, while the girls' schools range from 233·5 to 187·4, a difference of 46·1, i.e. 11·5 per cent. Nor are the high ranges due to isolated exceptions, as will be seen from Table 6.2. In contrast, the difference between the average attainment of all co-educated girls and that of all segregated girls is only 5·8, i.e. 1·5 per cent. But the distribution of the averages is best appreciated from the table.

From the table[1] we see that for boys the average mark of co-educational schools ranges from 230·6 to 168·6, a difference of 62·0, i.e. 15·5 per cent, and that of boys' schools ranges from 238·4 to 188·1, a difference of 50·3

[1] In assessing these averages readers should bear in mind that they are affected by many forces which are outside the control of the school, for example factors related to social class.

or 12·6 per cent. In contrast, the difference between the average of all boys in boys' schools and that of all co-educated boys is only 2·3 per cent.

Similarly in English literature, the average mark in co-educational schools (girls' group) ranges from 226·9 to 156·1, a difference of 70·8,

TABLE 6.2 *Average marks in English language of co-educational and single-sex schools: Northern Ireland Senior Certificate (Ordinary level), 1959 (Dale check)*

Maximum 400

Girls' groups[1]

C 237·1	G 215·4	C 207·3	C 201·1	G 194·3
G 233·5	C 215·0	G 206·4	C 200·9	G 191·2
C 232·1	G 214·3	C 205·8	C 199·8	G 190·0
C 230·1	C 213·9	C 204·8	C 199·2	C 189·6
G 229·4	G 213·7	G 204·3	G 198·0	C 188·0
C 225·9	G 209·8	C 203·8	C 196·6	G 187·4
C 222·3	C 209·3	G 202·3	C 196·1	C 180·7
G 221·1	C 209·2	G 201·2	C 195·0	

Boys' groups

B 238·4	C 211·5	B 205·2	C 196·4	B 188·1
C 230·6	C 210·3	C 203·6	C 195·9	C 187·4
C 222·9	B 210·0	B 201·5	C 193·9	C 187·3
B 221·9	C 210·0	C 200·7	C 192·1	C 176·5
C 219·4	B 208·2	B 200·6	C 192·1	C 170·8
B 218·9	C 207·1	C 200·3	C 191·6	C 168·6
C 211·6	C 206·3			

[1] C = co-educational schools, G = girls' schools, B = boys' schools.

being 17·7 per cent, while that of the girls' schools is 229·3 to 160·7, or 17·2 per cent. On the other hand the difference between all segregated girls and all co-educated girls is only 4·3 per cent. The same picture is to be seen in the boys' groups. The range for co-educational schools is 216·6 to 119·6, a difference of 97·0 or almost 25 per cent, but the lowest school average is an isolated one from a small school. If, however, we substitute the next lowest average at 144·1 the range is still 18·1 per cent. The highest average for boys' schools is 212·4 and the lowest 143·3 (disregarding a two-candidate entry which averaged 126!), the range being 17·3 *per cent*. But the overall difference between segregated and co-educated boys is only 0·5 per cent.

Dale's survey

In a comparison of raw scores the co-educated girls do almost as well as their matched pairs from girls' schools, both in English language and English literature, the differences being minimal, and in view of the several handicaps of the co-educated girls, outlined previously, it certainly cannot be said from this evidence that the co-educated girls make worse progress than those from girls' schools in these subjects.

Although the co-educated boys did less well than those from boys' schools in English language in 1949 the difference was not statistically significant and was turned into a statistically highly significant advantage for the co-educated boys in the much larger sample of 1950. In English literature the co-educated boys did better in both years, their advantage in 1949 being statistically significant and that in 1950 being highly significant. As the groups were closely matched we can say that for this survey the co-educated boys made better progress in English literature and minimally better progress in English language. Taking the two sexes together the co-educated pupils have a clearly discernible advantage.

The quality of the staffing is an unknown variable, but it would be very surprising if the girls' schools had less highly qualified staff than the co-educational schools in English and unexpected if the corresponding boys' schools were less well staffed than the co-educational.

Conclusions

An overall appraisal of the research position is difficult. In Tyson's enquiry (two years) the co-educational schools were slightly superior in raw scores; in King's doubtful[1] enquiry they were slightly inferior. In Sutherland's research, confirmed by Dale's check, they were also slightly inferior, but in Dale's enquiry (1949–50) they have a clearly discernible advantage. It is also necessary to state yet again that the co-educated pupils were handicapped by being, on average, of lower social class, and usually of lower average intelligence level, though these factors were largely controlled in Dale's survey. Except in this 'matched samples' survey the co-educated girls were several months younger, and a greater percentage of them in Northern Ireland took the shorter course. In view of these unwanted variables it would certainly be highly dangerous for anyone to interpret these small differences between the mixed and single-sex schools as meaning that pupils make better progress in single-sex schools *because these schools are single-sex*. How, also, could such a statement be reconciled with Tyson's results and with the general picture which emerged from chapter 1? It is also probably

[1] As explained earlier this enquiry was designed for other purposes.

significant that in the comparison of 'raw' scores the co-educational schools do least well in English—the subject most affected by their social class disadvantage—and best in mathematics, the subject probably least affected by this factor. No suggestion is made that this is the only variable causing the contrast (staffing may be another) but it is difficult to conceive how such a force could be without any influence in view of the plethora of research which demonstrates this association between high social class and good progress in the grammar school and vice versa.

When one is immersed in the *minutiae* of research it is easy to forget to stand back and get an 'aerial photograph' of the position. In this appraisal, however, such a photograph is very rewarding. We see clearly, first the smallness of the *real* differences in English attainment between the two types of school; their practical significance may be almost negligible. If we study the scene for some time a certain pattern emerges, in which the differences between the two large groups appear of little consequence in comparison with the differences between schools within those groups. In a chapter which of necessity leaves many questions unanswered it seems fitting to conclude by asking yet another question. Why is it that the segregated schools have a better result in English in Northern Ireland than in the London or northern England researches, when compared with co-educational schools? If the authorities, both in government and universities, provided the funds and facilities, the answer to this and many more important questions would soon be known. The result would not be Utopia, but we would at least know a little more about the likely consequences of major decisions.

7

R. R. Dale and P. McC. Miller

Comparative progress in university[1]

Introduction

It seems reasonable to hypothesize that students from single-sex schools going to work and often to live in a co-educational institution for the first time might be distracted from their first-year studies by the presence of the opposite sex.

Research on this topic appears to have been limited to a comparison of student academic attainment at the end of the first year at university, without regard to the relative entry attainment level of students from co-educational and single-sex schools. McCracken (1969) at Leeds analysed the first-year results of students for three successive years (over 5,500 students) and found no consistent pattern of difference between students from the two types of school, though those from single-sex schools had slightly fewer failures in two years out of the three. In view, however, of the doubts about the comparability of the entrance standards of the students from the two types (single-sex schools including for example those from the direct grant schools which take highly selected pupils from a wide radius) the findings are of little value for assessing the comparative *progress* of students from co-educational and single-sex schools.

In the present enquiry a preliminary examination has demonstrated that in our data the women make better progress than the men in *first-year studies* (Miller and Dale, Nov. 1972) and there is a curvilinear relationship between attainment and the 'location of the school' variable, students from city schools making best progress and those from towns of 15,000 to 60,000 population the worst progress (Dale and Miller, June 1972). These factors receive attention in the procedure outlined below.

Procedure

The method of analysis was by the comparison of matched samples of students from co-educational and single-sex schools who entered four colleges of the University of Wales in 1965–6, 1966–7, 1967–8 and Swansea 1968–9. The numerous unwanted variables were treated by (a) exclusion, (b) separation, (c) matching of students in pairs—the

[1] Part of a research project financed by the Social Science Research Council.

principal technique—and (d) 'balancing' the total numbers on each side for other known variables. In this way examining boards other than that of the Welsh Joint Education Committee were excluded, as were students not taking *at least* one of eight specified subjects at university. These were French, history, geography, applied mathematics, pure mathematics, physics, chemistry and botany. The faculties of arts and science were separated[1] and students were divided into four categories or 'levels' according to performance in the Advanced level examination.

Students from co-educational schools were matched with those from single-sex schools on population of school area (four categories), sex, social class, university institution, average grades, best subject and number of attempts in the Advanced level examination. Almost all sat three subjects but where a selected student sat only two he was paired with a similar student. However, in order to obtain a sufficient number of pairs the exact matching was relaxed after a core sample (of 126 pairs) had been selected, with the proviso that the difference in one direction for any variable was 'balanced' by one in the opposite direction. For example, if a co-educated male was matched against a female from a girls' school there had to be an opposite case of a co-educated woman matched against a man from a boys' school; there were 14 such pairs out of a total of 221 pairs, or 442 students. A similar process was carried out by 'balancing' the numbers of students for university institution, for location of school, and for attainment on entry (with minimal difference of grades). For social class the matching and also the balancing had to be relaxed on a somewhat larger scale, resulting in a slightly smaller proportion of the co-educated than of the single-sex educated being from the higher social classes. As previous examination of the data had satisfied us that there was little difference between the performance of the different social classes among these students and the social class matching was merely precautionary the writers were not unduly worried by the relaxation. In order to avoid the possibility of unconscious bias affecting the results all matching was done on the basis of objective rules with the university grades unknown to the matchers.

There resulted eight opposing samples, one for each category (level) of A-level performance within each faculty. The points allocation for student attainment on entry ranged from 1 for grade A to 7 for fail, in each subject, and the comparison was made on average grades. Students sitting twice were given their average grades for the two examinations. The cut-off points for the levels were 1·67, 2·33, 3·0, and worse than 3·0. The criterion by which the progress of the co-educated students was compared with those from single-sex schools, after selecting the pairs for equality on entry attainment, was their comparative attainment at the end of the first year. This was measured by calculating the

[1] Geography and economics were included in arts.

stanine grade (a measure of 'place in class', ranging from 1 to 9) of each student in each subject, taking his or her average grade and calculating the overall average scores for the opposing groups. In both entry and first-year data the *smaller* scores indicate the better grades. The entry grades of the co-educated students and those from single-sex schools were exactly equal in arts and virtually equal in science.

Results

The comparisons of the performance of the two groups in the examinations at the end of the first year at the university are presented in Tables 7.1 and 7.2.

TABLE 7.1 *Arts: progress of co-educated and single-sex educated students:*[1] *matched pairs analysis (first-year examinations)*

Entrance level	No. of pairs	Mean difference A-level	Mean first-year stanine grades		Mean difference of co-ed and s/sex stanine grades
			Co-ed	S/sex	
Level 1	16	Nil	3·67	4·49	+0·82
Level 2	37	Nil	4·86	4·55	−0·31
Level 3	38	Nil	5·59	5·46	−0·13
Level 4	28	Nil	5·38	5·20	−0·18
Extra cases[2]	4	Nil	5·00	5·33	+0·33
Total	123	Nil	5·05	5·00	−0·05

NOTE: *t* value for the overall difference is 0·31.
[1] The larger the stanine grade the worse the performance. A minus difference means advantage to single-sex.
[2] To increase numbers students near to the level boundaries were matched across them (maximum difference at entry 0·33); the opposite sides were then balanced according to entrance attainment.

In the arts faculty (Table 7.1) the students from co-educational and single-sex schools make virtually the same average progress, the negligible superiority of the students from single-sex schools being clearly highly unreliable statistically and of no practical importance. In the science faculty (Table 7.2) the co-educated students have a larger superiority, consistently in the same direction at all levels, and though this difference fails to reach the accepted standard of statistical significance it is quite substantial.[1]
[1] *t* = 1·48.

TABLE 7.2 *Science: progress of co-educated and single-sex educated students: matched pairs analysis (first-year examinations)*

Entrance level	No. of pairs	Mean difference A-level (minus is single-sex advantage)	Mean first-year stanine grades		Mean difference of co-ed and s/sex stanine grades
			Co-ed	S/sex	
Level 1	3	−0·11	1·78	2·22	+0·44
Level 2	8	−0·04	3·89	4·83	+0·94
Level 3	15	−0·03	4·67	5·20	+0·53
Level 4	68	+0·02	5·18	5·32	+0·14
Extra pairs	4	+0·17	4·08	4·33	+0·25
Total	98	+0·01	4·85	5·12	+0·28

NOTE: *t* value for the overall difference is 1·48.

TABLE 7.3 *Pass/fail analysis by students: co-educated and single-sex educated: matched pairs*

No. of students:	Arts		Science	
	Co-ed	S/sex educated	Co-ed	S/sex educated
Failing				
1 subject	16	20	23	15
2 subjects	4	4	5	15
3 subjects	0	1	6	6
0	103	98	64	62
Totals	123	123	98	98

In order to examine further both the amount and nature of the differences a pass/fail criterion was used, producing Table 7.3. This method brings the results of the two faculties into line with each other, the co-educated students now having a negligible and unreliable superiority in the arts faculty, and a distinctly larger one in science. The nature of the difference is more clearly expressed by opposing bad failures to the others. Out of some 98 students from single-sex schools about 10 more failed badly in science (i.e. in 2 or 3 subjects) than among those from co-educational schools with which they were so carefully matched (Table 7.4). The difference reached statistical significance on a chi-square test for matched pairs at the 0·05 level. The data is further

TABLE 7.4 *Science: poor and good performance: matched pairs analysis*

	Pair in which co-educated member satisfactory (3 or 2 subjects passed)	Pair in which co-educated member poor (None or 1 subject passed)
Pair in which single-sex educated member satisfactory (3 or 2 subjects passed)	70	7
Pair in which single-sex educated member poor (None or 1 subject passed)	17	4

NOTE: The difference is statistically significant. Chi-square — 4·167 allowing for correlation.

TABLE 7.5 *Pass/fail analysis by subject: co-educated and single-sex educated, matched pairs*

	Subjects taken	Passes	Fails
Faculty of Arts			
Co-educated	369	345	24
Single-sex educated	369	338	31
Faculty of Science			
Co-educated	294	243	51
Single-sex educated	294	231	63
Totals			
Co-educated	663	588	75
Single-sex educated	663	569	94

interpreted by the pass/fail analysis by subject rather than by student, in Table 7.5.

In Table 7.5 we see that in the faculty of arts the co-educated sample had slightly fewer *subject* failures (24 to 31) and in the faculty of science, out of 294 subjects sat on each side by the matched pairs, there were 63 failures among those educated in single-sex schools and 51 amongst the co-educated. This is not a dramatic difference but neither is it negligible and it is certainly worthy of further investigation.

Discussion

The tentative finding that in this sample students from co-educational schools are less liable to first-year failure in science than their counterparts from single-sex schools who were of similar attainment on entry, might seem to have confirmed the hypothesis that students from single-sex schools find it difficult to adjust to life and work in a co-educational institution. Such an interpretation could, however, be erroneous, as there may be other explanations for the difference found, even if its existence is confirmed by other research.

The first problem is to discover why a gap exists in science and not in arts. Two possible hypotheses are that either the laboratory facilities or the sixth form teaching (or both) are superior in single-sex schools; the co-educated students would be handicapped at A-level and would need to be of somewhat superior ability to their opposite numbers from single-sex schools to reach the same standard; once at the university the co-educated students, now enjoying equal facilities, would do better than their rivals. Fortunately we know that the laboratory explanation is unlikely to be true, as estimates were available from part of the sample about such provision in the schools students came from,[1] and within this part-sample the co-educated students appeared, surprisingly, to have rather the better facilities. In addition a partial correlation for 141 Swansea co-educated and single-sex educated students combined, between their estimates of laboratory provision and their university grades, with A-level attainment held constant, yielded coefficients which were small and inconsistent for the three sciences.[2] Students' estimates of the ability of their science teachers, obtained as for laboratory provision, produced small and inconsistent differences for the three sciences, between co-educational and single-sex schools. Assessment by partial correlation, as above, between students' estimates of their teachers' ability and university grades with A-level attainment held constant,

[1] Physics 30 schools, chemistry 37, biology and botany 23.
[2] Physics $N = 41$, $r = 0.027$; chemistry $N = 50$, $r = 0.204$; biology $N = 50$, $r = 0.16$.

again gave very small inconsistent coefficients.[1] Clearly these facts reduce the possibility that the teachers or laboratory facilities variables are the explanation.

Another factor relevant to this discussion is that research has repeatedly found that most failures and poor performances at university are not due to lack of ability but to factors affecting motivation; this runs counter to the argument that the extra failures among science students from single-sex schools were caused by their ability being lower than that of the co-educated students with whom they were paired on attainment.

TABLE 7.6   *Incidence of first-year failure in arts: women students from co-educational and single-sex schools, matched sample*

Social class:	Co-educational schools						Single-sex schools					
	1	2	3	4 & 5	0	Total	1	2	3	4 & 5	0	Total
No. of subjects failed:												
0	19	19	18	6	3	65	13	22	12	7	2	56
1	0	5	0	3	2	10	8	6	3	2	0	19
2	0	1	1	1	0	3	1	1	0	0	0	2
3	0	0	0	0	0	0	0	1	0	0	0	1
Totals	19	25	19	10	5	78	22	30	15	9	2	78
% fail	0	24·0	5·3	40·0	40·0	16·7	40·9	26·7	20·0	22·2	0	28·2

As the above hypotheses appear to be unlikely explanations for the difference between the findings in arts and in science, we must turn to other possibilities. The difference in the proportions of the sexes in the two faculties might seem to be a likely cause, but all except a few members of the opposing samples were paired by sex, and the remainder balanced by sex. Moreover the disappearance of the gap in arts (as compared with science) between the mean stanine grades of the students from co-educational schools *versus* those from single-sex schools is not due to the greater proportion of women in that faculty, as the co-educated women fared better than their counterparts, while for the men there was a small difference in the opposite direction.

The small social class imbalance in favour of those from single-sex

[1] Physics $N = 41$, $r = -0.252$; chemistry $N = 50$, $r = -0.031$; biology $N = 50$, $r = 0.130$.

schools seems another obvious explanation, the better cultural background of students from single-sex schools having a more powerful effect in arts than in science. In view of the data in Table 7.6, however, this theory would appear to be ruled out. The only hint of such an effect might be under social class 4/5 for co-educated women, where 4 out of 10 fail in at least one subject, but this is countered by the minute fail rate of 5 per cent for class 3, while the theory is finally demolished by the failure rate of 41 per cent for social class 1 women from girls' schools. An incidental and curious discovery, however, is that the women in social classes 1 and 2 from girls' schools did far worse in arts than the men of those classes from boys' schools (0·01 level), yet there was no hint of such an effect on the co-educational side. It is remotely possible that this is a significant difference which has arisen by chance out of so many differences existing in the data, but it seems well worth consideration by other researchers. The women were not matched with the men, but the entry standards of the two sexes were almost identical.

It will be seen that the difficulties of interpretation are manifold. Of the theories examined the one put forward in the hypothesis—the influence of the type of schooling—seems to conform best to the evidence of the data, but there may be other explanations which have not been thought of. Though a difference in favour of co-educational students has been found at the level of 'bad failures' in science (P < 0·05), and a consistent lead in science for co-educated students at all levels (significant at the 0·1 level only with a one-tailed test), the first task of research in this field is to replicate the study with a different and if possible larger sample in order to confirm or query this tentative finding. It might be possible to collect at the same time such data as might contribute towards an explanation of the underlying cause if confirmation is given.

Another interesting incidental finding is that among the women in halls of residence who were in the Swansea intensive sample from which the matched sample of this chapter was selected, failures both in science and arts, including the bad failures, tended to be concentrated in one hall (significant at 0·01 level), though there was near equality between this hall and the others in the entrance standard of students. The prevailing atmosphere in such halls can of course help or hinder academic work, but from the example given it seems as if it might well sometimes overrule or weaken the effect of other variables that researchers are investigating, while its freakish incidence would make the prognostication of student progress more difficult. In the present case careful enquiries produced 'over-socialization preventing work' as the most likely cause.

Part II

Attitude to school work and school subjects
A miscellany of papers

This section is not an exhaustive analysis of the attitudes of pupils towards the subjects of the curriculum, whether boys' attitudes are compared with those of girls or the attitudes of co-educated pupils compared with those of pupils from single-sex schools. As the sub-title states, it is a miscellany of papers on these topics, some written expressly for the book while others are revisions of articles published in journals during the last ten years. They merely have the common theme that they are concerned with the interests and attitudes of pupils towards the subjects of the curriculum, in relation to the co-education controversy.

8

The surveys

Several chapters in this section are based on new material obtained from projects which were described in chapter 1 of the first volume of this series and to a lesser extent in chapter 1 of volume II. The explanation of these projects is therefore not given here in full, but in order to assist those readers who are unacquainted with the first two volumes they are briefly described.

Second College survey

In the Second College survey some 900 men and some 800 women from colleges of education and university departments of education scattered throughout England and Wales were asked to complete a questionnaire[1] (years 1949–50, 1964–5). Each of the items was answered on a five or seven-point scale. The questionnaire was administered under examination conditions with large groups, so that the percentage of returns was almost 100. Replies were private and anonymous in order to encourage students to write frankly. For a representative part of the sample data were secured on parental occupation.[2] An important aspect of this and the two other main questionnaires was that respondents were encouraged to make a comment after the principal questions.

'Both schools' survey

The sample used for the 'Both schools' survey, as its name implies, was composed of ex-pupils of secondary schools (excluding secondary modern) who had attended both a co-educational and a single-sex school. They were all students in colleges of education again scattered widely throughout England and Wales. There were 175 men and 620 women drawn from 71 participating colleges. A more detailed questionnaire, again requesting answers on a five-point scale, was administered under similar conditions to those of the Second College survey. To minimize undue influences in any direction the students were asked to place the

---

[1] This and the other questionnaires are placed in Appendix 1.
[2] Because some chapters are enlargements of articles written over a period of time, this is sometimes called 'social class' and sometimes 'occupational class'.

completed questionnaire in an envelope and seal it before handing it in. The mass administration of the questionnaire resulted in a very high percentage of returns, and in any case it should be noted that any abstention would be an abstention from both the co-educational and single-sex school statistics, because the student had attended at least one of each type of school. Most of the questions were about the particular school which the student had attended and the wording of these questions was identical for both the co-educational and single-sex school.

Data were obtained about: type and sex of secondary school (even if more than two), length of attendance, order of schools attended, boarder or day pupil, occupation of parent, sex, age, length of stay at college of education, type of college, and details about the school playing fields. Schools were classified as either 'first' or 'last', those in the middle being classed as 'first' unless the pupil had a year in the sixth.

Schools project

A research questionnaire and paper and pencil tests of temperament were given in 1964 to pupils in 42 co-educational and single-sex grammar schools in South Wales and the West Riding of Yorkshire. Twenty pupils were chosen alphabetically from each single-sex school and similarly 20 boys and 20 girls from each co-educational school. The schools were matched in triples for social background. The tests and questionnaire were administered under examination conditions by the writer and a research assistant and were repeated two years later. The questions asked were of a similar type to those of the previous two surveys.

Unfortunately a wrong administrative decision caused a comprehensive school to be included in the sample and this had later to be excluded because some of the pupils in the sample could not read sufficiently well to do the tests, and a later examination of the valid IQ scores showed them to be below the average of any other school. This also caused the omission of the two single-sex schools which were tripled with it for social background. For the 1966 testing another triple of schools had to be excluded because two of the 1964 single-sex schools were amalgamated into a co-educational school.

The project was originally designed as a pilot study, preparatory to the taking of a national sample of schools, and had consequent limitations imposed upon it by restrictions of time and money; the end result is that the sample of 14 schools of each type, ultimately reduced to 12, though useful, is none the less small. The tripling of the schools for social background helps to reduce the danger implicit in the small number of schools, but recourse must be had to the general pattern of the results from all of the surveys for confirmation or otherwise. It would be foolish not to recognize that there are many different reasons why schools might be good or bad and the chance inclusion of two or three very bad—or abnormally good—schools in one of the samples could seriously affect the results.

Tables showing the comparative levels of the samples in intelligence and social class are given in Appendix 2 (Tables A2.1 and A2.2). Here it must suffice to say that the detailed analysis of the occupational class composition of the samples shows that in the 1964 full sample the single-sex schools had a somewhat higher social class entry. Similarly girls in girls' schools were superior to the co-educated girls in intelligence at both 11 plus and 15 plus.[1] The boys in boys' schools were also slightly superior in intelligence at 11 plus but there was virtual equality between the two groups in the 15-plus category. The position was changed a little in the smaller *longitudinal sample* where the co-educated girls were of a slightly lower social class composition at the age of 11 plus and 13 plus, with approximate equality at ages 15 plus and 17 plus. The co-educated boys were lower in social class composition in all groups. Again in the longitudinal sample the two boys' groups were approximately equal in intelligence at all ages but the co-educated girls were inferior except at the age of 15 plus, when they were equal (Tables A2.3 and A2.5).

The 'check' sample

As some of the early results from the Schools project showed smaller differences between the opposing girls' groups than those found in earlier surveys a 'check' investigation was made amongst all girls in each school who were in the 11-plus age group and had *not* been included in the Schools project. A 15-minute questionnaire containing the more important questions and a few additional ones was administered to large groups in each school by the writer and a research assistant. There were 1,122 girls from 24 schools.[2] In spite of the pairing of the co-educational and girls' schools for social background the girls' schools had a small but not serious advantage in the social class of their pupils (Table A2.6 in Appendix 2).

In all the above survey tables the totals will vary because of 'blanks' and in some cases because a percentage of the pupils do not take a subject.

[1] Significant beyond the 0·05 level.
[2] One school of the 28 was omitted because it became co-educational and another because it was the only comprehensive school; this entailed the omission of the two 'matching' schools.

Boys versus girls surveys

Part II includes two chapters on the comparative interest of boys and girls in two subjects of the academic curriculum. The research as a whole has deliberately excluded any systematic assessment of this aspect of the co-education problem, but these two chapters are presented as illustrations of what still needs to be done. As the samples affect only those chapters, the description of them is given there.

9

Attitudes to school studies

What is it that motivates a child to learn? Curiosity, career, pride in success, imitation, competition are some of the answers. This chapter endeavours to assess whether another factor, the pupil's environment in a co-educational secondary school, might give him a greater desire to learn than if he were placed in a school for one sex only. Since the forces motivating an individual to learn are many and various and of different intensities and since they change somewhat from day to day, from teacher to teacher, and from subject to subject, the task of deciding the ultimate balance of these forces is indeed complex.

Crucial to the outcome are major factors such as good or bad teaching, the pupil's level of intelligence in relation to the work he is asked to do, the attitude of his parents to his schooling, and his capacity for sustained work with books. A comparison of co-educated pupils with those from single-sex schools in their attitude to academic work must therefore have regard to these factors, some of which may be as powerful as, or even more powerful than, any change in attitude to work which might be brought about by the co-educational environment.

With this approach as the background we can then ask what fundamental and inescapable differences there are between the two types of school which might affect the pupils' attitude. Obviously two such differences are the presence of the opposite sex of pupil and opposite sex of teacher. (Girls' schools who have male teachers on the staff are moving towards the co-educational principle.) Some opponents of co-education fear that the presence of the opposite sex of pupil will create a distraction from academic work, while protagonists of co-education point out that the friendly competition between the sexes is a healthy stimulant to good achievement. The first emphasize the difficulty of catering for the differing interests of the two sexes, the second point out the broadening effect contributed by the presence of both the feminine and the masculine point of view in class discussions. This enrichment of the instruction is also the view taken by a sample of 71 teachers in France who had taught in both types of school (Breuse, 1970).

To this is added the question of the effect of a mixed staff on boy and girl pupils together. Do the boys like or dislike being taught by a woman? Do girls, correspondingly, like or dislike being taught by a man? From which sex does boy or girl learn most effectively?

At a more detailed level we can ask whether men teach mathematics and science, on the average, better than women—and whether women teach arts subjects better than men. Again, using a broader outlook, we ask ourselves whether the mixed staff would produce a more harmonious or a less harmonious atmosphere in the staff room and in the school. What also is the effect of the presence of both boy and girl pupils on the discipline of the school? Do either of these last two factors have an influence on the pupils' attitude to work?

In this complex field of research a few tentative answers have been given in the two previous volumes, and an attempt has been made in the first part of this present volume to avoid some of the complexity by assessing the outcome of the pupil's studies—i.e. the progress they made. Using the less direct approach we can ask the ex-pupils and pupils of the two types of school—and especially those who attended both—to make an overall appraisal of the attitude to academic work in these schools with regard to their own careers there. In doing this, however, we must always remain aware of the other fundamental forces which are acting on the situation. Since we know that both intelligence and social class are correlated positively and strongly with attainment and also that single-sex secondary schools (excluding secondary modern) have for many years had a pupil intake rather higher in intelligence and of rather higher social class (Tables 2.2 and 2.3) than co-educational schools it would be expected that the former would have a somewhat higher level of attainment and that the pupils in these single-sex schools would show a greater interest in, and liking for, academic work. It has already been shown in the first section of this book that boys in single-sex schools have a lower average level of attainment at the Ordinary level of the GCE than co-educated boys and do not make as good academic progress in relation to their ability. Girls in girls' schools, though *slightly* superior to co-educated girls *on raw scores*, are not by a long way as superior as one would expect from their advantages in intelligence or social class, their selective entry in individual examination subjects, and their usually older age when sitting the examination. The question which now arises is whether a comparison of the attitudes towards the work of pupils in co-educational schools with those prevalent in single-sex schools will provide more evidence about the forces which produce the situation we find. This topic was investigated through the 'Both schools' enquiry and the Schools project. In the former the opposing groups are necessarily equal on social class and intelligence level, but in the latter, in spite of the matching of schools by neighbourhood, there remains a small advantage to the single-sex schools in both factors. This difference will be kept in mind during the analysis.

Procedure was by the inclusion of various items on attitudes to academic work, in several of the surveys, asking for answers on a five or seven-point scale, and giving pupils in two cases the opportunity of making a free response. The first of these enquiries was the 'Both schools' survey.[1]

'Both schools' survey

GOOD TEACHING

In the 'Both schools' survey the ex-pupils were asked, 'Do you agree or disagree with the following statement about your co-educational school? Good quality of teaching.
Agree strongly/Agree/Doubtful/Disagree/Disagree strongly.'

TABLE 9.1   *Good quality of teaching (male ex-pupils)*

'Both schools' survey

	Replies from male ex-pupils about 'first' schools				Replies from male ex-pupils about 'last' schools			
	Co-ed schools		Boys' schools		Co-ed schools		Boys' schools	
	N	%	N	%	N	%	N	%
Agree strongly	9	10·8	22	18·5	18	17·5	19	26·7
Agree	44	53·1	54	45·4	65	63·1	36	50·7
Doubtful	18	21·7	30	25·2	15	14·6	7	9·9
Disagree	10	12·0	8	6·7	4	3·9	8	11·3
Disagree strongly	2	2·4	5	4·2	1	0·9	1	1·4
Totals	83	100	119	100	103	100	71	100

NOTE: None of the differences between co-educated boys and those educated in boys' schools is statistically significant.

The same question was asked about their single-sex school. These ex-pupils were in a better position to judge than usual as they had attended both a co-educational and a single-sex school, though in one of these as a junior and in the other as a senior. The results are given in Table 9.1.

[1] A sample of 175 men and 620 women students in colleges of education who had each been educated in both a co-educational and a single-sex secondary school (excluding secondary modern).

As the ex-pupils were more enthusiastic about their last school attended than about their first, and more of them finished up in a co-educational school, the results for 'first' and 'last' schools were kept apart. The men who attended their boys' school first were slightly more pleased by the quality of the teaching than were those who attended their co-educational school first, but the former gave estimates for the teaching in their co-educational ('last') schools which were rather better than those given by the opposing group for their single-sex ('last')

TABLE 9.2   *Good quality of teaching (female ex-pupils)*

'*Both schools*' survey

	Replies from female ex-pupils about 'first' schools				Replies from female ex-pupils about 'last' schools			
	Co-ed schools		Girls' schools		Co-ed schools		Girls' schools	
	N	%	N	%	N	%	N	%
Agree strongly	49	16·4	73	18·0	67	18·7	57	21·9
Agree	184	61·8	204	50·4	208	57·9	132	50·8
Doubtful	45	15·1	94	23·2	68	18·9	49	18·8
Disagree	12	4·0	29	7·2	12	3·4	19	7·3
Disagree strongly	8	2·7	5	1·2	4	1·1	3	1·2
Totals	298	100	405	100	359	100	260	100

NOTE: The difference between the co-educated girls and those from girls' schools is statistically significant for 'first' schools at the 0·01 level.

schools; none of these differences is statistically significant. Two points are worth noting. First, that this is one of the few instances where the boys' schools have the advantage for the positive reply 'Agree strongly'; second, that there is a distinct advantage to the co-educated seniors in the 'Disagree' and 'Disagree strongly' categories where they have only 5 per cent of their number as against 13 per cent in the corresponding boys' schools. Summing up, there is little difference between the two sides.

The results from the female ex-pupils are in Table 9.2.

The data in Table 9.2 indicate that the women who were in their co-educational schools as juniors gave significantly higher estimates of the standard of teaching there than did those who were juniors in girls' schools. The slight difference between the senior groups is in the same direction; though, by statistical convention, it may have occurred by chance it receives support from the juniors' result.

In neither the data for men nor for women is there any support for the idea that the standard of teaching is better in single-sex schools, though because of the sprinkling of direct grant and prestigious city schools in the segregated schools samples, this is what might have been expected. Yet it is inadvisable to place complete reliance on the results from one question and from one sample even though its members attended both types of schools, and both pupils and schools were quite large in number. As there was, however, no time available to follow this up we pass on to the next question. It explores a different facet of the same topic, but the two facets are inter-related.

EXAMINATIONS AND PRESSURE OF WORK

Here the ex-pupils were asked whether they agreed or disagreed with, 'The intense pressure of work for examinations worried me'. Replies were on the same five-point scale as for the previous question. As senior pupils facing external examinations would probably be more anxious

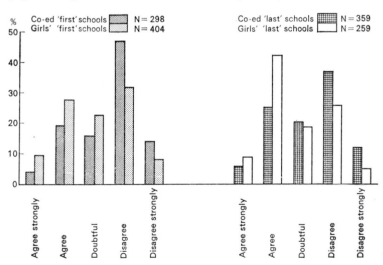

NOTE: The differences between co-educational and girls' schools are significant at the 0·001 level both for 'first' and 'last' schools.

FIGURE 9.1 *Pressure of work for examinations worrying (female ex-pupils): 'Both schools' survey*

than the junior pupils the results for 'first' and 'last' schools were again separated. In both these sections the ex-pupils estimated that the pressure of examinations was more worrying in their boys' than their co-educational schools, the *difference* being greater for 'first' schools though falling a little short of statistical significance (Table A2.11).

The results on the female side were more clear-cut (Figure 9.1).

The pressure of work for examinations worried these ex-pupils far more when they were in girls' than when they were in co-educational schools. Whereas 23 per cent of them confessed to being worried as juniors in co-educational schools this figure rose to 37 per cent for those in girls' schools; the same percentages on the senior side were 31 for the co-educational and 51 for those from girls' schools. The discussion of the meaning of this result is reserved until the concluding section of the chapter, and we pass on to a closely related question.

PRESSURE OF WORK MADE ME ANXIOUS

The question is so nearly related to the previous one and on the whole so similar in outcome that it adds only a little to the picture and the tables are therefore placed in the appendix (Tables A2.12 and A2.13). The addition referred to is that in this instance the difference between the co-educated juniors and those from boys' schools widened and became statistically significant (almost at 0·01 level), the co-educational ex-pupils giving a lower estimate of being worried than their opposite numbers. The differences reported for the previous question for both junior and senior girls were fully confirmed.

After giving their estimates the respondents could add a free response as a comment on or qualification to their estimate. As the full treatment of the responses, similar to that given in other instances, would unduly prolong this chapter, detailed analysis of the men's replies is omitted, making it possible to give classified summaries and fairly extensive quotations for the women, since the largest difference between the two sides is to be found here. First, however, a few responses from the men are quoted because of their *general* interest, though some also are relevant to the theme of the book.

Co-educational school

(Very anxious) 'After travelling a great distance to and from school I was often too fatigued to concentrate effectively on homework.'

(Anxious) 'In some subjects—especially maths—not in other subjects.'

(A little anxious) 'This was especially so because of the competition between the sexes for examinations and homework.'

(A little anxious) 'The work during the term did not worry me very much, but was always worried about exams. Used to have acute stomach upsets at exam time.'

(No effect) 'It was not the pressure of work that led me to be apathetic; it was the attitude of the teachers who only seemed interested in the three pupils who were Oxford/Cambridge candidates.'

One ex-pupil clearly regretted his slackness:

(No effect) 'The result of "No effect" was no GCEs!'

Boys' school

(Very anxious) 'If you couldn't get it done they were down on you like a ton of bricks.'

(Very anxious) 'Penalties for failing to work were rather severe, and there was a lot of work to do.'

(Very anxious) 'It was difficult to get all the work in in time. Punishment was rather severe for failure to produce homework.'

(Very anxious) 'Exams were all that ever counted and this was continually drummed in.'

(Anxious) 'Only with regard to physics.' (Mathematics and physics were the only subjects named.)

(Anxious) 'Sink or swim attitude.'

(Anxious) 'Through attitude of teachers.'

(A little anxious) 'By this time I was naturally anxious in the rat-race that exists in London schools.'

(A little anxious) 'I often stayed up late to complete my homework. Thus I was often tired and strained at school.'

The only 'direct comparison' comment was:

(Anxious) 'There was much more preoccupation with exams than in the co-ed school.' (Co-ed first.)

The classified list of free responses from the women who attended 'first' schools is presented in Table A2.14 in Appendix 2; that for 'last schools' attended is in Table 9.3.

TABLE 9.3   *Free responses on anxiety about work (females, 'last' schools)*
'Both schools' survey

Estimate	Comment	Co-ed schools	Girls' schools
Very anxious	higher standard than previous school		4
	great emphasis on exams	1	3
	unable cope—became ill		1
	exams—inferiority complex		1
	at first, then apathetic		1
	work deteriorated here		1
	pressure from home		1
	Sciences—no grounding like boys	1	
Anxious	standard higher, worked harder	3	1
	great pressure		3
	exam success school's main aim	3	
	exam time worrying	8	10
	exams unnecessary pressure		4
	frantic with worry before A-levels		1
	had work harder than boys for A-levels		1
	helpful staff eased anxiety		1
	high standard to maintain	2	
	difficulty coping, illness	3	
	particularly maths	1	
	worrying disposition	3	1
	because lack of pressure	2	
	other	3	
A little anxious	a little anxious; at times	11	3
	a very little, pressure not great	9	
	exams only, mainly	29	10
	exam time especially	26	8
	great emphasis on results	2	3
	if staff or subject disliked, poor at it	6	3
	exams own pressure, necessary sixth	5	
	always anxious pressure work, excessive homework		2
	wanted to do well	9	1

Table 9.3 (continued)

Estimate	Comment	Co-ed schools	Girls' schools
A little anxious	teachers strict about work	3	
	although staff helpful	2	
	standard higher than first school	3	2
	received less encouragement		1
	no time anything else	1	
	but enjoyed work	1	
	but got over it by sixth	3	
	worrying disposition	6	1
	settling down new school		2
	others	4	
No effect	no effect	13	3
	little pressure	5	
	did not work hard, school lax re homework, easygoing staff	4	
	little competition, nobody bothered		2
	work well spread	2	
	no pressure—work to be enjoyed	6	1
	some pressure, not worried		3
	teachers helpful at A-level	1	
	work had to be done, right for exams	2	1
	except when exams near	5	1
	was used to faster pace	1	1
	not harder than at co-ed		1
	much less than single-sex	1	
	by upper sixth used to the work	3	
	could not be bothered	1	
	others	7	1

The free responses, for the purpose of quotation, have those for 'first' school combined with those for 'last' school, and are limited to the 'Very anxious' and 'Anxious' categories. The number of these responses quoted in each category is strictly in proportion to the *estimates* given for that category. For example 3 per cent of the ex-pupils estimated 'Very anxious' for their co-educational schools and 18 per cent for their girls' schools, and the free responses quoted under this heading are therefore in the proportion 3 to 18, the actual numbers being 2 and 12. (A somewhat similar result would have been reached if the number of *free responses* had been used as the basis.)

Co-educational schools

(Very anxious)
Most responses mentioned examinations, but the two selected relate most closely to the theme of the book.

'I became extremely ill due to nerves under pressure of work and working with the opposite sex.'

'We had to take science subjects in which we had no grounding as the boys had. We were therefore doing double the amount of work.'

(Anxious)
'The pressure was for exams, the ideal to please the public eye.'

'There was a large stress on exams and much status to be gained from being in certain streams.'

'The pressure for exams was tremendous. The school was still trying to make its name as a co-ed and examination results were important to it.'

'Particularly in maths. The teacher was an elderly spinster with a quick temper which soon showed when poor work was produced, quite naturally I suppose, but this fear of her temper made me dread the lessons and I believe hindered my learning.'

'The main aim of the school was to get pupils through exams and this caused anxiousness in many people.'

'The school laid great stress on O- and A-levels—sometimes this was frightening.'

'I had a minor breakdown from the beginning of trial A-levels.'

'The anxiety of the headmaster to prove the point that co-educational schools were correct made him more than press the need for good O- and A-level results.'

'I disliked failing.'

'I was worried about my exams because I found it difficult to work and to learn facts.'

'At A-level it became impossible to cope.'

'Girls worked hard to keep up with boys. I think both sexes were worried that the other sex might do better in exams etc.'

Girls' schools

(Very anxious)
'When work worried me the problem grew to enormous proportions because I felt that the staff were inaccessible. I dare not ask about something I did not understand as I imagined it would make me even more of an inferior being.'

'Threats of what would happen if we did not pass exams.'

'The staff invariably showed more concern for girls of high intellectual ability. No real interest in the individual, therefore work became of utmost importance.'

'The only aim of the school seemed to be to get as many pupils to get as many GCEs as possible.'

'I remember crying frequently because I could not finish homework or do revision for exams.'

'I felt I had to keep up so I used to work far too hard and the result was illness and loss of time at school.'

'To the extent that I was unable to cope and became ill with anxiety. Afterwards I went on at my own speed and just did not worry. I was under pressure from home as well.'

'Created a feeling within me that I would rather fake an illness than go to school on the day of a test.'

'I am terrified by all exams—put extra pressure on myself.'

'Yes, I was in a nervous condition when I left.'

'Very anxious when I was younger but eventually I became apathetic and just took things as they came, not working as hard as I should have.'

'I changed schools just before O-level (from co-ed to all girls) and failed miserably—inferiority complex—constant worrying about exams.'

(Anxious)
'Split up into groups on examination results. High academic tradition.'

'Fearful of not keeping up standard in a rather specialist field.'

'Because future depended upon GCE work.'

'One-upmanship was a great part of the school life. If you did badly in exams you were humiliated.'

'Very much geared to keeping people in the right stream.'

'There was nothing else to do except work or skip round the paths. I was not academically minded and this made me fret.' (Boarding)

'Just before A-levels I was absolutely frantic with worry—almost hysterical at one point.'

'I found it a strain keeping up with the mathematics and this teacher was particularly unapproachable. In other subjects I was not anxious at all.'

'Gave extra work as said no one would pass exams—told all very unintelligent.'

'The place terrified me.'

'Girls will work hard if pushed. Tended to push too much for my liking.'

'General atmosphere during examination time became very tense.'

'If one could not do one's homework the teacher was unpleasant and did not always explain the work.'

'It had this effect on me because the teachers were not very good. Maths teacher very frequently made stupid errors on the board and insisted she was correct—she had a good degree as well.'

'Possibly because it was a much larger school than I was used to, everything seemed important.'

'The helpful staff eased the anxiety.' (Boarding)

'At this stage I was extremely anxious about work—I do not feel this was particularly because of pressure felt.'

'If didn't get about average mark lost confidence in capability to do it.'

The only free responses which made a direct comparison between the co-educational and girls' school attended were:

About co-educational schools

(No effect)   'I was more affected by work in my previous school.'

About girls' schools

(Very anxious)   'I worked badly despite the fact that I was able to work well before attending this school.'

(Very anxious)   'Work and teachers of a much higher standard than previous school. Maths teacher very nasty. I settled down after one year.'

(Very anxious) 'Ability of pupils was higher than in co-ed school: more serious and concentrated work necessary.'

(Anxious) 'We found we were working for A-levels far harder than the boys with whom we had been in the same class. We wondered whether this was necessary.'

(A little anxious) 'I was certainly concerned that I should do my work well—there was strong competition not met with in the co-ed.'

(A little anxious) 'My work had tended to go down in standard in co-ed school so I had to catch up.'

(A little anxious) 'Only a little anxious because the school was single-sex only up to the fifth form. More stress in sixth form—mixed.'

(No effect) 'There was very little pressure of work compared with my previous school.'

We pass on to the results from another question put to the 'Both schools' sample: 'Do you consider that the amount of homework to be

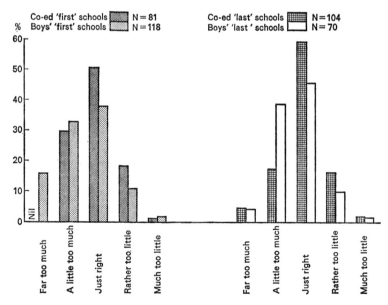

NOTE: The differences between co-educational and boys' schools are significant (for 'first' schools P < 0·001 and for 'last' schools P > 0·025).

FIGURE 9.2 *Amount of homework (male ex-pupils): 'Both schools' survey*

done in the school was: Far too much/A little too much/Just right/ Rather too little/Far too little?' The results for the males can be seen in Figure 9.2.

The estimates of the male ex-pupils about the co-educational schools they attended are well balanced around 'Just right', while those about their boys' schools lean rather heavily towards the 'too much' categories.[1] In keeping with this tendency for the boys' schools estimates to be inclined towards 'too much' these schools have slightly smaller percentages than the co-educational on the 'too little' side, the bulk of the difference being adjusted in the 'just right' category. The emphasis on 'too much' homework would seem to link up with the stricter discipline that characterizes boys' schools, but no evidence has been found to indicate that it results in higher attainment—rather the reverse, which is a point of no little interest.

Opportunity was given for the inclusion of free responses, but when these are split up into those from 'first' and those from 'last' schools there are too few for any worthwhile classification. However, a few comments are made. The responses reinforce the verdict of the estimates, the principal difference between the opposing types of school being the greater number of complaints about too much homework when in the boys' schools. Apart from this, individual remarks of interest about the co-educational schools were that the presence of keen girls helped, that it was a good balance with social life, that they were trusted to work but it was often abused and that there was little opportunity for original work. One ex-pupil evidently stood up for his rights, asserting that if there was too much homework it didn't get done! Much to be commended was the following practice: 'Homework was never set on Wednesday nights, these being regarded as nights for private outings, i.e. when parents could take their children out without disrupting homework.'

Remarks about the boys' schools were more frequently concerned with the great stress of examinations, with the school's main aim being academic and with the homework restricting outside interests and leaving no free evenings. One individual, however, said that the amount was left to the pupils' discretion, another that homework was a necessary evil, and two thought there should have been more homework. One ex-pupil from the senior forms regretted that there was no time or opportunity to meet the opposite sex. The responses that made a direct or clearly implicit comparison between the schools were as follows:

'Just right. Rather more than in co-ed, and discipline was such that one had to do it.'

[1] For 'first' schools $P < 0.001$ and for 'last' schools $P < 0.025$.

'A little too much, but it did me good. Never had as much at co-ed schools.'

'A little too much—school curriculum left no time for social enjoyment as I enjoyed at co-ed school.'

'Too little—relative to my previous (single-sex) school there was less homework than I was accustomed to.'

'With the change-over [to amalgamated schools] the burden on the teachers became greater and homework less. This resulted in somewhat poorer examination results than previously.'

The experience of two ex-pupils was different from the above:

'It seemed a lot to do in VI A English. The presence of girls keen on the work helped my own enthusiasm.'

'Little too much (co-ed). The main reason for this was that when I started in 4th year co-ed I found the standard appreciably higher. Had to work very hard to catch up.'

The estimates made by the female ex-pupils are in Figure 9.3.

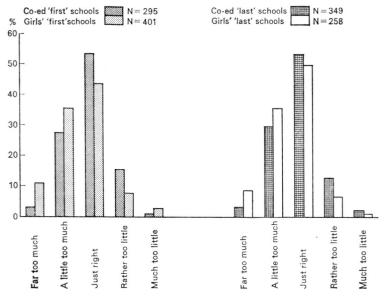

NOTE: The difference between the estimates for the co-educational and girls' schools are statistically highly significant both for 'first' and 'last' schools.

FIGURE 9.3 *Amount of homework (female ex-pupils): 'Both schools' survey*

The opinion of the women ex-pupils is the same as that of the men, namely that there tended to be too much homework in their single-sex schools. In contrast a majority of the women thought homework was 'just right' in their co-educational schools though they were more inclined than the men to consider it to be too much rather than too little.

The numerous free responses in this instance add little to the evidence, merely underlining the difference between the schools which is shown by the estimates in Figure 9.3. No classification of them is given, but the salient features are the larger amounts of homework said to have been set in the girls' schools—three to three and a half hours each night is mentioned several times, with no time to read around a subject or engage in hobbies, but some ex-pupils believed it to be necessary to get good results and others blamed themselves for lack of sufficient ability to do the homework more quickly. There were the following 'direct comparisons' comments, taking first those based on co-educational schools.

Co-educational schools

'Just right, having come from a school where a great amount of homework was done.'

'Just right. In single-sex did $2\frac{1}{2}$ hours every night.'

'I was surprised at not having nearly as much homework as I had been used to.'

'The amount of homework seemed to decrease when the two schools began to be mixed.'

'Much less than single-sex.'

'In the previous school we had more homework; the amalgamation brought with it upheaval and interruption, homework took a far less important place.'

'Rather too little. I was doing A-levels and compared with the other school it was much less. We were left on our own much more.'

'Rather too little. I spent my 6th form in a co-ed school and I had as much work in the two years as I had in six months at my single-sex school.'

'Although I was older than when I attended single-sex school, we had less homework. We worked much harder during the day however.'

'Rather too little. In secondary school (single-sex) we did far more homework than in the grammar.'

'Rather too little—this is compared to the other school, which gave more than normal.'

'Compared with my previous school we sometimes had very little homework.'

'Rather too little, but offset by fact that we had a long working day and worked under high pressure in school hours.'

'Far too little. The truth of this reply is evident in relation to examination results as compared with a nearby single-sex school where much homework was compulsory.'

One young lady, however, thought differently:

'I did as much as I needed to reach a standard. This was considerably more than I had done at the single-sex school.'

A last quotation is not a comparison, but has a general interest and will probably take many a reader back to schooldays:

'A little too much—we were given piles of work, but everyone copied the few who had done it five minutes before the lesson.'

Girls' schools

'Far too much. When I moved to co-educational school I had far less homework.'

'Far too much. I got more homework at the grammar school (single-sex) because I was taking A-levels.'

'A little too much. Similar work set as in co-ed, especially for A-level.'

'A little too much. We had rather a lot for the first year. I found the work and atmosphere more easy going in my co-educational school.'

'A little too much. Depends what value you set on academic standards. I did far better in examinations than at co-ed. Five O-levels at co-ed, three good A-levels here (single-sex).'

'Just right. We worked hard and gave good results. All of us lost ground at grammar school (co-ed).'

'Just right. Was more than in my previous school.'

A few of the ex-pupils had to work harder in their co-educational schools or found the standard higher there:

'Far too much. Not quite as much as for O-level studies in previous school. I still hadn't sufficient time to spend with my parents or pursue my own hobbies.'

'Just right. There was less work to be done than in the co-ed school but then the course was narrower.'

'Rather too little. There wasn't the pressure of work as I had in my previous school.'

'Rather too little. Standard of education seemed to be rather lower.'

The following comment about a girls' school gives a factor which affects co-educational schools much more because of their rural situation:

'A little too much. Long travelling hours which many pupils had left them too tired to work well evenings, and little spare time.'

A rather curious point of view is presented here:

'Far too much. Amount of homework set showed the dislike the staff had of pupils leading a separate life outside.'

Summary

With regard to the comparison of the quality of teaching in co-educational and single-sex schools the male ex-pupils gave opposite trends for schools attended first and those attended last, neither statistically significant, whereas the female ex-pupils considered the teaching better in the 'first' co-educational schools (statistically highly significant) and slightly better in co-educational schools attended last, than in their girls' schools. One needs to be somewhat cautious about the size of the difference for the two 'first school' groups and its interpretation, as the result could have been influenced by such factors as the 'halo effect' of the greater happiness of the girls when in co-educational schools, their belief in the greater friendliness of the teachers and even by the girls' expressed liking for male teachers. However, the fact that these female ex-pupils believed so strongly that their teaching was better (for junior pupils) is of importance in its own right. Certainly also the result should give cause to protagonists of girls' schools to hesitate before claiming that teaching is better in girls' than in mixed schools.

The joint result of the two questions on the pressure of academic work is emphatic. Both the females and males are highly positive that they were more worried by the pressure of work in their single-sex than they were in their co-educational schools. In the results on the amount of homework, also, the estimates for the co-educational schools tend to be balanced around 'just right', while those for the single-sex schools stress the 'too much' categories, the difference being statistically highly significant.

The teachers in boys' and girls' schools might argue that the 'consumers'—even as ex-pupils who have passed most of their examinations and are intending teachers—are not the best people to judge what amount of homework is best for a child. But the issue is not as simple as that. For example, the co-educated pupils appear to feel less pressure and have less homework to do, and if it is argued that the amount is inadequate how does it come about that—taking all factors into account —their results at O-level are at least equal to those of the pupils from single-sex schools? The greater pressure and additional homework would be expected to produce superior results—but they do not appear to do so. Though the greater happiness of these pupils in their co-educational schools might have made their work-load lighter, one would not have expected it to have made so much difference. The argument is also two-edged because even if the work-load only *appears* to be lighter, this is surely a good characteristic of a school.

The results from this 'Both schools' survey should be more dependable and more valid than those from the other main samples, because these ex-pupils were able to look back on the two types of school they attended. We now turn to the results obtained from present pupils.

Schools project

Present pupils in the 42 grammar schools of this project, reduced to 36 in the second testing, completed a questionnaire which contained a number of items about their work in school. Each item asked for an estimate given on a five-point scale. At the first administration the pupils were 11 plus and 15 plus, and there was a repeat administration to the same pupils two years later. The estimates were analysed in the following ways, comparing co-educated pupils with those educated in single-sex schools:

(a) Overall average estimates at age 11 plus, 13 plus, 15 plus and 17 plus. For pupils aged 11 plus the analysis was often omitted because they had been at the schools only a short time; that for pupils aged 17 plus was somewhat tentative because of the decided differences in policy from one school to another (and, one suspects, from one type to another) over the admission of pupils to the sixth form.

(b) The preparation of distribution tables showing the increase or decrease of the estimates of all individuals for each item, from the first to the second testing.

(c) Co-educated pupils were matched with individuals from the relevant single-sex schools, on intelligence score and socio-economic class, and their estimates compared at 13 plus and 17 plus. The matching on intelligence was rather rough as the scores available had a range of only 0 to 10, but it was necessary owing to the imbalance favouring especially the girls' schools. A similar imbalance in social class distribution favoured both boys' and girls' single-sex schools.

Unfortunately there was another difficulty with this sample in the peculiar circumstance that the drop-outs at age 13 plus (i.e. those who for one reason or another did not appear in the testing room for the second testing) were less anxious about school than the average on the co-educational side and more anxious than average on the single-sex side (Table A2.7). Remarkably, this happened for boys as well as for girls, and disturbs the representativeness of the samples, as the drop-outs approached 10 per cent of the total, handicapping the co-educational schools in the comparison at age 13 plus, and affecting the longitudinal analysis also.

To have reported the results from all three methods of analysis would have imposed an unnecessarily wearisome task on the reader. Instead the methods have been collated and found to give similar results; these are reported, with indications of divergences when necessary. In this report of the Schools project results any difference which is reliable (i.e. 'statistically significant') is marked with an asterisk, those 'highly significant' with two asterisks and so on.

HOMEWORK AND GENERAL EFFORT

The first section related to this topic contained the items: 'I try my hardest in school work: Nearly always/Often/Sometimes/Occasionally/ Rarely.'
'I do my written homework: Nearly always/Often/etc.'
'I do my learning homework: Nearly always/Often/etc.'
'I do my reading homework: Nearly always/Often/etc.' (1964 only)
The results of the last item were not checked by means of the matched samples.

The girls

The analysis of the girls' estimates is confined to those from girls aged 13 plus, 15 plus (where applicable) and for most items, 17 plus. Few of the differences were sufficiently large to be statistically significant. The results for 'I try my hardest in school work' slightly favoured the co-educated girls aged 13 plus and the difference increased at 17 plus[1] but there was no difference at 15 plus. For written homework a slight advantage to the girls' schools at 13 years of age was countered by a

[1] $t = 1 \cdot 116$.

strong opposing trend at age 15, which approached statistical significance. The difference in favour of the co-educated girls at 17 years of age became still greater in the matched sample.* The item on 'learning homework' yielded a difference at age 13 which was substantial though not statistically significant, the co-educated girls being rather better at getting this work done, a difference maintained in the matched sample, and at age 15 this difference was still greater.* Here 49 per cent of the girls in co-educational schools said they 'always' did their learning homework, compared to 37 per cent of girls in girls' schools. A smaller difference in the same direction occurred at age 17 in the 'matched' sample. For 'reading homework' there was a further change of trend, a slightly greater number of the 15-year-old girls from girls' schools than of those from co-educational schools estimating that they 'nearly always' or 'often' did their reading homework. This item was not included for 13- and 17-year-olds.

The boys

The parallel samples of boys answered the same items; no difference was statistically significant. Of the seven possible comparisons three were even, one gave a minimal and two a slight advantage to the co-educational schools and the seventh, for written homework, indicated that the boys aged 13 plus and 17 plus from boys' schools, for whatever reason, were rather more zealous about doing their *written* homework.[1] The co-educated boys, however, at both these ages had the more favourable estimates on 'learning homework'.[2]

A point of some little interest is that it is on the item concerned with *written* homework that the boys' schools do best, and this may be a result of the rather stricter discipline in these schools, where the written work would be tangible evidence that it had been done, whereas there would not be the same clear proof about the learning homework, and it is here that the co-educational schools had some advantage. Though all in all there is a slight advantage to the co-educational schools, only two of the differences reached statistical significance, both favourable to the co-educated girls.

THE NATURE AND EFFECT OF SCHOOL WORK

Two additional and related items were, 'The intense pressure of work at school worries me', and 'To what extent do you consider your school keeps a fair balance between school work and other aspects of school life?' (1966 only). The results from the girls are taken first.

[1] $t = 1.471$ and 1.326 respectively in the matched sample.
[2] $t = 1.253$ and 1.496 respectively in the matched sample.

The girls

Though the difference between the distribution of the estimates given by the samples of girls aged 13 plus for the item on 'Intense pressure' is statistically significant this is difficult to interpret because it is partly the result of conflicting rather than complementary tendencies, and the results are therefore given in full (see Table A2.15). A study of the table will show that although some 39 per cent of the co-educated girls aged

TABLE 9.4   *Balance between school work and other aspects (girls)*

Schools project

	Replies from girls aged 13 plus				Replies from girls aged 17 plus			
	Co-ed schools		Girls' schools		Co-ed schools		Girls' schools	
	N	%	N	%	N	%	N	%
Far too much work	12	5·6	15	7·1	3	2·6	14	11·7
Rather too much work	40	18·6	43	20·3	20	17·4	32	26·7
Balanced	151	70·2	135	63·7	83	72·1	51	42·5
Rather too little work	8	3·7	16	7·5	8	7·0	13	10·8
Much too little work	4	1·9	3	1·4	1	0·9	10	8·3
Totals	215	100	212	100	115	100	120	100

NOTE: The difference between the estimates of co-educated girls and those from girls' schools falls short of significance for the 13-year-olds but is highly significant for girls aged 17 plus (P < 0·001).

13 plus agreed with this statement, compared with the 32 per cent of girls from girls' schools, within this group an opposite tendency occurred in that only 6 per cent of the former agreed *strongly*, and 10·3 per cent of the latter. Similarly this general trend (of 39 and 32 per cent) changes direction at the other end of the distribution, where 35 per cent of the co-educated said they disagreed or disagreed strongly that the pressure worried them as against 33 per cent from the girls' schools.[1] As the differences between the two distributions do not form a consistent

[1] The amount of the chi-square is therefore made up from two opposing trends.

logical progression we can discount the statistical significance of the resulting chi-square. That the difference is a small one is supported by comparing the mean scores obtained when we give the estimates weightings or 'scores' on a scale ranging from five to one; the means are almost equal. Though this weighting is admittedly somewhat arbitrary it would be quite capable of revealing any decided trend in one direction, and that it does not show such a trend provides strong support for the above argument. The results from the matched sample agree with this finding in that the co-educated show minimally less worry. At age 17 appreciably more of the girls from girls' schools than from co-educational schools agreed or agreed strongly that the intense pressure of work worried them, and logically this time, fewer girls from girls' schools disagreed strongly that it worried them. This trend was repeated in the matched sample.[1]

The item on the balance between school work and the other aspects of school life gave results at 13 plus in which rather more co-educated girls than those from girls' schools thought there was a better balance, the latter giving slightly more stress to both 'too much' and 'too little'. At age 17 plus the co-educated girls were much more strongly of this opinion than were the girls from girls' schools, 72 per cent of the former estimating 'Balanced' as against the 43 per cent of the latter (Table 9.4).

The boys

The boys from boys' schools aged 13 plus felt the pressure of work minimally less than those from the co-educational schools, and slightly less in the group aged 17 plus, neither difference approaching dependability. When the opposing groups were matched in pairs on social class and intelligence this difference unexpectedly increased for the older boys, but was still not statistically significant.[2] This is a result which is difficult to understand, as one would have expected the tighter control in boys' schools to have produced the opposite effect. It is possible that the difference is produced by the presence of female teachers in the mixed school, as the results from the girls' schools suggest that they are more hard-driving.

There was no clear-cut result from the item on the balance between work and other aspects of school life; the co-educated boys, however, gave estimates which showed a better balance than those of their opposite numbers, at both 13 and 17 years of age, neither difference being large enough to be reliable.

[1] $t = 1.265$.
[2] Chi-square $= 7.436$ for 4 DF.

Attitude to school work and school subjects

Taking these two related items together the results for the boys are so inconclusive that the full data are not presented.

ENJOYMENT OF SCHOOL WORK

Another group of questions was about the enjoyment—or the reverse—of school work: 'Taking the subjects all together, how much do you *enjoy* your school work?'

'Our lessons are made more enjoyable because teachers and pupils are ready to share a joke.'

'We have lots of interesting discussions in class.'

These items were answered on a five-point scale and there was an opportunity for comment after each one. They were included only in the 1966 questionnaire; results are therefore available only for pupils aged 13 plus and 17 plus.

The girls

At the age of 13 plus there was a scarcely perceptible advantage to the girls' schools, but at age 17 plus the estimates of the co-educated girls showed appreciably more enjoyment, especially for the full sample*

TABLE 9.5   *Enjoyment of school work (girls)*

Schools project

| | Replies from girls aged 13 plus | | | | Replies from girls aged 17 plus | | | |
| | Co-ed schools | | Girls' schools | | Co-ed schools | | Girls' schools | |
	N	%	N	%	N	%	N	%
Enjoy much	78	37·8	81	38·6	65	58·0	50	42·4
Enjoy a little	85	41·2	85	40·4	27	24·1	41	34·7
Jogging along	24	11·7	31	14·8	17	15·2	16	13·6
Dislike a little	16	7·8	10	4·8	2	1·8	8	6·8
Dislike much	3	1·5	3	1·4	1	0·9	3	2·5
Totals	206	100	210	100	112	100	118	100

NOTE: At the age of 17 plus the greater enjoyment of the co-educated girls is statistically significant (P < 0·05).

(Table 9.5) though not significantly so with the reduced numbers of the matched sample.[1]

'Readiness to share a joke' produced results showing a greater readiness in the classrooms of the co-educational schools, the difference between the two types of schools being rather greater at the age of 17 plus than for those aged 13 plus. Though at both ages it was a little short of statistical significance, the direction was the same and each result gives strong support to the other[2] (Table 9.6).

TABLE 9.6   *Teachers and pupils ready to share a joke (girls)*

Schools project

| | Replies from girls aged 13 plus | | | | Replies from girls aged 17 plus | | | |
| | Co-ed schools | | Girls' schools | | Co-ed schools | | Girls' schools | |
	N	%	N	%	N	%	N	%
Agree strongly	39	18·3	44	20·5	25	21·7	24	20·0
Agree	131	61·5	114	53·0	77	67·0	68	56·7
Doubtful	35	16·4	37	17·2	7	6·1	9	7·5
Disagree	4	1·9	14	6·5	6	5·2	16	13·3
Disagree strongly	4	1·9	6	2·8	0	0	3	2·5
Totals	213	100	215	100	115	100	120	100

NOTE: Greater readiness of co-educated girls and their teachers to share a joke falls a little short of statistical significance at both ages.

The item on interesting discussions in class unexpectedly produced inconclusive results, with a minimal advantage to girls' schools for pupils aged 13 plus and equality at age 17. The full results are therefore not given.

The boys

At the age of 13 the co-educated boys enjoyed their work slightly more than did boys from boys' schools, but at age 17 this tendency was

[1] $t = 1·537$ for the matched sample.
[2] Became statistically significant in the matched sample: $t = 2·457$.

reversed.[1] For 'sharing a joke', however, the co-educated boys aged 13 thought there was greater readiness to share a joke than did the opposite group,* but the groups of 17-year-olds showed equality (Table 9.7).

TABLE 9.7   *Teachers and pupils ready to share a joke (boys)*

Schools project

| | Replies from boys aged 13 plus | | | | Replies from boys aged 17 plus | | | |
| | Co-ed schools | | Boys' schools | | Co-ed schools | | Boys' schools | |
	N	%	N	%	N	%	N	%
Agree strongly	45	20·0	47	21·7	45	33·8	50	36·5
Agree	140	62·2	116	53·4	77	57·9	79	57·7
Doubtful	31	13·8	31	14·3	9	6·8	4	2·9
Disagree	8	3·6	19	8·8	2	1·5	3	2·2
Disagree strongly	1	0·4	4	1·8	0	0	1	0·7
Totals	225	100	217	100	133	100	137	100

NOTE: The difference between the estimates of co educated boys aged 13 plus and those from boys' schools is statistically significant (P < 0·05).

As with the girls the item on 'having lots of interesting discussions in class' produced an inconclusive result, with an advantage to the co-educational schools at 13 years of age,[2] but equality after the 17-year-olds. This brings us to the last of the items in this section: 'I'm rather afraid to speak out in class.'

AFRAID TO SPEAK OUT IN CLASS

This item was included in an attempt to get some specific information about an argument used sometimes by the protagonists of single-sex schools—that girls would be inhibited from answering questions and taking part in discussions because of the presence of boys. As also the writer's earlier analyses of research on the comparative attainment of the two types of school had uncovered several hints that the co-

[1] $t = 1·509$ for age 17 years in the matched samples.
[2] $t = 1·471$ for the matched sample.

educated boys might not be as superior—or might sometimes be a little inferior—in French to boys in boys' schools (though in view of the number of unwanted variables the 'hints' are only tentative possibilities), this reversal of the usual trend might conceivably be at least partly due to the co-educated boys, especially when their voices were changing, being reluctant to make an effort with French pronunciation in front of an opposite sex who on the average tend to be more at home in this aspect of the work.

TABLE 9.8   *Afraid to speak out in class (girls)*

Schools project

	Replies from girls aged 13 plus				Replies from girls aged 17 plus			
	Co-ed schools		Girls' schools		Co-ed schools		Girls' schools	
	N	%	N	%	N	%	N	%
Always afraid	16	7·5	6	2·8	9	7·9	4	3·3
Often	63	29·6	51	23·9	27	23·7	27	22·5
Sometimes	87	40·8	101	47·5	42	36·9	45	37·5
Hardly ever	31	14·6	36	16·9	24	21·0	29	24·2
Never	16	7·5	19	8·9	12	10·5	15	12·5
Totals	213	100	213	100	114	100	120	100

NOTE: Though the greater fear of speaking out in class expressed by the co-educated girls aged 13 is not by convention statistically significant the difference between the two groups of this age is not negligible, and the slight difference between the groups aged 17 is in the same direction.

Though the results in both the full and the matched samples were far from conclusive there was a slight tendency for them to be in the expected direction, especially with the girls. Those aged 13 from co-educational schools expressed rather more reluctance to speak out in class than their opposite numbers did, but this difference was too small to be reliable. At 17 years of age there was again some advantage to the girls' schools (Tables 9.8 and 9.9). Co-educated boys aged 13 had a minimal advantage, but those aged 17 were rather more reluctant to speak out than were the sample of boys from boys' schools. Both results were repeated in the matched sample, reaching the accepted standard of reliability for boys at 17 years of age. The effect of this factor, if it exists,

TABLE 9.9 *Afraid to speak out in class (boys)*
Schools project

| | Replies from boys aged 17 plus | | | |
| | Co-educational schools | | Boys' schools | |
	N	%	N	%
Always afraid	1	0·8	0	0
Often	30	22·6	21	15·3
Sometimes	43	32·3	50	36·5
Hardly ever	43	32·3	46	33·6
Never	16	12·0	20	14·6
Totals	133	100	137	100

NOTE: The difference increased and became statistically significant in the matched sample.

would depend in part on the teaching method used. If indeed it is confirmed that the presence of the opposite sex in class, though welcomed by pupils and by teachers, has some restricting effect on 'speaking out in class' or on oral work, this would need specific attention in teacher training. However, the free responses provided some additional evidence.

Free responses

The free responses of the girls on the reasons for being 'afraid to speak out in class' are tabulated in Tables 9.10 and 9.11, where for simplification the categories 'Always', 'Often', and 'Sometimes' are combined. The wording 'speaking out in class' confers a rather wide meaning to the item; this is because it was felt desirable to include discussion as well as the asking and answering of questions. Several questions instead of one would, however, have given us more informative and more precise results.

In view of what has already been said about the girls' estimates (5-point scales) on this topic the data in Tables 9.10 and 9.11 seem rather unhelpful. Taking the two sexes together only four replies out of 362 attribute the fear to the presence of boys and two of these were from girls' schools! (For financial reasons boys sometimes attend the sixth forms of a girls' school to study one or more subjects.) We can therefore discount any *strong* and widespread reluctance to speak out in front of boys rather than in front of their girl peers. However, the difficulty having at least been voiced it is possible that other girls might either feel this more mildly or even unconsciously and record it under a more comprehensive heading. Yet this cannot be detected in the free responses of either the 13- or the 17-year-old girls. Out of almost

TABLE 9.10 *Afraid to speak out in class: free responses of girls aged 13 plus*

Schools project

Always + often + sometimes	Co-ed schools	Single-sex schools
afraid to be wrong,		
look foolish, be laughed at	39	56
embarrassed, lack confidence	40	22
friends made me laugh	1	
nothing to say, don't know	3	1
stammer	2	1
opportunity rare		1
depends on teacher	10	11
with head		1
fear of teacher, criticism	5	6
depends on subject (or teacher?)	12	12
dislike disagreeing		2
depends what I have to say		2
rude comments from boys	1	
others, general	9	6
Total	122	121

identical totals of responses the 13-year-old co-educated girls express embarrassment, lack of confidence, 'afraid to be wrong', look foolish or be laughed at in 79 of them and girls from girls' schools in 78, while at age 17 the figures are 37 for both sides! On the other hand the co-educated girls did show in the estimates a somewhat greater reluctance to speak out. If the difference is due to the presence of boys in the classrooms of co-educational schools—which seems the most likely explanation—its size is not large enough to create serious problems, though it should not be ignored. Breuse (1970) also found some similar diffidence in individuals in his Couvin enquiry (p. 86).

In view of findings in the preceding volumes it would seem unlikely that the greater embarrassment or lack of confidence among the co-educated girls could be due to the teachers, nor is there any hint of it in

TABLE 9.11 *Afraid to speak out in class: free responses of girls aged 17 plus*

. *Schools project*

Always + often + sometimes	Co-ed schools	Single-sex schools
afraid to be wrong,		
look foolish, be laughed at	31	29
embarrassed, lack confidence,		
hate it	6	8
don't understand,		
don't know what to say	1	1
dislike giving views, afraid,		
dislike or disagree	1	4
feel inferior		1
stutter	2	
depends on teacher	6	3
depends on subject (or teacher?)	2	6
teachers find fault, sarcastic,		
lack understanding	2	1
not fluent in English	1	
little practice		1
depends on mood	3	2
only with head	1	
don't know why afraid		1
depends on strength of view		1
less than previously	2	
depends on sex of class		2
more so with boys	1	
Total	59	60

the free responses. A further point is that learning to speak out in front of boys might be viewed as part of the 'education for life' which the ex-pupils insist is given much more by the co-educational than by the girls' schools.

The free responses of the boys' groups are given in Tables A2.16 and A2.17. Here we find only two small voices possibly hinting at a dislike of speaking out in front of girls, out of 306 replies, though neither is specific. 'When speaking French' and 'Depends who is in class' need not imply that girls are in mind—though they well may be. So much for the strong, direct or widespread fear of speaking out in front of girls; neither do the other categories of response provide any support for the idea, as at 13 years of age rather fewer of the co-educated boys' responses admit embarrassment or 'fear of being wrong, looking foolish' etc than do those boys in boys' schools, while at 17 there is equality if both categories are taken together, but here the numbers are small. It is curious, however, in view of the argument set out earlier, that French should be the subject singled out by a boy in a co-educational school, and this topic will be examined again in a later chapter. In passing we see that fear of speaking out because of the teacher (or subject, which may mean teacher) is more prevalent among the boys in boys' schools (30 ex 160) than among co-educated boys (17 ex 146). The expected pattern is here maintained, though not between the girls' groups, where there was equality.

The 'Check' survey

Only two of the items in this chapter were presented to the 1,122 girls aged 13 in the 'Check' survey. These were those on the enjoyment of school work and sharing a joke with the teacher in class. There was no difference in the distribution of the estimates for co-educated girls and those from girls' schools for either of the items. Yet the slightly superior social class of the girls in girls' schools and their probably larger superiority in intelligence should, failing any force in opposition, have produced for them the greater success in their work, leading to greater enjoyment of school work and therefore greater readiness on the part of the teacher to share a joke with them.

Other relevant research

The only other large-scale work that this writer has been able to discover on the comparative attitudes of co-educated and single-sex educated pupils towards work is contained in a valuable book edited by Pidgeon and published by the National Foundation for Educational Research (1967). One of the attitude scales they administered to the national sample of schoolchildren (in age groups commencing at 13) was on attitudes towards school and school learning. As Pidgeon rightly points out in his concluding chapter, the samples from co-educational secondary schools cannot validly be compared with those from single-sex schools because of the imbalance produced by such forces as the unselective comprehensive schools being mostly co-educational and the highly selective direct grant schools being almost entirely single-sex. It so happens, however, that in spite of what one would normally regard as serious handicaps for academic progress—their lower intelligence and social class levels—the co-educated pupils have higher mean scores on attitude to school work in most age groups up to O-level.

Attitude to school work and school subjects

TABLE 9.12 *Means and standard errors of means on 'school and learning'*
attitude scale, by population and sex[1]

Possible range of scores: 0 to 22

	Replies from boys in				Replies from girls in			
	Co-ed schools		Boys' schools		Co-ed schools		Girls' schools	
	Mean	S.E.	Mean	S.E.	Mean	S.E.	Mean	S.E.
13-year-olds	9·38	0·12	9·22	0·13	9·56	0·13	9·10	0·12†
3rd formers	9·19	0·13	9·23	0·12	9·62	0·14	9·22	0·13*
15-year-olds	9·76	0·18	9·19	0·21*	9·94	0·20	8·88	0·24†
O-level candidates	8·65	0·19	8·58	0·12	8·85	0·21	8·71	0·15
A-level mathematicians	8·14	0·17	8·58	0·10*	8·05	0·32	8·60	0·24
A-level non-maths	8·91	0·25	8·54	0·09	8·45	0·17	8·50	0·10

NOTE: A high score expresses enthusiasm for school and the experience it provides, and a low score the reverse.
[1] Reproduced by permission of D. A. Pidgeon, J. Hall and the NFER.
* indicates co-educational/single-sex difference statistically significant at 0·05 level; † co-educational/single-sex difference statistically significant at 0·01 level.

The younger schoolchildren from co-educational schools showed more enthusiasm for school than did similar groups in single-sex schools and this is also true for boys in the sixth who did not take mathematics, though for similar girl sixth formers there was virtual equality between the two groups. In the case only of those pupils taking an A-level in mathematics were the pupils from single-sex schools more enthusiastic; it is possible that for the boys this may be due to the distinctly better mathematics staff in boys' direct grant and maintained grammar schools and in the case of the girls to the possibly finer 'selection' of candidates. As, however, pupils in modern and comprehensive schools (mostly co-educational) were more enthusiastic about school than those in grammar and direct grant schools, which is rather surprising, we are in very deep water and must await other interpretative evidence.

General summary and comment

The results of so many questionnaire items have been presented that the reader may have difficulty in summing them up to arrive at a judgment.

A summary is therefore given of all those findings which reached a reasonable level of certainty, i.e. that of accepted statistical significance, though to avoid a too artificial rigidity mention is made of a few findings which fall near this line and find support from related findings. The summary is as follows.

GIRLS

'Both schools' survey

1 Those who first attended a co-educational school gave higher estimates for the quality of the teaching there than those who attended a girls' school first gave about that school (P < 0·01).
2 Both as junior and senior pupils many more of the respondents estimated that the intense pressure of work for examinations worried them more in their girls' than in their co-educational schools (P < 0·001 in both cases).
3 Similarly, as juniors and seniors more of them estimated that the pressure of work made them anxious in their girls' schools than in their co-educational schools (P < 0·001 in both cases).
4 Both as juniors and seniors more of the respondents thought that the amount of homework was too much in their girls' schools compared with their co-educational schools (P < 0·001).

Schools project

1 The co-educated girls aged 17 gave more favourable estimates about doing their written homework (P < 0·05).
2 The co-educated girls aged 15 plus gave higher estimates than girls from girls' schools about doing their learning homework (P < 0·05), the trend at 13 plus being the same.
3 On the item 'the intense pressure of work worries me' there was (by chi-square) a statistically significant difference at age 13 in favour of girls' schools; this was, however, unsound logically, as sometimes occurs in this test, and the weighted means of the opposing students were equal. (At age 17 the difference was in the opposite direction and logically sound, though not significant.)
4 Co-educated girls aged 17 plus agreed much more than those from girls' schools that there was a good balance in their school between work and other activities (P < 0·001). The same trend was present but less strong for the girls aged 13.
5 Co-educated girls aged 17 gave higher estimates of enjoyment of school work (P < 0·05).
6 Co-educated girls aged 13 plus and 17 plus gave higher estimates than those from girls' schools about the readiness of teachers and pupils

to share a joke. (A little short of significance, but reaches this level for girls aged 17 in the matched sample.)

7 More of the co-educated girls aged 13 plus were afraid to speak out in class (not significant, but a small clear difference that needs investigation).

Pidgeon's project

Co-educated girls tended to show more enthusiasm for school, up to the O-level of the GCE, than did girls from girls' schools. After that age the samples are not comparable.

BOYS

'Both schools' survey

1 For 'first' schools the pressure of examinations tended to be more worrying in the ex-pupils' boys' schools than for those who attended co-educational schools first. (A little below statistical significance.)

2 For 'first' schools, on 'pressure of work made me anxious', the co-educated ex-pupils gave lower estimates than their opposite numbers (almost at 0.01 level). There was a similar non-significant trend for 'last' schools.

3 The pressure of homework was much greater in boys' schools than in co-educational ($P < 0.001$ for first and 0.05 for last schools).

Schools project

1 The boys aged 13 plus from boys' schools tended to report doing their written homework more often than did those from co-educational schools (not significant but substantial).

2 The boys aged 13 plus from boys' schools considered their teachers were less ready to share a joke than did the co-educated boys ($P < 0.05$).

3 Co-educated boys aged 17 appeared to be more reluctant to speak out in class than were the sample of boys from boys' schools (a moderate difference in the full sample but statistically significant in the matched sample).

Pidgeon's project

Co-educated boys tended to show more enthusiasm for school, up to O-level GCE, than did boys from boys' schools. After that age samples cease to be comparable. But see comments in text about the opposing samples.

Comment

An overview of the material in this chapter leads to the conclusion that, on the evidence presented, the chief danger would seem to be over-pressure in girls' schools—occasionally seriously so—and maybe under-pressure in some co-educational schools. Protagonists of girls' schools used to put forward the argument that girls are more susceptible to strain than boys and would be more liable to be overworked in a co-educational school; *this is no longer tenable* as it seems likely that girls would be more liable to be over-strained in a girls' school, maybe because the zeal and perhaps over-conscientiousness of women staff is not—or has not been until recently—tempered by the broader outlook and, as the women might say, the less insistent zeal of men.

More of the women ex-pupils estimated there was too much home-work in their girls' schools, while the amount was satisfactory in their co-educational school. Similarly for 'the intense pressure of work for examinations'. Those female ex-pupils who attended their co-educational school first also judged the teaching to be better at their co-educational school. More of the girls in the co-educational schools appeared to do their written and learning homework regularly; at some ages this difference was large enough to be statistically significant. The co-educated girls also gave higher estimates for enjoying school work and sharing a joke with the teacher, and judged there was a better balance between academic work and other activities than the girls from girls' schools judged about their schools. In this Schools project, however, there was a tendency for these differences about academic work to be largest at ages 15 and 17; in the check survey for girls aged 13 there was equality between the two sides on both enjoyment of school work and sharing a joke with the teacher. Pidgeon's survey gives general support to the findings in that his co-educated girls, at several ages, had more favourable mean scores on attitude to school work.

On the male side the summing up is not so simple. On the quality of teaching an advantage to boys' schools for 'first school attended' was more than balanced by an opposite tendency in 'last schools attended'. As on the female side, more of the male ex-pupils thought that the pressure of work in their boys' schools made them anxious, compared with their co-educational schools, and they also concurred that the amount of homework was too much. However the boys of the Schools project produced an opposite trend on anxiety, very slight at 13 years of age and slight at 17 except in the matched sample, in which the difference was surprisingly substantial, though not statistically significant.

For written homework the boys' schools had an advantage, countered by a similar difference in favour of the co-educational schools on 'learning homework'. On 'reading homework' (age 15 only) there was virtual equality. The co-educated pupils gave rather better estimates than those from boys' schools on the balance between work and other activities (slight), sharing a joke with the teacher and having interesting discussions in class, but the pupils aged 17 in boys' schools appeared to enjoy their work more (approached significance in the matched sample). To round off this section, Pidgeon's survey found the co-educated boys in secondary schools to have the more favourable mean scores on attitude to school work.

To sum up, the co-educational schools have a decided advantage for both sexes in the results of the 'Both schools' survey and that of Pidgeon, while in the Schools project the co-educated girls have a smaller though distinct advantage, and the co-educated boys a somewhat smaller one which is occasionally reversed in the 17-year-old sample. The reasons for the difference between the results from these two samples have been examined elsewhere, but the principal ones may well be:

1 In the 'Both schools' survey the ex-pupils were able to compare their experiences in the two types of school, and would not be so influenced by loyalty to one school or by fear of the staff or head reading the replies.

2 The 'Both schools' survey represented many more schools than did the Schools project, which represented only 13 schools of each kind in the first instance, reduced later to 12. This small number was strictly a pilot survey and was too liable to drastic fluctuation by the chance inclusion of one or two specially good or bad schools of each type. The attempt at 'tripling' the schools to equalize the social backgrounds also gave rise to uneasiness. (One headmistress kindly volunteered the information, after the field work, that she knew that the quality of entrants to her girls' school, an older establishment, was better than that of the co-educational school with which it was paired, and expressed surprise at the pairing, which had been left in the hands of an independent official. Nor should the official be blamed for this as the task was difficult.)

3 As detailed previously (cf. Table A2.7) the 13-year-old co-educated drop-outs from the testing were better than average on 'anxiety to school' while those for the single-sex schools were worse than the average. This applied to both sexes and would produce some bias against the co-educational schools in the rest of the sample aged 13.

4 A *theoretical* possibility is that the norms of many attitudes such as 'happiness in school' may, for lack of sufficient comparison, evolve for each separate community, and only when both types of school had been sampled would a more accurate norm be established. For example, a pupil might estimate himself as 'happy' in one type of school, but on going to another type find he was much happier, and realize that in the previous school he had been only 'fairly happy'. In this way the norms

for pupils who had known only a single-sex *or* a co-educational school would be closer together than the separate norms given to these two types of school by pupils or ex-pupils who had attended both. This may be a principle which affects much of life and has an influence on the results of some research. (It may even extend to the marking of examination papers in school batches.) An apt title for it might be '*the law of the sheltered norm*', or more precisely 'each separate institution or sample tends to develop its own norm'.

Left to the end because its outcome is different from that of the others is the item, 'I'm afraid to speak out in class'. Though the size of the difference between the co-educational and single-sex schools on this item is not large it is consistent at ages 13 and 17 for girls and at 17 for boys (slightly reversed for boys aged 13). In spite of what has been said about the sample of the Schools project this looks like a true difference, probably due to co-education. If it exists an awareness of it could lead to conscious steps to improve the reactions of both sexes. The constant practice of speaking out in front of the opposite sex in the classroom is of course not only a necessary part of co-education but also a necessary part of education for social life in the world.

10

Attitudes to arithmetic and mathematics

Most of us can remember something of our struggle with mathematics—the hesitancy and for some the fear which accompanied the uncertain oral answer, though there was sometimes also the joy of achievement. The stress of this prolonged 'test situation' has already been illustrated, together with its generalized psychological effects. Mathematics is the *bête noire* of many girls and of some boys, while French affects the two sexes in reverse manner. There is evidence that strong dislike of mathematics or of French (or Latin) is a characteristic of many severe deteriorators in secondary schools (cf. Dale and Griffith, 1965) and the distaste sometimes causes a pupil to hate school and most things attached to it.

We are concerned here with a related question—whether co-educational schooling, as opposed to single-sex schooling, has any effect on attitude to the subject. Mathematics has been selected not only because of its key position and strong influence but because it is the subject in which the co-educated pupils appear to do best as opposed to pupils from single-sex schools. It has been mentioned that this may be due to the social class handicap of the co-educational schools affecting them least in this subject, and also that with the co-educated girls better teaching may play a part, but the superiority seems so pervasive that other factors may be involved. This may be more clearly appreciated in the case of the boys, as the co-educated boys do better at O-level although their teachers are less well qualified. Enquiry into attitudes to the subject in the two types of school may give us more insight into the problem and the research was therefore extended to include this in a strictly exploratory way. The writer had not the resources of manpower and finance or even sufficient time to make a rigorous investigation into every small aspect of the controversy. Sometimes it was, so to speak, a trial bore-hole in what seemed a likely place, to determine whether a full-scale investigation might make a rich strike. Occasionally the trial bore produced so richly that a more scientific proving of the field was unnecessary; occasionally the bore was unrewarding, but more often its outcome was an invitation to further exploration.

This chapter is mainly concerned with two items relating to interest in arithmetic and mathematics, which were included in the Schools project questionnaire. Present pupils in some 40 schools were asked to underline the answer which was true for them in the item: Mathematics —Like much/Like a little/Neither like nor dislike/Dislike a little/Dislike much. Similarly for arithmetic, but these items were set only to pupils aged 11, 13 and 15. Written comments were invited. The item on arithmetic was repeated for a larger sample of 13-year-old girls in the Check questionnaire, without giving the pupils opportunity for free comment (for lack of administrative time).

For reasons set out in chapter 9 the main analysis was concentrated on the results of the 13-year-old pupils, and included a straight comparison of the liking for the subject shown by pupils of that age (and sometimes by those aged 15), a longitudinal analysis comparing changes of liking between 11 and 13 years of age, and in addition balanced samples and a matched pair procedure, both of which equalized intelligence and social class. All four methods were affected by the imbalance in the drop-outs, mentioned in chapter 9, which handicapped the co-educational schools. Nothing could be done about this. To avoid confusion and repetition some collation of the results from the various procedures is used in reporting the results. The girls' replies are taken first.

The girls

Because of the trend of the results in arithmetical and mathematical attainment the co-educated girls had been expected to express a greater liking for the two subjects than that expressed by the girls from girls' schools. Instead, at 13 years of age there was a minimally greater 'liking score' among the girls from girls' schools for both arithmetic and mathematics and the same minimal difference was repeated in a 'change over time' analysis between the ages of 11 and 13 (Table 10.1). These differences, however, disappeared and became complete equality when the two groups of pupils were 'balanced' for verbal intelligence and social class and opposed at 13 years of age. Analysis by a matched pairs technique confirmed the equality. The results from the same item (arithmetic) on the Check questionnaire, with a different sample of 1,122 girls of the same age from the same schools, again gave almost exactly the same distribution of the interest scores on each side, although this sample contained advantages in social class and intelligence for the girls' schools.

What is the explanation of this result? The question cannot be answered fully from the information available, but a few points can be made with certainty. It has already been shown that in the Check survey the sample of girls from girls' schools tends to be of slightly higher social class (Table A2.6) and like the sample from the Schools project,[1] involving the same schools, should have a rather higher

[1] Girls' schools significantly higher intelligence level (Table A2.1).

intelligence level; these factors acting alone should produce higher interest levels for the girls' schools. That they do not do so, or in some analyses only minimally, may be of some significance.

The effect of the imbalance among the drop-outs, commented on previously, also comes into consideration. In addition there is the evidence that one of the pairings of schools was less than fair to the co-educational school concerned. (The effect stemming from this would not be entirely removed by 'balancing' individuals for social class and intelligence score because of the influence of the dominant social class

TABLE 10.1   *Change in interest between 11 and 13 years (girls)*

Schools project, longitudinal sample

	Arithmetic: change in interest score between 11 and 13 years (scale range 1 to 5)									
	+4	+3	+2	+1	0	−1	−2	−3	−4	Totals
Co-educated girls	2	3	13	26	72	51	27	18	3	215
Girls in girls' schools	0	5	17	29	74	50	24	14	2	215
(chi-square = 1·588)										

	Mathematics: change in interest score between 11 and 13 years									
	+4	+3	+2	+1	0	−1	−2	−3	−4	Totals
Co-educated girls	1	6	13	36	67	49	23	14	5	214
Girls in girls' schools	1	10	18	38	60	44	27	14	3	215
(chi-square = 2·834)										

NOTE: A plus sign indicates greater interest.

attitudes in each school.) Lurking in the background all the time is the query arising from the smallness of the number of schools on each side and the possibly wide range of ability among the teachers.

Further examination of the data produced an additional influence. In recent years girls' schools, unable to recruit sufficiently well-qualified women mathematicians, have been appointing men instead. Such men tend to be popular in girls' schools, possibly partly because of their rarity, with the result that girls take more interest in the subjects they teach. Fortunately possibilities of this kind had been anticipated; the distributions of male and female teachers were checked in both the co-educational and the girls' schools, so that they could be linked with the

interest scores of their pupils. This was done for the largest sample—
that of the Check survey, resulting in Table 10.2.

In Table 10.2 there are two principal features, first, that the girls
taught by the male teachers in the girls' schools show more interest in
arithmetic than do the girls taught by female teachers in the same group
of schools, second, that the co-educated girls taught by male teachers
have *lower* interest scores than do the girls from girls' schools taught by

TABLE 10.2   *Attitude to arithmetic by sex of teacher: girls aged 13 plus*

'*Check*' *questionnaire*

	Replies from pupils taught by men				Replies from pupils taught by women			
	Co-ed schools		Girls' schools[2]		Co-ed schools		Girls' schools	
	N	%	N	%	N	%	N	%
Like much	56	18·5	46	23·6	33	22·9	112	23·4
Like a little	119	39·4	81	41·5	58	40·4	169	35·4
Neither like nor dislike	58	19·2	37	19·0	32	22·2	99	20·7
Dislike a little	44	14·6	23	11·8	11	7·6	69	14·4
Dislike much	25	8·3	8	4·1	10	6·9	29	6·1
Totals	302	100	195	100	144	100	478	100
Weighted means[1]	3·45		3·69		3·65		3·56	

[1] The higher the mean the greater the interest. Though the means should be
viewed with some caution because of the arbitrary weighting of the scores,
with their large numbers they are more informative than chi-square, which
for all co-educated *versus* all single-sex educated students was low and not
statistically significant.
[2] Six teachers only.

males, but those co-educated girls taught by women show *higher* interest
scores than do the girls from girls' schools who are taught by women.
The figures agree with the theory that the interest of girls in these girls'
schools in arithmetic is increased by the popularity of male teachers in
these schools, but the theory is not actually proved because, for

example, the male teachers might, by chance, be especially good, or the women teachers of arithmetic in the girls' schools not as good as average. No statistical test was made as the number of male teachers in girls' schools (6) was too small.

However, the balance of forces which produced this situation at 13 years of age, in this sample, probably persists to the age of 15 as at this age the girls in girls' schools showed a greater interest in arithmetic (almost statistically significant), and though the lead would be less if the differences in intelligence and social class were removed, this would probably not account for the whole of it (cf. Tables A2.1 and A2.2).

The problem is further complicated when the girls' estimates of interest in mathematics at 15 years of age are analysed by social class (Table A2.18). In this table the greater interest shown by the 15-year-old girls in girls' schools is entirely (and heavily)[1] due to social class 3 (daughters of skilled manual workers), classes 1 and 2, and 4 and 5 having the opposite tendency. This irregularity appears not to be due either to the higher incidence of the farming class among the pupils from social class 3 in the co-educational schools nor to the chance incidence of very good *or* male teachers in the girls' schools that had a large proportion of pupils from class 3 (and vice versa for the co-educational schools). There seemed to be a need to draw attention to this lack of consistency among the social classes, but the writer can in this case offer no explanation.

From evidence which will be presented about the comparative interest in other subjects it seems possible that in the co-educational schools there may be some *additional* polarization of interest by an interaction of sex and subject, the older girls tending to draw away from science and mathematics because the boys are better, and the boys correspondingly to draw away from literary subjects (such as French) in which the girls are better. Thus, in the subjects considered in this chapter—arithmetic and mathematics—one force making for a greater interest in the subject among girls in girls' schools, compared with *girls* in co-educational schools, may be this polarization effect. There seem, however, to be a number of factors involved, not all pulling in the same direction. For example, if the present finding at the age of 15 is replicated (there was equality at age 13 with intelligence and social class controlled), how does one explain the comparatively good showing of the co-educated girls in mathematical attainment at O-level? The answer might be that although the presence of boys in the class might increase the doubts of the girls about their ability, causing them to express less interest, yet this very presence could raise the girls' standard of attainment, through competition and also through an unconscious absorption of the boys' approach to mathematical problems.

[1] Statistically significant.

In all these considerations there is a danger that the immediate problem might loom too large; if we step back and consider the picture as a whole a truer balance is obtained. We are reminded that the principal factors producing a good level of interest and attainment, in any subject, are the ability, enthusiasm and personality of the teacher, given a reasonable equality in the intelligence level of the pupils. The large amount of variation in the level of interest between schools within each type and the overlap of the two is illustrated by the following table, though in order to ensure that there were sufficient numbers in each school the full sample had to be used, so that the imbalance of intelligence and social class makes a co-education/single-sex comparison inadvisable.

TABLE 10.3   *School mean scores for liking mathematics: girls aged 13 plus*

Schools project 1966 (range 1 to 5)
(C = co-educational; G = girls' school)

1	G	4·15	13	G	3·38
2	G	3·94	14	C	3·33
3	C	3·87	15	C	3·32
4	C	3·85	16	C	3·25
5	G	3·70	17	G	3·24
6	C	3·58	18	G	3·24
7	C	3·56	19	G	3·0
8	G	3·56	20	C	3·0
9	G	3·55	21	C	2·94
10	C	3·50	22	C	2·76
11	G	3·45	23	C	2·75
12	G	3·42	24	G	2·69

NOTE: The sample from the girls' schools is of rather higher intelligence and social class.

The boys

The expected pattern of the interest scores of the two opposing groups of boys would be a greater liking for arithmetic and mathematics among the co-educated boys, first because of the better progress they make, second because of the possible extra polarity effect in co-educational schools due to the sex/subject interaction, i.e. boys do better at mathematics than girls do, and it also tends to be regarded as a boys' subject, therefore the boys' expressed liking for the subject is increased by the presence of girls in their classes. This is the pattern we find.

In a longitudinal analysis examining the change in the liking for arithmetic between the ages 11 and 13 the co-educated boys started off with slightly more liking and the difference became considerable by the age of 13[1] (Table 10.4). In this analysis, however, the boys' schools had an appreciable in-built social class advantage in the sample (see Table A2.5). When this is removed by a matched pairs comparison at age 13 the difference in favour of the co-educated boys is again statistically significant.[2]

TABLE 10.4   *Interest in arithmetic at 11 and 13 years (boys)*

Schools project, longitudinal sample

| | Replies from boys aged 11 plus | | | | Replies from boys aged 13 plus | | | |
| | Co-ed schools | | Boys' schools | | Co-ed schools | | Boys' schools | |
	N	%	N	%	N	%	N	%
Like much	84	37·8	83	38·3	68	30·7	56	25·8
Like a little	60	27·0	50	23·0	76	34·2	58	26·6
Neither like nor dislike	40	18·0	39	18·0	42	18·9	42	19·4
Dislike a little	31	13·8	33	15·2	25	11·0	37	17·1
Dislike much	8	3·4	12	5·5	12	5·2	24	11·1
Totals	223	100	217	100	223	100	217	100

NOTE: At age 13 the co-educated boys have the statistically more favourable result.

As might be expected, mathematics follows the same trend, though not quite so markedly, and in the matched pairs analysis the greater liking shown by the co-educated boys did not quite reach the level of statistical significance.[3]

In assessing these results considerations to be kept in mind are the nature of the drop-out problem, which handicapped the co-educational schools, and the question of the smallness of the sample with only 13 schools on each side. We cannot be certain that the teachers 'opposing' each other are approximately equal overall in teaching ability, though the findings of the survey of the qualifications of teachers of mathematics show that the boys' schools normally have the better qualified

[1] Statistically significant at 13 plus; chi-square = 9·8 for 4 DF.
[2] $t = 2·385$.
[3] $t = 1·869$.

staff (chapter 4); if this holds good in the present sample the greater interest expressed by the co-educated boys would be all the more surprising and would also strengthen the suggestion of greater polarization among boys in co-educational schools. On the girls' side, however, the survey in chapter 4 found the teachers in the girls' schools to be less highly qualified than those in the co-educational schools; if this is also true in the present sample the greater interest shown by the older girls in girls' schools is (despite their various advantages) also more surprising and again strengthens the polarization argument. The results still take a natural place in the pattern which has been slowly evolving throughout the research. Within the general pattern this smaller one begins to emerge in this and the following chapter; these two chapters therefore give support to each other. It remains to be seen what effects the new methods of teaching mathematics will have on the findings, but there seems to be no obvious reason for any substantial changes except possibly a rise in the general level of interest.

The free responses of the boys and girls, though valuable in other respects, differentiate little between co-educational and single-sex schooling in the salient points made. Mathematics appears to arouse more keen hatred on the one hand, and real enjoyment on the other, than most other subjects. Apart from this, pupils concentrate mainly on the method of teaching or their own difficulty in understanding, and the two types of school are distinguished only by the number of the favourable and unfavourable comments; these replicate the result obtained from the estimates.

Attitudes to English literature, French and physics

English literature

The comparison of the attainment of co-educated and single-sex educated pupils has given us fairly clear expectations about the relative keenness of interest of these opposing groups in the various subjects of the curriculum, especially for the boys. In English literature, however, the expectations are less clear, possibly because in this subject the social class handicap of the co-educational schools acts more strongly on their attainment, so that even the co-educated boys do not have the same consistency in their lead that they have in most other subjects. If, however, the accentuation in co-educational schools of the polarization of interests by subject/sex interaction holds good in this subject (i.e. girls lean towards arts and boys towards science) and if there is nothing to counteract it, we would expect the co-educated boys to be less favourable to English literature than boys from boys' schools, and the girls' groups vice versa. Such an accentuation of this subject/sex interaction may be caused, at least partly, by the discouragement of the boys at the greater success of the girls in the same classes.

First come the girls' estimates.

THE GIRLS

In the longitudinal sample, measuring the comparative rate of change in the two types of school between the ages of 11 and 13, the girls from co-educational schools started off with interest estimates similar to those of the girls in girls' schools and finished at 13 years of age with a just discernible difference in favour of the girls' schools (Table 11.1). If this change is translated into actuarial terms it means that, on the average, 24 more from the girls' school sample of 205 girls than from the opposing sample increased their 'liking' score by one point of a five-point scale. Yet this analysis contained the far from negligible imbalance in social class and in intelligence level in favour of the girls' schools. When this was removed by a matched pairs analysis a state of complete equality was reached. However, all the caveats that were mentioned in the preceding chapter on mathematics apply here also, especially that concerned with the drop-outs (see Table A2.7), which should have given an advantage to the girls' schools.

At age 15 an analysis of the estimates of the 280 girls on each side yielded slightly greater interest among the pupils from girls' schools, which would have disappeared if intelligence and social class had been controlled.[1]

TABLE 11.1 *Interest in English literature at 11 and 13 years (girls)*
Schools project, longitudinal sample

	Replies from girls aged 11				Replies from girls aged 13			
	Co-ed schools		Girls' schools		Co-ed schools		Girls' schools	
	N	%	N	%	N	%	N	%
Like much	86	42·0	77	37·5	94	45·8	99	48·4
Like a little	64	31·2	77	37·5	60	29·3	63	30·7
Neither like nor dislike	34	16·6	29	14·2	27	13·2	24	11·7
Dislike a little	17	8·3	19	9·3	17	8·3	13	6·3
Dislike much	4	1·9	3	1·5	7	3·4	6	2·9
Totals	205	100	205	100	205	100	205	100

NOTE: Neither difference between the co-educated and girls' schools groups is statistically significant.

There appears here to be little sign of polarization of subject liking according to sex. It may be, however, that this force exerted a pressure but was neutralized or balanced by other factors which have not yet been discerned.

The two groups were so close together that their free comments also failed to distinguish between them; these comments are therefore omitted.

THE BOYS

In the rate of change analysis between 11 and 13 years of age there was near equality between the opposing samples in their estimates for liking

[1] Lack of time precluded the preparation of a matched sample or the use of a similar technique.

TABLE 11.2   *Change in interest towards English literature between 11 and 13 (boys)*

Schools project, longitudinal sample

	Change in interest score (scale range 1 to 5)									
	+4	+3	+2	+1	0	−1	−2	−3	−4	Totals
Co-educated boys	1	10	17	48	81	41	13	9	4	224
Boys in boys' schools	2	10	19	39	80	42	16	8	0	216

NOTE: A plus sign indicates greater interest. The difference is minimal. The advantage of the boys' schools in social class and drop-outs has not been removed.

English literature (Table 11.2). The very slight advantage of the boys' schools would disappear if account were taken of their social class superiority, the advantageous nature of their drop-out problem and the fact that rather more of their boys dropped the subject. Equality also resulted in the balanced sample and in a matched pairs analysis. There is again no overt evidence of any subject/sex interaction turning the co-educated boys against English literature; it could still be exerting an influence, as with the girls, and be neutralized by some force acting in the opposite direction, such as the greater richness of lessons in English literature when pupils of both sexes are taking part, but this is in the realm of speculation.

The free comments again fail to offer anything new about the main theme.

French

French was selected for inclusion in the school subjects investigated in this enquiry because, during the writer's previous studies, there had been indications that French was not as definitely 'in pattern' as were almost all other school subjects. These indications concerned the slightly lower attainment of co-educated boys in this subject compared with those from boys' schools, so that the following *girls'* results came as something of a surprise.

THE GIRLS

At the start of their secondary school career the co-educated girls liked French a little less than did the girls in girls' schools, but by the age of

13 the co-educated girls had clearly the more favourable estimates (Figure 11.1). Viewed another way—by examining the increase or decrease in this liking recorded by each individual, we arrive at Table 11.3

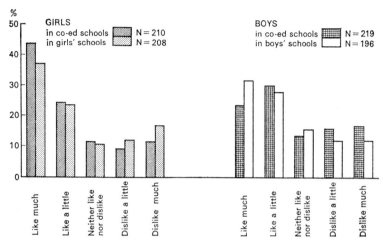

NOTE: Neither the difference between the girls nor that between the boys is statistically significant. Fewer boys in boys' schools took the subject compared with those in co-educational schools.

FIGURE 11.1 *Interest in French at 13 years (girls and boys): Schools project, longitudinal sample*

which makes the trend clearer. Additionally, when intelligence and social class are equalized by the matched pairs technique the difference in favour of the co-educated girls becomes almost statistically

TABLE 11.3 *Change in interest in French between 11 and 13 (girls)*

Schools project, longitudinal sample

	Change in interest score (scale range 1 to 5)									
	+4	+3	+2	+1	0	−1	−2	−3	−4	Totals
Co-educated girls	3	6	14	32	76	35	24	12	8	210
Girls from girls' schools	2	7	6	18	73	46	24	19	13	208

NOTE: A plus sign indicates greater interest. The difference in favour of co-educated girls is almost statistically significant.

significant.[1] At the age of 15 the greater liking shown by the co-educated girls is statistically significant (Table 11.4) in spite of the intelligence and social class imbalance.

TABLE 11.4   *Interest in French at 15 years (girls)*
Schools project

| | Replies from girls aged 15 | | | |
| | Co-educational schools | | Girls' schools | |
	N	%	N	%
Like much	103	39·5	76	27·4
Like a little	78	29·9	97	35·1
Neither like nor dislike	35	13·4	35	12·6
Dislike a little	21	8·0	35	12·6
Dislike much	24	9·2	34	12·3
Totals	261	100	277	100

NOTE; The greater liking of the co-educated girls is statistically significant (chi-square = 10·893 for 4 DF).

Here we may again be seeing a polarization effect by sex, girls' liking for French being increased by their juxtaposition with the boys in the classroom. The argument might take the following line. The girls are rather better at the subject, on the average, than the boys and this increases their liking; there also tends to arise the idea that languages are girls' subjects, whereas science is for boys. Curiously, in Tyson's survey, French, German and Latin were, apart from mathematics, the only subjects in which the co-educated girls either did better than or held their own with the girls from girls' schools.[2]

The free responses of the girls, while interesting in themselves, add nothing definite to the co-education/single-sex controversy except that there is a slight tendency for more of the girls from girls' schools than from co-educational to think they have not the ability to learn French—a belief directly opposite to the facts—while rather more co-educated girls find the subject easy or interesting. These two beliefs could arise, as mentioned above, from the co-educated girls finding themselves more

[1] $t = 1·838$.
[2] In Sutherland's survey the corresponding subjects were Latin and alternative mathematics.

successful than the boys and therefore being encouraged. Yet after a diligent reading of all the comments of the 13- and 15-year-old girls from co-educational schools, none could be discovered which even hinted at a possible polarization effect by sex of pupil. On the whole, however, such hints would be more likely to come from the boys than from the girls, in this subject.

Incidentally, French, like mathematics, appears to arouse strong feelings, even in the girls, e.g.:

'French is wonderful.' (Male teacher)

'I hate french emensly.' (*sic*)

'I can't stick French and get embarrassed in class.'

'Hate teacher.' (Male)

and amusingly,

'I like the language very much but I don't like the masculine and feminine.'

THE BOYS

If the theory of increased polarization according to sex and subject is to hold good the boys in co-educational schools should—contrary to expectations founded on such findings as their greater happiness compared with the happiness of boys in boys' schools—show less liking for French than do the latter. This is again what we find. At 13 years of age the boys in boys' schools show an appreciably greater interest in French than do the opposing group (though social classes 1 and 4 go the opposite way) and this persists even when the opposing samples are balanced on intelligence, though neither result is statistically significant (Figure 11.1). In Figure 11.1 we see that the boys from boys' schools have a pronounced lead in the 'like much' category and have clearly fewer in both 'dislike' categories. In the matched sample this lead becomes statistically significant.[1] This appears to be a tendency which is of some importance for teachers of French in co-educational schools, but it needs to be placed in proper perspective. At the age of 11 plus the boys in boys' schools started off with a substantially more favourable attitude to French, although there had been little time for polarization to exert an influence, and much of the more favourable attitude is probably due to the effect of social class factors. Between that time and 13 years of age the lead had been increased only by an amount equivalent to 11 boys in

[1] Pritchard (1935) has similar findings. The popularity of French among school subjects varied from fifth to eighth among his boys' school groups but fell to tenth in his mixed school groups.

some 200 improving their liking by one point in the five-point scale. This is derived from Table 11.5.

The more favourable attitude of the boys from boys' schools is also present at the age of 15 and is then statistically significant not only overall but also for social classes 3 and 4/5 taken separately, with classes 1 and 2 going in the same direction (Table 11.6). The results in Table 11.6 demonstrate that social class cannot be the factor creating the more favourable attitude in boys' schools, nor can intelligence, as at this age the two groups are almost equal in both factors. Accentuated polarization seems the most likely explanation, with the co-educated girls having a more favourable attitude to French than girls from girls' schools and co-educated boys having a less favourable attitude than their opposite numbers.

For some reason these differences in attitude do not appear to result in a consistent tendency for boys to do much worse in French than do boys

TABLE 11.5 *Change in interest in French between 11 and 13 years (boys)*

Schools project, longitudinal sample

| | Change in interest score (scale range 1 to 5) | | | | | | | | | |
	+4	+3	+2	+1	0	−1	−2	−3	−4	Totals
Co-educated boys	4	8	15	28	64	46	27	21	6	219
Boys in boys' schools	4	3	8	28	70	45	20	11	7	196

NOTE: A plus sign indicates greater interest. The boys in boys' schools are rather more finely selected.

in boys' schools and the reverse for girls, though in Tyson's survey French was the only subject in which the co-educated boys were inferior, before allowing for their various disadvantages; apart from English this was also the position in Sutherland's survey. The interest of the co-educated boys in French may be affected by an intensification of boys' stereotyped attitude that French is a 'cissy' subject or at least not a boys' subject. The intensification may be due to the juxtaposition with girls and the boys' consequent feeling of inferiority in French, especially in oral work (cf. Stevens (1962), p. 58). It seems possible that this attitude may exert a pressure against the progress in French of the co-educated boys and even occasionally help to make the co-educational mean mark lower (in raw scores) than that of the opposing group. This lower interest might, however, be countered by other forces, such as

TABLE 11.6 *Interest in French at 15 years by type of school and social class (boys)*

Schools project

Social class	Replies from boys in co-educational schools					Replies from boys in boys' schools				
	1 & 2	3	4 & 5	Total[1]	N	1 & 2	3	4 & 5	Total[1]	N
	%	%	%	%	N	%	%	%	%	N
Like much	23·1	21·1	14·3	20·5	53	24·5	31·5	30·6	28·4	77
Like a little	28·5	23·6	16·6	24·0	62	31·2	29·9	30·6	30·3	82
Neither like nor dislike	16·5	18·7	28·6	19·8	51	16·0	14·2	8·3	14·4	39
Dislike a little	16·5	6·5	28·6	13·6	35	16·0	11·0	5·5	12·5	34
Dislike much	15·4	30·1	11·9	22·1	57	12·3	13·4	25·0	14·4	39
Total	100	100	100	100	258	100	100	100	100	271

[1] Includes 2 unclassifiable.

NOTE: The greater interest in boys' schools is statistically significant, and consistent for South Wales and Yorkshire samples, and for social classes.

emulation of the standard of the girls. As, however, the generally superior progress of the co-educated boys in most subjects seems to be reduced in French, it looks as if this research may have isolated the cause, though it was not designed to prove the connection nor has it done so.

It was hoped that the boys' free comments might elucidate the problem, but the nearest to the polarization effect was merely one comment from a boy in a boys' school!

(Like a little) 'I don't want to take the arts so why bother with the language?'

It would seem that if polarization exists it is probably a background force, because the co-educated boys who disliked French or who were 'neutral' concentrated their reasons on the immediate situation in the classroom, thus giving 'poor teacher', 'dislike of teacher', 'poor ability' as comments and to a much lesser extent 'dislike of speaking or answering questions in French because poor at it', and 'dislike of grammar' for the same reason. As it seems impossible to clarify the position further with the available data we pass on to the next subject of the curriculum —physics.

Physics

Physics is another subject which might show an extra polarizing effect, according to interest by sex of pupil, in co-educational schools. If this force exists it would be expected to reduce the interest of the co-educated girls and increase that of the co-educated boys. This is again what we find, though there were difficulties in the test administration which affect the findings about the girls.

THE GIRLS

In the Schools project the girls were asked to underline that category of liking for physics which was 'true for the individual', but they were also asked to omit this item if they had never taken physics. Unfortunately many of the girls in girls' schools took general science in which were included topics taught in physics, and they endorsed the item; other girls omitted the item because they took only general science and not physics. At first this seemed such a muddle that the results would have to be scrapped, but as they yielded one of the relatively few findings strongly in favour of the girls' schools it was decided to retain them, with a statement about their limitations. The decision was also influenced by the fact that the results seemed to have a practical use in spite of the confusion.

The usefulness lies in the demonstration that the girls in girls' schools in this survey had a more favourable attitude to their mixture of general science and physics than had the co-educated girls to physics.[1] Girls are interested in people and living things rather than mathematics and inanimate objects, and this, allied to additional polarization, presents the co-educational schools with a considerable problem. It would be misleading to condemn co-educational schooling for this alone, because its other advantages are so varied and so pronounced, but the problem should be faced.

The change in liking for the subject, between 11 and 13 years of age, is substantial (Table 11.7). The advantage to the girls' schools is to be seen most clearly in the negative or 'loss' part of the scale, but note that this advantage will have been increased by the operation of the intelligence and social class biases, by the school drop-out problem, maybe by the popularity of male science teachers in girls' schools, and very much by the restriction of the sample—although there are equal numbers in the full opposing samples *only 53·7 per cent of the girls from girls' schools gave a 'science' estimate compared with 77·6 per cent of the co-educated girls*. However, even when the intelligence and social class factors were equalized, by 'balancing' in one instance and matching in

[1] A small minority of the co-educated girls took general science.

pairs in the other, the greater liking shown by the girls in girls' schools at the age of 13 was statistically significant.[1]
Provided the results are not misread as physics versus physics, they make their point. *In my judgment* some advantage to the girls in girls' schools would persist even if the school drop-out problem, the more

TABLE 11.7 *Change in interest in physics between 11 and 13 years*

Schools project, longitudinal sample

	+4	+3	+2	+1	0	−1	−2	−3	−4	Totals
Co-educated girls	2	5	12	20	37	38	24	15	6	159
Girls from girls' schools	2	5	4	23	33	21	10	9	3	110
Co-educated boys	1	4	8	23	54	20	4	4	2	120
Boys from boys' schools	3	4	5	23	44	24	8	7	6	124

Change in interest score (scale range 1 to 5)

NOTE: A plus sign indicates greater interest. The change in liking favouring the girls' schools is not statistically significant. Those taking science are 77·6 per cent of the co-educated girls and only 53·7 per cent of girls from girls' schools.

refined sample in girls' schools, and the possible popularity effect of male science teachers in girls' schools, were allowed for in the comparison.[2] On the other hand it is not certain that the girls' schools would still have the greater liking if they took only physics and not general science. As one of these girls writes:

(Like much) 'Find general science intriguing, especially biology and dissection.'

In other words it is not so much the physics she enjoys as the biology. However, four comments from co-educated girls suggest the possibility of polarization by sex:

(Dislike much) 'I don't think girls should be forced to do physics.' (13-year-old)

[1] $t = 3·668$ for matched pairs.
[2] Pritchard (1938) again has a somewhat similar result. His girls' secondary school groups placed chemistry fifth in order of popularity of school subjects and girls in co-educational schools placed it eighth. There were few, if any, male teachers of chemistry in girls' schools at that period.

The other three comments are from co-educated girls aged 15.

(Dislike a little) 'I do not think it is a girls' subject.'

(Dislike much) 'I think it is better for boys to take it than girls.'

(Dislike much) 'I feel it is for boys although it could have its uses.'

Feeling among some co-educated girls runs strong:

(Dislike much) 'I hate physics: it is boring and useless.'

(Dislike much) 'Terrible, but interesting for some.'

(Dislike much) 'The complicated equations get me down.'

(Dislike much) 'I just could not understand any of it.'

To avoid misunderstanding it should be recorded that the detestation is equally strong among a section of the girls in girls' schools, e.g.:

(Dislike much) 'I hated it.'

(Dislike much) 'Took it for one year and dropped it as fast as I could.'

(Dislike much) 'I don't take it now but the thought of it makes me sick.'

(Dislike much) 'No interest and I was made to take it—I hate it.'

(Dislike much) 'I can never understand what we are talking about.'

The following quotation is not relevant to the theme of the book, but the writer cannot refrain from quoting it. The comment is by a 15-year-old girl in a co-educational school.

(Dislike much) 'I dislike it because some countries use their knowledge of it in wrong ways. It is not relevant to my career.'

Though out of its section a boy's comment from a co-educational school matches the previous one:

(Dislike much) 'The most boring subject ever to have been imposed on suffering youth. Probably responsible for mods and rockers riots.'

One comment from a co-educational school may be hinting that a little masculine help with the difficulties of physics is thankfully received:

(Like much) 'I like physics a great deal because my friend and I get helped and it is a complete change from other subjects.'

The foregoing is balanced by a remark from a girl aged 15 in a girls' school:

(Like a little) 'It all depends whether we have our mistress or master taking us.'

The table of classified quotations is not given because it differentiates very little between the attitudes of the pupils in the two types of school.

THE BOYS

As hypothesized, the boys in co-educational schools recorded a greater liking for physics than did the boys from boys' schools, with almost

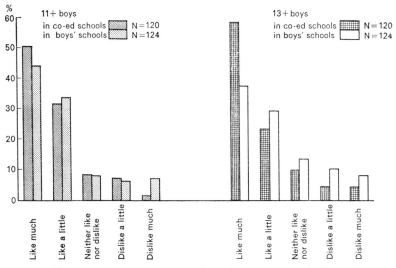

NOTE: The greater interest of the co-educated boys aged 13 plus is significant at the 0·025 level.

FIGURE 11.2 *Interest in physics at 11 and 13 years (boys): Schools project, longitudinal sample*

equal proportions of boys taking the subject. The change in liking between the ages of 11 and 13 may be seen in Table 11.7.

Figure 11.2 indicates that the co-educated boys started off at 11 years of age with a slightly greater liking for physics than had boys in boys' schools, and that this difference increased until by the age of 13 it was substantial; the change itself was short of statistical significance. At the later age, however, 58 per cent of the co-educated boys 'liked physics very much' compared with only 38 per cent of the boys from boys' schools, while the grouped percentages expressing dislike were 8 to 20,

TABLE 11.8   *Interest in physics at 13 years (boys)*
Schools project, balanced sample

| | Replies from boys aged 13 | | | |
| | Co-educational schools | | Boys' schools | |
	N	%	N	%
Like much	86	55·1	62	38·3
Like a little	36	23·1	52	32·1
Neither like nor dislike	18	11·5	19	11·7
Dislike a little	10	6·4	16	9·9
Dislike much	6	3·9	13	8·0
Totals	156	100	162	100

NOTE: The greater interest of the co-educated boys is statistically significant (chi-square = 10·872 for 4 DF). The opposing numbers are unequal because there were some blanks.

and this difference between the two types of school was in itself statistically significant. Table 11.7 shows that whereas the liking for physics increased slightly in the co-educational schools it decreased markedly in the boys' schools.

In the 'balanced sample' the greater liking of the co-educated boys at the same age became statistically significant (Table 11.8). The trend of this result was steadily consistent for all social class groups (with classes 4 and 5 combined). The result was replicated in the matched sample.[1]

At age 15 greater liking was again expressed for physics in the co-educational schools; though the difference in their favour was not sufficiently large to be statistically reliable, it was consistent for each social class and for the Welsh and Yorkshire schools. This was of course a different sample of boys and the social class imbalance had not been removed.

The comments of the pupils are fascinating and varied but they add little to the present comparison. A few are quoted for their general interest.

Co-educational schools

(Like much)   'Because it is interesting, exciting.'

(Like much)   'Because of the experiments and it is exciting.'

[1] $t = 2·513$.

(Like much) 'I enjoy learning about the world around me.'

(Like much) 'I like all science. One finds out unbelievable things.'

(Like a little) 'Until now I have liked it but our new master cannot teach for toffee.'

(Like a little) 'The teacher tries to be what he isn't.'

(Neutral) 'It is rather hard to pick up unless you are a genius.'

(Dislike much) 'I dislike it because we do not do any practical work. It is all dictation.'

Boys' schools

(Like much) 'I have always liked magnets and electricity. I find it fascinating.'

(Like much) 'Made easier by having a very good master.'

(Like much) 'Very interesting and a subject of the modern age.'

(Like a little) 'Too much emphasis on theory. No practical demonstrations.'

(Like a little) 'Used to like, but getting fed up because the new physics master is crap and doesn't know what he is talking about.'

(Dislike a little) 'Although proficient in physics I have always had a dislike of scientific thought in general.'

(Dislike much) 'Who wants to know about the Leclanché Cell, Daniel Cell, magnetic fields etc? Stupid subject.'

General comment

The chief points that arise from this chapter and the previous one are the greater expressed interest of the co-educated boys in mathematics and physics, and of the co-educated girls in French, compared with pupils in single-sex schools, and the lower expressed interest of the co-educated girls in mathematics (age 15 only) and in physics compared with their rivals' general science, combined with the lower interest scores of the co-educated boys in French. In English literature the comparison brought equality in the case both of boys and of girls. On the whole there is support for the thesis that there is a tendency for interest in school subjects in co-educational schools to polarize for the boys round mathematics and the physical sciences, and for the girls round literary and language subjects, though biology could be an exception.

Finally, the theory that co-education may *increase* the tendency for boys to prefer science and girls arts receives some support from a county survey,[1] the Department of Education and Science,[2] and from correspondence in the educational press.[3] The Ministry simply stated that 'almost twice as many girls from single-sex schools as from mixed schools, in proportion to the number of girls in each type, went on to read mathematics or science at a university'.[4] The Gloucestershire survey made in 19 grammar and 2 comprehensive schools reported that girls did about 25 per cent fewer science subjects at A-level in mixed schools, while boys in mixed schools did more science than boys in single-sex schools. In a letter to the press, King (1971) published an analysis of the subjects taken at A-level in 18 grammar schools, of which six were co-educational, six were for boys and six for girls. The figures showed a greater polarization of the sexes, in choice of subject, in co-educational schools, though no test of significance was applied. However, that this tendency in a co-educational school can be successfully countered is illustrated by further statistics published in the same newspaper in a letter from the head of one of the only two co-educational direct grant schools in this country. In 1971, at A-level some 44 per cent of the 56 girl candidates took full arts courses, 36 per cent full science and 20 per cent mixed courses. The figures for the boys were not so favourable, as they had 10 doing full arts courses (with 8 more doing mixed courses) out of 49 boys who were A-level candidates.

Some caution is needed here. For example the basis used by the Department of Education and Science for calculating the proportion of girls who go on to read science at a university could be misleading, e.g. it might be inferred that the co-educational nature of the schools is the only reason for the small proportion of co-educated girls reading science compared with the proportion from girls' schools, though, as has often been repeated, the co-educational schools are more rural, and admit a much larger proportion of the 11-plus age group each year, therefore their pupils tend to be of lower social class and tend to have a lower average level of intelligence. The co-educated girls could not therefore be expected to gain the same proportion of university places as the girls' schools do, and this is especially so in science where the successful candidates, in spite of their lower A-level grades, are possibly of rather higher intelligence level than those in arts (Entwistle, 1971). It may be,

---

[1] Gloucestershire Education Committee: Report of Science Advisory Group, 1971 (cf. TES, 1 October 1971).
[2] Department of Education and Science: Annual Report, 1967 (cf. TES, 1 October 1967).
[3] *Times Educational Supplement*, Norris, D., 10 September 1971; Higginson, M., 1 October 1971; and Johnston, L., and King, R., 15 October 1971.
[4] The Crowther Report (1959), Table 49, p. 253, gives a similar result, but the limitation outlined later is equally relevant.

also, that the presence of male teachers of mathematics and the physical sciences in many girls' schools may have been acting as a stimulus to the number of girls in these schools who take sciences in the sixth. (In co-educational schools the presence of male teachers would be considered more 'normal'.) An appropriate close to the section is the query whether the changes of method in Nuffield science and Nuffield mathematics— and other breaths of change—will have any effect on the interest of girls in these subjects.

Only in French does there seem to be evidence that lower interest among the co-educated boys might—in combination with other forces— sometimes bring their O-level attainment slightly below that of boys in boys' schools. Yet even here the 'other forces' are the lower average intelligence level and lower social class of the co-educated boys—which are not necessary accompaniments of co-education. Another aspect of the somewhat low level of interest in French among the co-educated boys is that it would appear to link up with another finding—the rather greater reluctance of the co-educated boys to 'speak out in class'. It remains to be seen whether the present greater emphasis on oral methods in the teaching of French will sweep away the reluctance or intensify it. In case this analysis gives an exaggerated view of the situation it should be said that overall there is no evidence that the co-educated boys make less progress in French than boys from boys' schools, after differences in intelligence and social class are taken into account.

The pupil's direct interest in a subject is not the only force which contributes towards his or her level of attainment. A recognition of the usefulness of the subject can also be powerful (Long, 1949); this might, of course, affect quite strongly the pupil's 'interest' in a subject—and it could be this utilitarian aspect[1] which produced the equality found in English literature between the estimates of the co-educated groups and those from single-sex schools. Again, liking or disliking the teacher can have a strong effect on the liking for that teacher's subject; some of the liking for the teacher could be reflected in the recorded interest in the subject but some might well be reserved for the teacher and help to cause good attainment, even though the level of direct interest in the material was not high.

[1] Although English literature in itself may not be considered utilitarian by some, in practice it is included as English in the timetable, and will be considered by many to be in consequence a key subject.

12

Type of school and attitude to physical activities

The boys

Advocates of the segregation of the sexes for education at the secondary stage have sometimes claimed that educating the two sexes together turns the boys into 'cissies', i.e. makes them effeminate. Supporters of co-education have refuted the charge vigorously, but both accusers and defendants have had no facts whatsoever with which to sustain their arguments. This study seeks to make a start in providing those facts, but it makes no claim to provide a complete answer. Its approach is limited to one aspect of the question and depends on the hypothesis that the degree of manliness or masculinity of boys may be tested *in part* by their attitude towards boys' organized physical activities. It is conceded that there may be a very small minority of individuals of whom this is not true but it is posited that these would be submerged in the analysis by the vast majority of normals and that this small minority would be present in fairly equal proportions in boys' and co-educational schools. As an alternative to this last point it might be maintained that boys with personalities which led them to dislike organized physical activities would tend, if they had the choice, to go to a co-educational rather than to a boys' school. As will be seen later, even if this minor and unsupported hypothesis is conceded it has no effect on the direction of the outcome. In addition the results have their own intrinsic interest, quite apart from the above argument.

SECOND COLLEGE SURVEY

Procedure

The first attack on the problem was through a questionnaire which was administered to about 900 male intending teachers who were ex-pupils of grammar schools. In this chapter we are concerned with only four of the questions, namely:
'Did you like playing football at school?'
'Did you like playing cricket at school?'
'Did you like gymnastics at school?'
'Did you like athletics at school?'
Respondents were asked to indicate their answers on a seven-point

TABLE 12.1 The attitude of male ex-pupils towards organized physical activities in their schooldays[1]

Second College survey

	Football				Cricket				Gymnastics				Athletics			
	Co-ed schools		Boys' schools		Co-ed schools		Boys' schools		Co-ed schools		Boys' schools		Co-ed schools		Boys' schools	
	N	%	N	%	N	%	N	%	N	%	N	%	N	%	N	%
Liked very much	185	53·3	231	41·1	128	37·4	183	32·2	102	30·1	131	23·4	94	27·2	148	26·2
Liked much	61	17·6	108	19·2	60	17·5	99	17·5	83	24·5	114	20·3	82	23·8	113	20·0
Liked a little	61	17·6	106	18·9	82	24·0	143	25·3	86	25·4	149	26·6	109	31·6	167	29·6
Undecided	6	1·7	19	3·4	14	4·1	31	5·5	15	4·4	28	5·0	17	4·9	42	7·4
Disliked a little	13	3·7	44	7·8	31	9·1	49	8·7	30	8·8	64	11·4	24	7·0	43	7·6
Disliked much	10	2·9	25	4·4	16	4·7	32	5·7	8	2·4	30	5·3	11	3·2	24	4·2
Disliked very much	11	3·2	29	5·2	11	3·2	29	5·1	15	4·4	45	8·0	8	2·3	28	5·0
Totals	347	100	562	100	342	100	566	100	339	100	561	100	345	100	565	100
Average score[2]	5·94		5·48		5·43		5·22		5·38		4·91		5·41		5·17	

[1] 913 intending teachers.

[2] Obtained by giving a weighting of 7 to 'Liked very much', 6 to 'Liked much', etc, then multiplying by the number of respondents in each of the seven sections, adding the seven totals and dividing by the overall number of respondents. The weighting is arbitrary but it yields a reasonably valid comparison of large groups which can be appreciated at a quick glance.

scale by ticking the appropriate word, namely, 'Very much/Much/A little/Undecided/Disliked a little/Disliked much/Disliked very much'. The numbers of men placing themselves in each category were then found and the distribution of preferences for the men from boys' schools was compared with that for the co-educated men. The results were as shown on Table 12.1 on the previous page.

The table shows that the smaller of the two groups—the co-educated men—is about 350 in number. The institutions in which these men were students were scattered throughout England and Wales; hence the students must have come from a very large number of schools. Their replies and those of the larger group can be taken therefore to be reasonably representative of this type of ex-grammar school pupil. In the comparison between men from boys' and men from co-educational schools the principal results embodied in the above table are as follows. In all four physical activities the men from the mixed secondary grammar schools had the better attitude, and the difference between the boys' school and the co-educated group is statistically significant in three out of the four activities—only in the case of cricket does it fail to rise to this level, though the difference lies consistently in the same direction.[1] We have, therefore, a series of results which form a coherent pattern, with nothing which is in the least discrepant. (For the purists the *t* tests have all been confirmed by chi-square.)

The consistency of the pattern is maintained in an aspect with which this enquiry was not primarily concerned, that is in the relative popularity of the four organized physical activities. Taking the boys from boys' schools separately we see in the bottom row of Table 12.1 that football is easily the most popular,[2] cricket next, with athletics about equal to it, and fourth comes gymnastics. The results of the boys from co-educational schools show exactly the same order, and again the difference between football and cricket is large, while that between cricket and athletics is negligible; the only change is that for boys in co-educational schools the gap between athletics and gymnastics has almost vanished, though this change might be due to chance. In the case of boys in co-educational schools the popularity scores for cricket, athletics and gymnastics are so close together that the differences are not statistically or practically significant.

[1] As the *t* ratio is only a little below the 'conventional' significance level (at 1·803) and the difference is in the same direction in all four cases, it is reasonable to maintain that this also is not a chance result. With football and gymnastics the significance level is well beyond 1 per cent, with athletics well beyond 5 per cent.

[2] The difference between the average scores in football and cricket is highly unlikely to have occurred by chance alone (less than 1 in 100). For boys' schools also the difference between gymnastics and cricket would be highly unlikely to have occurred by chance, and that between gymnastics and athletics, though not as large, would occur by chance much less than 1 in 20 times.

A further point should be added. In the question 'Did you like playing football at school?' the word football was used in its overall sense to mean either rugby or 'soccer' (the meaning given in the Oxford Dictionary), and seemed to cause no difficulty in the pilot test. This meaning could also be inferred from the fact that questions on the three other major sports activities—cricket, gymnastics, and athletics—were asked in the same section. Four or five respondents, however, during the test proper crossed out 'football' and put 'rugby'. Their answers of course would be exactly in line with what the researcher wanted. We cannot, however, be sure whether other rugby enthusiasts placed the same narrow interpretation on the word without crossing it out, and hence did not give 'football' as high an enjoyment value as they would have given for 'rugby'. Though we think this number would be small, and though this interpretation is given some support from the consistency of the results, we cannot be sure of this, and have included an amended question in a further questionnaire to another sample. The chief effect of the fault, if any, would be to decrease slightly the recorded 'enjoyment value' for football. If it had any effect on the difference between the co-educated men and those educated in boys' schools it is scarcely conceivable that this large difference would vanish and even change direction if the question were amended, especially in view of the persistent pattern of higher 'enjoyment values' for the co-educated men in the other three activities.

While research was in progress the writer decided that the different distribution of social class among boys in boys' schools, compared with those in co-educational schools, might affect the comparison of the popularity scores. From the half-way stage onwards therefore data about the pupils' parental occupational class was obtained.[1] Owing to the small numbers in social class 2 it was combined with class 1; similarly with classes 4 and 5. The results for football and cricket are shown in Table 12.2.

It will be seen at a glance that in five of six comparisons between boys' and co-educational schools the latter have the higher average score; in the sixth case, classes 4 and 5 (football), the numbers in both types of schools are too small to give adequate reliability to the figures, and the isolated exception to the general trend may be due to chance fluctuation. We can say, therefore, that unless the proportions of the occupational classes are extremely different in the two types of school, the difference in the popularity scores between the school samples is not due to social

---

[1] The occupational class categories were those used by Peaker in the Early Leaving Report. Class 1 includes professional, administrative, managerial and teachers, class 2 clerical workers, class 3 skilled manual workers, class 4 semi-skilled, and class 5 unskilled.

TABLE 12.2   *Football and cricket: average popularity scores by school and occupational class*

Second College survey

Occupational class	Football				Cricket			
	Boys' schools		Mixed schools		Boys' schools		Mixed schools	
	N	average score	N	average score	N	average score	N	average score
1 & 2	77	4·95	54	5·85	76	4·66	54	5·07
3	115	5·28	69	5·80	113	4·81	69	5·06
4 & 5	20	6·15	17	5·88	20	5·50	17	5·88

class. Only if classes 4 and 5 were heavily under-represented in the boys' schools sample compared with that from co-educational schools could there be any possibility of the lower score of the boys' schools being due to social class factors, and as the proportions of classes 4 and 5 calculated from Table 12.2, are about 7 per cent in the boys' school sample and 12 per cent in the mixed, this possibility is ruled out. Similar results for gymnastics and athletics are presented in Table 12.3.

TABLE 12.3   *Gymnastics and athletics: average popularity scores by school and occupational class*

Second College survey

Occupational class	Gymnastics				Athletics			
	Boys' schools		Mixed schools		Boys' schools		Mixed schools	
	N	average score	N	average score	N	average score	N	average score
1 & 2	79	4·41	52	5·21	77	5·12	53	5·21
3	114	4·57	67	5·18	115	4·97	69	5·33
4 & 5	20	4·80	17	5·12	18	4·89	17	5·41

In Table 12.3 we see again that within each occupational class division the sample of boys from co-educational schools records a more favourable attitude, this time to gymnastics and athletics, than does the sample from boys' schools. Moreover, as the lowest average of the co-educational schools is higher than the highest average recorded by any social class group in the boys' schools, it is obvious that in the case of these sports also, the more favourable attitude of the co-educational school sample cannot be due to any difference in their social class composition compared with the sample from boys' schools.

Comment

There is a general tendency for classes 4 and 5 to record more favourable attitudes than the other occupational classes; this occurs in five cases out of eight, with two instances showing virtually no difference, and the remaining case (athletics in the boys' school sample) showing a very small difference in the opposite direction, possibly due to chance factors. There is also a less well-marked tendency for classes 1 and 2 to have the least favourable attitude, class 3 slightly more favourable and classes 4 and 5 most favourable of all. It is tempting to see this at first sight as a difference due to differences in social class 'milieu' and atmosphere, but class 3, and to a greater extent classes 4 and 5, children are more highly selected than those from classes 1 and 2. Though the selection is by academic ability, there is a small positive correlation among schoolchildren between academic ability and ability in games. Another point is that as these respondents are representative of only one type of grammar school leaver, we need further research before the findings of this enquiry can be safely generalized.

In assessing the significance of the results it is necessary to be cautious because sometimes there are hidden factors at work which are difficult to detect. For example most co-educational grammar schools are situated in small towns and there are few in the cities (though the distribution is now changing), whereas most of the city schools are single-sex. It may be, therefore, that the co-educational grammar schools tend to be better provided with playing fields than the boys' schools are, though on the other hand the greater age and sometimes wealth of the boys' schools may operate in the opposite direction. Although such a factor, if it exists, could conceivably affect the popularity scores in football and cricket and even athletics, it would be unlikely to have much effect on attitudes to gymnastics. Unfortunately the only evidence which seems to be available about the comparability of playing-fields provision is from the small-scale survey of 42 grammar schools in the Schools project, and a similar one in the 'Both schools' survey; in both there was a small difference in favour of co-educational schools, but such a difference would be far from large enough to account for the greater popularity of games in the schools of the Second College survey (see Table A2.19). Though the question of comparable provision cannot be ignored it can be said, none the less, that up to the present the data give no support to the argument that educating boys together with girls makes them more effeminate or turns them into 'cissies'.

It is interesting to see that in all occupational classes, in both boys' and co-educational schools samples, with one insignificant exception, football was more popular than cricket, but as these games are played in different seasons the finding is not of any practical significance. Of greater interest is the extraordinary consistency of the results, stemming from the administration of a questionnaire. The pattern produced by all four physical activities, by the two types of school and by all three occupational class groups, is such that it provides strong evidence against the argument that the questionnaire is imprecise. It is true that the questionnaire, when inadequately prepared and unwisely used, justifies the condemnation, but is this not also true of the attitude scale and any other technique? Unfortunately, however, shortage of time for the administration of the questionnaire prevented the writer from asking the students to add free responses, a technique which proved so valuable in other parts of the surveys.

SCHOOLS PROJECT

So far we have assessed the experience and attitudes of ex-pupils. This has its advantages—the wide scatter and large number of schools, the more mature outlook and the removal of school pressures, fear of answers being seen—but there are also disadvantages. Some critics would raise the objection that these ex-pupils may not recollect their school experiences sufficiently clearly, and others may say that they were limited to one type of pupil. To the first point one could reply that these students, who had been in school only two or three years before, would scarcely have forgotten whether or not they had liked playing football there, and to the second that the limitation of the sample to intending teachers, from each school, should minimize any bias—such as that due to occupational class—which might be present in samples thoroughly representative of the pupils in each type of school. However, in order to allay doubts an opportunity was taken to incorporate in a questionnaire to present pupils additional items similar to those used in the previous section.

This Schools project is described fully in the first chapter of volume I of this work, but for readers who have not seen that volume an outline is given at the beginning of part II of this volume. The questionnaire was administered under examination conditions to 42 schools in South Wales and the West Riding by the writer and a research assistant. The study was longitudinal with two years in between the testings. The longitudinal sample is used here because it was thought that a measurement of change in attitude would reduce (though not remove) any bias between the samples due to factors such as social class. In spite of a serious attempt being made to get the co-educated and single-sex schools matched independently by administrators in 'triples' there is incontrovertible evidence that in a few cases the scales were tipped unintentionally in favour of the single-sex schools, e.g. it is acknowledged by all concerned that in one area parental choice favours the older-established (and at one time higher status) single-sex schools.

The boys gave their answers on a five-point scale to three questions: 'Do you like playing football (either rugby or soccer) at school?' and two others on gymnastics and athletics. The scale ranged from 'Like much' to 'Dislike much'. Unfortunately there was no time available for the pupils to add free responses to these questions.

The results were not conclusive, though the differences found between the co-educated and single-sex educated pupils were almost always in the same direction as those found in the Second College survey. With the boys the change in the popularity of football between the ages of 11 and 13 was virtually the same for the two groups (N = 223 and 213), while the co-educated boys aged 15 converted an almost statistically significant lower popularity score into clear equality when they were 17 plus (N = 133 and 137). In athletics and gymnastics the co-educated junior boys were equal in score with boys from boys' schools at 11 plus but their liking for these pursuits was clearly greater than that of the rival group at the age of 13 plus, though the difference was not statistically significant. For gymnastics the senior co-educated boys gave lower popularity scores at 15 plus than did those from boys' schools (almost statistically significant) but by the age of 17 had changed their position to one of equality. In athletics also the co-educated senior boys had the better rate of change, though at age 17 they had only a slightly (non-significant) better attitude than boys from boys' schools. To summarize, in five out of the six comparisons the co-educated pupils had the more favourable 'rate of change', with equality between the groups in the sixth case.

In this project the investigators were able to classify the schools' playing field provision on the spot; there proved to be little to choose between them.[1] The sample of schools is too small to generalize from but it shows that difference in playing-field provision would be unlikely to affect this present survey.

THE 'BOTH SCHOOLS' SURVEY

In this survey, among 620 female and 175 male student teachers who had each attended a co-educational and a single-sex school, there was

---

[1] The rough classification was: co-educational schools Excellent 4, Satisfactory 5, Poor 1, Very Poor 2, while that of the boys' schools was Excellent 4, Satisfactory 4, Poor 3 and Very Poor 1.

only one question on games, namely, 'Do you agree or disagree with the following statement about your co-educational or single-sex school? The organized games were enjoyable.' Answers were on the usual five-point scale, beginning 'Agree strongly', but free responses had to be omitted. Again there was a tendency for respondents to give more favourable estimates about their co-educational schools, but the differences between these and the estimates for their boys' schools they attended were not statistically significant,[1] and the meaning of the differences is obscured by a *slightly* better provision of playing-fields for the co-educational schools (see Table A2.19). In this recent 'Both schools' project this small advantage on the co-educational side may be due to part of the sample moving from old boys' grammar school buildings to newly built co-educational comprehensive schools surrounded by their own playing-fields. Movement from co-educational to single-sex schools was smaller.

The girls

We know very little about the effect of the presence of boys on the interests of girls in a co-educational school. Does their presence make girls more 'masculine' in type or encourage them to be more feminine? Does the process exaggerate feminine characteristics to a point where they become faults or does it rather soften their regrettable tendencies until they almost become virtues? We know very little about the nature of these psychological effects. The field is vast and the writer has made a small beginning by attempting to discover whether a particular sample of girls in mixed schools had a more or less favourable attitude towards certain organized physical activities, i.e. gymnastics and athletics, than a corresponding sample from girls' schools.

SECOND COLLEGE SURVEY

Procedure

A questionnaire was administered to some 800 women who were ex-pupils of grammar schools. They were students in colleges of education and university departments of education, in roughly representative proportions. We are here concerned with only two of the questions, namely: 'Did you like gymnastics at school?' and 'Did you like athletics at school?' Answers were requested on a seven-point scale ranging from liking 'Very much', through 'Much' and 'A little' to 'Disliked very much'. The judgments given were again weighted seven for 'Very much' down to one for the opposite end of the scale. The percentages of

[1] Chi-square for 4 degrees of freedom was 3·334 and 2·693 (Table A2.20).

Type of school and attitude to physical activities

students expressing each judgment were found, and a comparison made between the distribution of scores in the group from girls' schools and that from co-educational schools.

The number of respondents replying was quite large—there were 300 in the smaller group and they came from institutions scattered all over England and Wales, and therefore from a large number of schools. From Table 12.4 it will be seen that 21 per cent of the girls in the sample from girls' schools and 29 per cent of those from the mixed

TABLE 12.4 *Attitude towards gymnastics and athletics: comparison according to schooling (women)*

Second College survey

| | Gymnastics | | | | Athletics | | | |
| | Co-ed schools | | Girls' schools | | Co-ed schools | | Girls' schools | |
	N	%	N	%	N	%	N	%
Liked very much	85	28·6	107	21·1	79	27·1	77	17·2
Liked much	59	19·9	103	20·3	45	15·5	88	19·6
Liked a little	68	22·9	145	28·4	87	29·9	136	30·4
Undecided	6	2·0	15	3·0	13	4·5	22	4·9
Disliked a little	39	13·1	63	12·4	27	9·3	56	12·5
Disliked much	18	6·1	41	8·1	16	5·5	37	8·3
Disliked very much	22	7·4	34	6·7	24	8·2	32	7·1
Totals	297	100	508	100	291	100	448	100
Means	5·01		4·84		4·97		4·71	

school sample said they 'liked gymnastics very much', but there was very little difference between the two groups in the proportions disliking gymnastics (rather more than a quarter of each group disliking the activity). With athletics the difference between the sample from girls' schools and that from co-educational was greater, only 17 per cent of the former saying they liked athletics very much, whereas 27 per cent of the co-educational school group gave this judgment, while at the opposite end of the scale 28 per cent of the girls' school sample showed some shade of dislike, and only 23 per cent of the group from co-educational schools. When the groups are compared statistically, by

179

calculating their mean scores from the weighted judgment scores and applying the t test to the difference between them, the more favourable attitude of the co-educational school group falls fractionally short of statistical significance in athletics ($t = 1 \cdot 92$) and the same test applied to the gymnastics mean scores falls further below significance at $1 \cdot 27$. We cannot deduce from these results that there is no difference between the average attitude scores of the two groups; in fact there remains a distinct probability, amounting almost to 19 chances in 20 for athletics, that those students from co-educational schools represented by this sample have a more favourable attitude than the contrasted group. What we cannot say is that this difference is 'statistically significant', because the convention exists that 'proof' begins when the odds are 1 in 20. Yet the fact that these differences are both substantial and in the same direction cannot be ignored; they give each other support. It is not unimportant also that differences in the same direction (i.e. with the co-educational school sample having the more favourable attitude) in the corresponding boys' groups were demonstrated in the previous section for football, cricket, gymnastics and athletics, three of these differences being statistically significant.

In passing we see that there is virtually no difference between the popularity of the two activities in the mixed school sample, and the small advantage shown by gymnastics over athletics among the student teachers from girls' schools is by inspection not statistically significant, nor is such a slight difference of practical significance. In weighing up these results, however, we need to bring the whole situation in review before us; clearly factors such as better provision for athletics of diverse types for girls, or a much greater emphasis on this branch of physical activity in the syllabus, might result in an increase in its popularity.

As the different proportions of occupational class in the two opposing samples might have affected the results, a further analysis was made, though unfortunately occupational class data were available for only part of the sample. The breakdown gave the results shown on the facing page.

In Table 12.5 there appears to be no consistent social class effect on the popularity scores, either in gymnastics or in athletics. In order, however, to see whether the differences between the two samples in their social class distribution were affecting the comparison, the social class proportions shown in the table for the sample from mixed schools were imposed on the sample from girls' schools, and the new number of pupils in each social class was multiplied by the mean score in gymnastics for this class. The change in the mean of the girls' schools was negligible. If we look at the results in another way, in five of the eight comparisons the mixed school sample had the more favourable attitude and in two its attitude was less favourable, while in the remaining case the scores were virtually the same.[1] It is noticeable that in the girls' schools' sample appreciably fewer respondents answered for athletics than for gymnastics, while in the sample from mixed schools there were almost identical numbers for these activities. Perhaps some girls' schools could not offer athletics because of lack of facilities, or did not encourage athletics even when a ground was available. Another possible explanation is that it was easier for individual girls to secure permanent exemption from athletics in a girls' school than in a mixed school.

TABLE 12.5 *Gymnastics and athletics: average popularity scores by school and occupational class*

Second College survey

Gymnastics				Athletics			
	Co-ed schools		Girls' schools		Co-ed schools		Girls' schools
Occupational class	N	average score	N	average score	N	average score	N	average score
1	158	4·72	59	4·25	134	4·48	58	4·5
2	44	4·61	33	4·76	38	4·68	31	5·0
3	143	4·72	88	5·22	132	4·53	86	4·79
4 & 5	18	4·22	18	5·06	14	4·64	18	4·06
Totals & means	363	4·68	198	4·84	318	4·54	193	4·67

Comment

Though the data expose a tendency for the sample of girls from mixed schools to show a rather more favourable attitude to gymnastics and athletics than the comparable sample from girls' schools, the difference verges on statistical significance only for the latter activity and is rather less reliable for gymnastics. This difference is not as large as was anticipated, and the reason for this may lie in the nature of the samples. Both of these consist of student teachers, hence the attitudes of the two groups towards organized physical activities might be closer together than are the attitudes of the two school populations as a whole. The answer will have to await the results of further research. A factor not taken into account is the possible difference in the quality of the

[1] In view of the lack of a social class pattern, the reliability of these differences was not calculated.

staffing for physical training in girls' schools compared with mixed; it is likely that the girls' schools would have a larger percentage of highly qualified teachers, and if this is so they should have had a beneficial effect on the attitudes of their students. Yet the difference in attitudes lies in the opposite direction. Another factor which was not controlled is the standard of playing-field provision for the two groups; here the influences would resemble those mentioned in the previous section.

SCHOOLS PROJECT

The questions for the girls in this project were concerned with hockey, gymnastics and athletics. As girls did not play hockey in some schools at 11 plus no analysis was made for that age, but at the age of 13 the co-educated girls had a rather better attitude to hockey than their rivals.[1] In attitude to gymnastics the change between 11 and 13 years of age was small, but in favour of the co-educated group, while in athletics the picture changed from a near equality at 11 to an almost statistically significant more favourable attitude by the co-educated girls at 13 plus.

For the senior girls there was, however, a very slightly better improvement in attitude to gymnastics (non-significant) among girls from girls' schools and in athletics the slightest of movements in the opposite direction. Both subjects, especially athletics, were somewhat more popular at the co-educational schools.

In attitude to hockey the co-educated girls were distinctly more favourably inclined, both at age 15 and age 17, though both differences fell somewhat short of conventional statistical significance.[2] An analysis of the changes in *individuals'* liking for hockey, between the ages of 15 and 17, revealed little difference between the co-educated girls and the opposing group,[3] but this result is not as definite as it might seem as there would probably be a 'ceiling' effect operating to reduce the co-educated score in that they had almost half their number on the maximum scores at 15 plus and these pupils could not of course go higher than this 'ceiling' and it would be easy for some to drop a grade or two. For comparison, one-third of the girls from girls' schools were on this ceiling.

There was little difference between the two types of school in the provision of playing-fields.[4] All in all the outcome, though rather more

[1] Not statistically significant, chi-square = 7·132 for 4 DF, 9·488 being needed by convention.
[2] See Table A2.21.
[3] See Table A2.22.
[4] Of the co-educational provision, 4 were classed Excellent, 5 Satisfactory, 1 Poor and 2 Very Poor, while for girls' schools 3 were Excellent, 6 Satisfactory, 2 Poor and 1 Very Poor.

favourable to the co-educated girls, could certainly not be generalized from the evidence of this survey alone.

'BOTH SCHOOLS' SURVEY

The 620 women ex-pupils of the 'Both schools' survey also replied to the item 'The organized games were enjoyable'. When a comparison was made between co-educational and girls' schools attended first the former had the more favourable estimates,[1] but for schools attended last the difference was small and not statistically significant, being however still in favour of the co-educational schools. There was a nearly complete equality in the classification of the playing-fields for the two types of school (see Table A2.19).

Overall conclusion

Here we merely need to draw the threads together, there having already been sufficient comment. There is no evidence whatsoever, as far as it can be judged from this criterion, that co-education tends to make boys effeminate. It seems likely that there is a rather greater interest in sports activities in co-educational than in single-sex schools, and the co-education factor would seem to be a likely reason, but the first statement has not been conclusively proved and the second is only an hypothesis. If co-education does have this effect it might be due to the interest taken by each sex in the sports activities of the other. An imponderable factor, but one which should not be dismissed lightly, is the influence of a tradition of success in inter-school games. In such competitions the co-educational schools would presumably have had to draw their teams from smaller numbers of each sex (and especially of seniors because of their smaller sixth forms).

[1] Statistically significant beyond the 0·01 level for 'first' schools; see Table A2.23.

13

Type of school and popularity of cookery and needlework

The controversy about the advantages and disadvantages of co-education at the secondary stage has raged furiously in the past, though in recent years it has assumed a quieter tone. The argument was furious, partly because entrenched interests thought themselves assailed and partly because absence of knowledge left the door wide open for polemics; assertions were made without evidence and refuted in a similar way, and only recently has a start been made in providing some of the facts. This enquiry attempts to discover whether the presence of boys in mixed grammar schools influences the attitude of the girls towards cookery and needlework; it tests the hypothesis that this factor should improve the attitude of the girls to these subjects.

Second College survey

It was decided to approach ex-pupils first, as they would be more mature in judgment and more considered in their replies than pupils in school and might provide evidence of any lasting effects. As it would have been difficult to have secured a representative sample of ex-grammar school pupils, the study was limited to one type of such pupil, namely teachers in training. The approach was by questionnaire; here we are concerned with only two of the questions. The students were asked, simply and directly, 'Do you like cooking?', 'Do you like needlework?' They were invited to reply on a seven-point scale ranging from 'Very much' through 'Neutral' to 'Disliked very much'. Two methods of scoring were used, the first a simple percentaging of the number of ex-pupils who were at each step on the scale, the second a weighting of the judgments on a scale from 7 to 1, commencing at 7 for 'Like very much', then finding the mean score.

The results are presented in Table 13.1. The means for girls' schools and mixed schools are virtually identical for cookery, and also for needlework, though at a rather lower level. The scatter of the preferences also shows an astonishing similarity from one type of school to the other when each subject is taken separately, a similarity which persists right through the range of the scale. The only difference of note is that between the popularity of cookery and needlework. This is the case in

TABLE 13.1   *Ex-pupils' attitude to cookery and needlework*

Second College survey

	Replies about cookery				Replies about needlework			
	Co-ed schools		Girls' schools		Co-ed schools		Girls' schools	
	N	%	N	%	N	%	N	%
Liked very much	154	38·4	252	40·1	128	31·8	196	31·3
Liked much	115	28·7	175	27·9	81	20·0	143	22·8
Liked a little	102	25·4	151	24·0	111	27·5	168	26·8
Undecided	8	2·0	24	3·8	13	3·2	8	1·3
Disliked a little	12	3·0	13	2·1	25	6·2	34	5·4
Disliked much	4	1·0	5	0·8	24	5·9	47	7·5
Disliked very much	6	1·5	8	1·3	22	5·4	31	4·9
Totals	401	100	628	100	404	100	627	100
Means	5·89		5·93		5·28		5.31	

both types of school, cookery having a superiority of 0·62 in girls' schools and 0·61 in mixed schools within a maximum score of 7·0. Both differences are statistically significant ($t = 7·27$ for the girls' schools, and 5·69 for the mixed). Of practical importance in the classroom is the proportion of pupils who dislike needlework (approaching one in five in both girls' and mixed schools) compared with the very much smaller proportion who dislike cookery (about one in twenty).

There is here no evidence whatsoever to sustain the hypothesis that the presence of boys in the school would encourage the girls to enjoy their cookery and needlework. When, however, the clinical situation is examined for hidden systematic bias it becomes clear that factors connected with social class might have affected the result. Girls' schools at present tend to have a rather higher social class intake than do mixed schools, and this is also true of our sample. Might not the children of the manual working classes have a higher—or lower—appreciation of these useful skills than the children of professional people? Fortunately information on the father's occupational class was available for a large part of the sample; the data were therefore re-classified, with the results shown in Table 13.2.

The pattern of the data reveals a tendency for the popularity scores to increase, in both types of school inversely to social class, in both subjects.[1] The one discrepant mean, that of needlework in social classes 4 and 5 in girls' schools, may well have been produced by the unreliability inherent in a small sample of twenty.

This systematic, though small, bias makes it essential to attempt to allow for it by placing the two types of school on the same social class

TABLE 13.2 *Popularity scores of cookery and needlework according to social class and type of school*

Second College survey

	Classes[1] 1 and 2		Class 3		Classes 4 and 5		Overall
	N	Mean	N	Mean	N	Mean	Mean
Cookery							
Women from co-ed schools	93	5·82	91	5·86	18	6·17	5·87
Women from girls' schools	206	5·82	146	5·97	18	6·28	5·90
Needlework							
Women from co-ed schools	93	5·43	91	5·32	19	5·42	5·84
Women from girls' schools	206	5·14	147	5·31	20	5·0	5·20

[1] The social class categories were those used by Peaker in the Early Leaving Report. Class 1 includes professional, administrative, managerial and teachers; class 2 clerical workers; class 3 skilled manual workers; class 4 semi-skilled and class 5 unskilled.

basis. To do this the mean score of the girls' schools was adjusted by superimposing on them the social class distribution of the mixed school, while retaining the original means of each social class in the girls' schools. This was done for cookery, but the difference between girls'

[1] The differences in cookery scores between social classes 1 and 2 combined as against 4 and 5 combined, pooling girls' and mixed schools, is significant beyond the 0·05 level. In needlework the similar difference, taking mixed schools only, is not significant.

and mixed schools means increased negligibly! A similar negligible change occurred when the calculation was reversed by superimposing the social class distribution of the girls' schools on to the mixed schools. In needlework, by inspection of Table 13.2 we can safely say that the above procedure would again have little effect on the result.

Comment

This survey is concerned only with a certain type of grammar school ex-pupils—those who became student teachers. For these no evidence has been produced to sustain the hypothesis that was being tested.

The small inverse association between social class and the popularity of cookery and needlework needs cautious interpretation. Three important factors are, first, that the social class element in the sample may have been diminished in importance by the limitation of the sample to one kind of pupil—student teachers. Second, and probably more important, that the sub-samples of each social class are not equivalent, the children of manual workers being much more finely selected—directly on attainment and academic ability, and indirectly on other factors— than the children of social classes 1 and 2. The rather higher scores of classes 4 and 5 may therefore be due to the more refined nature of their sample. Third, that the attempt to remove the social class variable by either calculating the means for each social class separately or by equating theoretically the social class distributions of the two types of school, though useful, probably does not entirely remove its influence, because an appreciable difference in social class distribution in any school might produce a difference in the prevailing attitude of all social classes towards a subject, thereby altering the mean scores before any comparison is made.

The pattern of the data in Table 13.2 shows the same remarkable consistency (one score excepted) as did the data in Table 13.1; this in spite of the use of the much-maligned questionnaire approach, briefly commented on in the previous chapter. Though the technique is simple it can be remarkably successful, provided that the questions are clear, unambiguous and not double-barrelled, that the anonymity of the respondents is guaranteed and they are well motivated, and that the administration is efficient and of such a type that collusion is avoided.

The Schools project

The trend of the findings of the Second College survey was checked by including the same two questions in a questionnaire administered to grammar school pupils and christened in the previous volumes the 'Schools project'. This was administered personally, under examination conditions, by the writer and a research assistant to some 2,240 pupils in 42 schools. We are first concerned, however, only with the girls who were aged 15 plus, 560 in number, from 28 schools. It should be noted that the questions were not directly about cookery or needlework lessons but 'Do you like cooking?' and 'Do you like needlework?'

With these 15-year-old girls cooking was decidedly popular, round about 88 per cent recording either 'Like much' or 'Like a little' (see Table 13.3). Whereas in the Second College survey there was a rough equality of popularity between the co-educated girls and those from

TABLE 13.3   *Liking for cookery and needlework (girls aged 15 plus)*

Schools project

	Replies about cookery				Replies about needlework			
	Co-ed schools		Girls' schools		Co-ed schools		Girls' schools	
	N	%	N	%	N	%	N	%
Like much	164	58·6	144	51·5	91	32·4	79	28·2
Like a little	87	31·1	100	35·7	85	30·4	94	33·5
Undecided	7	2·5	7	2·5	14	5·0	8	2·9
Dislike a little	11	3·9	18	6·4	43	15·4	50	17·9
Dislike much	11	3·9	11	3·9	47	16·8	49	17·5
Totals	280	100	280	100	280	100	280	100

girls' schools, here there is a consistent trend towards greater popularity among the co-educated girls, though this difference is not near the accepted level for statistical significance.[1] The trend was, however, consistent for all three parental occupational class groupings.[2] As there seemed to be no systematic difference between these occupational groups in the popularity of cookery the breakdown of data for this variable is omitted.

The results for needlework were a repetition of those for cookery but in a lower key. The occupation was less popular (though some 62 per cent of girls liked it either 'much' or 'a little') and it was only very slightly more popular among co-educated girls—the emphasis should decidedly

[1] Chi-square = 3·892 for 4 DF.
[2] Classes 1 and 2, white collar, class 3, skilled artisans and intermediate, classes 4 and 5, semi-skilled and unskilled manual.

188

TABLE 13.4   *Liking for cookery and needlework (girls aged 17 plus)*
Schools project

| | Replies about cookery | | | | Replies about needlework | | | |
| | Co-ed schools | | Girls' schools | | Co-ed schools | | Girls' schools | |
	N	%	N	%	N	%	N	%
Like much	60	52·2	46	38·3	39	33·9	34	28·3
Like a little	45	39·1	60	50·0	39	33·9	46	38·4
Undecided	0	0·0	2	1·7	4	3·5	3	2·5
Dislike a little	7	6·1	8	6·7	10	8·7	18	15·0
Dislike much	3	2·6	4	3·3	23	20·0	19	15·8
Totals	115	100	120	100	115	100	120	100

be on equality. Nor did an analysis according to occupational class produce anything of note. Of general interest is the very small percentage of pupils who were undecided in their attitude.

The same girls, apart from those who had left or were absent, were given the questionnaire again at the age of 17 plus (Table 13.4). The picture is similar to that seen two years previously except that the tendency for cookery to be more popular among the co-educated girls than among those in girls' schools has become more sharply defined, though the difference is short of statistical significance.[1] As frequently occurs in this research, the two distributions are characterized by a concentration of estimates in the 'Like much' category for the co-educated girls whereas the parallel concentrations for the girls in girls' schools is in the 'Like a little' section.[2] The same contrast, though slight, is found in the estimates of the two groups about needlework. In passing it is worth recording that, as in the Second College survey, needlework was much less popular than cookery and about one-third of the girls in both types of school expressed some measure of dislike for it.

General comment

The second study provides some evidence that cookery is more popular in co-educational schools, but the lack of confirmation in the findings of

[1] Chi-square = 6·07 for 4 DF.
[2] When 'Like much' is opposed to the rest (for cookery) the difference between the two types of school, though substantial, fails to reach statistical significance for the 15-year-olds, but does so for the 17-year-olds.

the earlier study enforce a verdict of 'likely, but not proved'. In addition, although in this sample of schoolgirls there is a tendency for cookery to be more popular in the co-educated group, this is only an association of two things and there is no proof that the greater popularity has been caused by co-education. In view, for example, of the relatively small number of schools and therefore, of cookery mistresses, the difference in popularity might have been caused by differences in the personalities of the teachers and not by the two types of schooling. On the other hand, the context of this one small piece of research in the constellation of findings in favour of the co-educational type of schooling makes it reasonable to assume that the cause of the difference found is likely to be the contrast in schooling and suggests that further research with a larger number of schools might produce a more conclusive result.

14

Attitudes of boys and girls to history[1]

Some educationalists believe that the interests of boys and girls are so different that at the secondary stage they need different syllabuses for many subjects. Others lay stress on the fundamental similarity of human nature in both sexes, minimize the differences, and suggest that there is a wide variation of interest within each sex. This study tries to ascertain the extent of the differences between the sexes and of variations within each sex with regard to the interest shown towards history in grammar schools.

The research of Ieuan Jones (1955) was carried out in four boys', four girls' and four mixed grammar schools in South Wales, among the form pupils of one fourth-year form in each school. There were 190 girls and 143 boys of average age fifteen. A questionnaire[2] was administered by the researcher and not signed by the pupils, who were assured that their replies would not be shown to the staff. It was divided into six 'aspects' of history: military, religious, social, 'cultural', economic, political and constitutional. Each of these had four sub-sections, the fourth always being biographical. The larger 'aspects' and the detailed topics were chosen from those common to the history syllabuses of the participating schools. Departures from what was considered to be the best arrangement of items had to be made to meet practical difficulties in the field work. For example, the economic aspect included as sub-sections, 'Relevant scientific discoveries' and 'Voyages of exploration'; these were too diverse for effective marriage. The 'cultural' section, similarly, contained sub-sections on crafts, painting and architecture, music, and relevant biographies. The work would also have been improved by the separation of political from constitutional history. In those instances where sections are now considered to be insufficiently homogeneous

[1] The research reported in this chapter was planned and supervised by the writer, and carried out by I. Jones, one of his research students; it is also based upon an analysis of all directly relevant theses listed in A. M. Blackwell's *Lists of Researches in Education and Educational Psychology*, published by the National Foundation for Educational Research; namely those by T. Cairns (1953), A. Hashim (1948), E. M. Uprichard (1947), A. Smyth (1946), C. Lambert (1944), R. Rallison (1939), D. Jordan (1937), J. Shakespeare (1934) and R. A. Pritchard (1928). The chapter was written by the author.
[2] See the addendum to the chapter.

emphasis has been placed on the results of individual sub-sections rather than on the section as a whole. Pupils were asked to represent their interest in each item by recording a numerical score on a five-point scale ranging in units of five, from +10 to −10. Provision was also made for free qualitative responses. Differences between means were tested for statistical significance by the small sample '*t*' technique, based conservatively on the small number of schools rather than on the relatively large number of pupils.[1]

The overall response to the 24 items for both sexes was well above the neutrality line. On the combined scale, which ranged from +240 to −240, the average score of the boys was 73·3 and of the girls 84·5, the difference not being statistically significant. The average score per item, on the scale +10 to −10, was 3·05 for boys and 3·5 for girls. In these overall averages, however, all the aspects received equal weighting, whereas in the usual syllabus the religious and 'cultural' aspects would be less prominent. Reducing the weighting of these two aspects would increase the overall averages; it would also bring the two sexes closer together as the girls scored more heavily than the boys on religious and 'cultural' aspects. This result was checked by requiring pupils to answer the question 'Do you like history as a school subject?' The same five-point scale was used, +10 meaning 'I like very much', +5 'I like' and so on. The average response for both sexes was rather higher than that for the 24 items combined, for reasons suggested above, and was almost identical for girls (5·42) and boys (5·35). The percentage of girls giving a favourable reply was 86·9 and of boys 84·6; 9·5 per cent of girls were negative, and 8·4 per cent of boys. Only three boys and not one girl expressed 'very great dislike'. One-third of each sex affirmed a 'very great liking'. The most marked feature of this part of the results is undoubtedly the similarity between the sexes in their total popularity scores. Such an overall similarity could, however, conceal appreciable differences in the response of the two sexes to various kinds of history. This problem is examined in the next section. We must keep in mind that the results of this section apply specifically to grammar school boys and girls who are about fifteen years old.

The relative popularity of the different aspects and of individual items is shown in Table 14.1.

It is surprising that military history was almost equally popular with the girls as with the boys, with no significant difference between them. When we look at the separate items, however, we see that while the girls are interested in the actual battles, the boys are rather more interested in them, and the girls on the other hand are perhaps slightly more interested than the boys in the causes and results of wars. Both

---

[1] A test to assess to what extent a difference between the means of two sets of scores might have occurred by chance.

TABLE 14.1   *The relative popularity of various aspects of history*

(Scale range +10 to −10)

Short title		Girls	Boys	Difference[1]
A	Military (all)	4·3	4·9	o·6B
1	Wars in Britain	4·0	5·8	1·8B
2	Wars in other countries	2·9	4·9	2·0B
3	Causes and results of wars	3·0	2·3	o·7G
4	Lives of generals, admirals etc	7·1	6·7	o·4G
B	Religious (all)	3·6	o·9	2·7G
5	Story of religion in Britain	5·2	o·35	4·85G
6	Christianity in other countries	o·8	−o·3	1·1G
7	Story of other religions	1·05	o·2	o·85G
8	Lives of great religious leaders	7·45	3·5	3·95G
C	Social (all)	5·5	3·5	2·0G
9	How people lived in Britain	7·2	4·4	2·8G
10	How people lived elsewhere	5·6	3·0	2·6G
11	Customs, games, sports etc	4·6	5·35	o·75B
12	Great social reformers	4·5	1·3	3·2G
D	Cultural (all)	2·4	o·6	1·8G
13	History of the arts	o·05	o·6	o·55B
14	History of the crafts	o·55	1·9	1·35B
15	History of music and literature	4·0	−1·4	5·4G
16	Great painters, writers, composers	4·9	1·4	3·5G
E	Economic (all)	1·4	4·4	3·0B
17	History of agriculture and industry	o·0	2·5	2·5B
18	History of trade, transport	o·95	4·3	3·35B
19	Science in agriculture, industry	o·55	4·3	3·75B
20	Great explorers, inventors etc	4·1	6·5	2·4B
F	Political, constitutional (all)	4·0	3·9	o·1G
21	Government in Britain	3·6	2·5	1·1G
22	Government elsewhere	o·5	o·8	o·3B
23	Political struggles etc	4·1	6·15	2·05B
24	Great rulers, statesmen	7·7	6·3	1·4G

[1] In favour of boys, B; girls, G.

sexes give a higher place to the lives of generals and admirals, etc. than to any of the other three items.

The four items of political and constitutional history produced a combined response signifying popularity for both boys and girls, and the pattern of response was similar for the two sexes. Both preferred political to constitutional history and both expressed keen interest in the lives of great rulers and statesmen.

Social history was popular with the girls and fairly popular with the boys. On the scale $+10$ to -10 (in units of 5) the boys averaged 3·5 and the girls 5·5; the difference is statistically significant, i.e. it is unlikely to have occurred by chance, but for practical purposes in the classroom the scores do not seem to be unduly apart. With regard to individual items the writer from his classroom experience would have expected the boys to have a rather higher score on the lives of social reformers. Only repeated experimentation could decide whether there is any fault here, and indeed decide whether the other findings are sound.

The 'cultural' aspect of history was only slightly popular with either sex, but the girls' score (2·4) was higher than that of the boys (0·6). Though the difference was small in relation to the scale range, it was statistically significant, and was mostly due to the liking of the girls for the history of music and literature (4·0), which was slightly unpopular with the boys ($-1·4$). The girls, more than the boys, appeared to enjoy biographies of artists, musicians, etc.

Sex differences were shown more clearly in the 'religious' and 'economic' aspects of history. With the former, though the ranking was close (fourth for girls and fifth for boys) the difference between the means was somewhat greater than in previous cases (girls 3·6, boys 0·9) and was statistically significant. The biographical approach to this aspect was, however, popular with both sexes. It was in the 'economic' section that the sex difference was greatest (girls 1·4, boys 4·4); girls ranked it last while boys ranked it second. Once again the biographical aspect was liked by both sexes, though more so with boys than with girls. This economic section included scientific inventions in industry, and it was in this item that the sex difference was most marked. In none of the four items did the girls sink below the neutrality line, though in the 'history of agriculture and industry' they reached it.

With only two of the 24 items was there an average response below the neutrality level for either sex. Boys expressed some dislike of the history of music and literature, and a very slight dislike of the history of Christianity in other lands.

An attempt was made to check the rank order of the six aspects as derived from their scores on the five-point scale, by later asking the pupils to arrange these aspects in order of preference. Unfortunately the titles, used without the numerous examples given in the main question-naire, did not in two cases suggest exactly the same content. The original 'political and constitutional' aspect appeared as 'history of governments', thus emphasizing the constitutional content, and being distinctly less popular. The original 'economic' aspect, not now specific-ally including relevant scientific inventions and exploration, also lost rank slightly with the boys. Otherwise there was a general confirmation of the rankings of the main investigation.

To the question, 'Would you like history lessons on the last 50 years?' there was a response rather above 'liking', with only a small difference between the sexes (boys 6·43, girls 5·32). The percentage of favourable replies was 86 for the boys and 80 for the girls. This was a response made when most of the pupils had received no direct instruction on the period.

It would be a great mistake to regard any difference between the mean scores of boys and girls, or between their rankings, as representing a clear-cut division between the sexes on any one of these aspects. In the first place the many small score differences, viewed in relation to the large possible range, are indicative of similarity rather than difference. Secondly, there is a wide range of scores between the school groups of each sex; for example in 'political and constitutional history' the girls' groups range from 4·7 to 0·6, and the boys' groups from 5·95 to 1·25; in the 'economic' aspect the girls' groups range from 4·2 to −0·2, and the boys' from 5·17 to 3·19. Thirdly, within each sex there is a wide individual variation; for example 25 girls gave military history as their first choice, while 22 gave it as their last, and 13 boys gave economic history as their last choice while 14 made it their first choice.

Fortunately we are able to compare these findings with those of Cairns (1953), who also attempted to ascertain the relative appeal of the principal aspects of history for the two sexes. His investigation was carried out in one mixed grammar school, two mixed secondary modern schools, one boys' technical school and one girls' commercial school, all in industrial parts of Durham. At each school about 30 boys and about 30 girls from the 12+ age group, and a similar number from the 14+ age group, took part. We should note here that Jones's pupils were slightly older (average age 15). The number of schools is small in view of the influence of the teacher on subject popularity.

The most reliable part of the work is a questionnaire of ten items. On this pupils expressed their reaction on a five-point scale, from +2 to −2, to various aspects of the history syllabus. Table 14.2 has been compiled by the writer from Cairns's results; it combines, however, pupils from three types of secondary school and two age groups. Jones on the other hand carried out his research only in grammar schools.

Both sexes ranked the 'romantic' aspect of history high in popularity, the boys having a very slightly higher score than the girls on 'Adventurous deeds in warfare and exploration', and vice versa on 'The lives and deeds of important men and women'. While the girls had a virtually identical score for these two items, the boys preferred the 'Adventurous deeds'.

'The history of your own town or district' was also ranked high by both boys and girls, with age having no apparent effect on the score. The girls, however, were slightly more strongly in favour of it than were the boys.

In response to the item which was next in popularity when both sexes

TABLE 14.2   *Interest in history (boys and girls)*

Cairns's questionnaire, average scores[1]

Topic		Boys' average	For	Against	Girls' average	For	Against
1	The lives and deeds of important men and women	1·11	149	10	1·48	181	1
2	The everyday life of ordinary people in other times	0·32	76	35	1·0	141	9
3	How trades and industries used to be carried on[2]	0·54	107	36	0·7	128	30
4	The development of things like ships, houses, tools, roads	1·2	153	10	0·42	97	43
5	The ideas people used to have about the world etc	0·61	113	30	0·61	114	33
6	Government and law, how Parliament grew etc	0·23	84	52	0·21	90	57
7	Difficulties and problems of kings and statesmen etc	0·70	115	27	0·84	183	24
8	The causes of all the problems that face the nations	0·28	89	51	0·12	85	63
9	Adventurous deeds in warfare and exploration	1·76	179	1	1·43	170	10
10	The history of your own town or district	1·15	152	12	1·44	175	6

[1] i.e. weighted scores in the scale $+2$ to -2. There were 191 girls and 186 boys. Neutral votes are omitted in the table, but are included in the averages, 'strong approval' is combined with 'approval' under the heading 'For' and 'strong disapproval' is combined with 'disapproval' under the heading 'Against'.
[2] For full wording see text.

were combined, 'The development of things like ships, houses, tools, roads', any sex difference would depend largely on the choice of examples; in this instance both sexes indicated their approval, but the boys were more enthusiastic than the girls.

Just below the last item, fairly popular and with little difference between the sexes, came 'Difficulties and problems of kings and statesmen of other days, and how they tried to overcome them'.

Still on the positive side of the popularity continuum, 'The everyday life of ordinary people in other times' was popular with the girls but at this age only slightly popular with the boys. Industrial history, 'How trades and industries used to be carried on, e.g. clock-making, mining, farming', received a similar ranking of slight popularity from both sexes, as did 'The ideas people used to have about the world and about how men should live together and behave towards one another'. For these last two items, however, approximately one-sixth of each sex recorded disapproval.

The attitude of both sexes to 'Government and law, for example, how Parliament grew, elections, methods of justice and various types of courts, rates, and taxes' was identical and merely tinged with approval, as was also their attitude to 'The causes of all the problems and difficulties that face the nations of the world nowadays'.

We see therefore that in eight out of the ten items the popularity voting of the girls is very similar to that of the boys. The remaining two items need further comment. 'The everyday life of ordinary people in other times', though more popular with girls than with boys, has more than twice as many boys voting for it as against it. Similarly, though the 'development' item is more popular with boys than with girls (possibly because of the examples chosen) yet the number of girls liking it is more than twice the number of those who dislike it. The emphasis throughout the results is on the broad similarity of the attitudes of the two sexes.

Teachers who read this with a view to applying their findings in the classroom should note that these averages, like those of Jones, sometimes conceal important differences between school groups of the same sex. For instance the popularity of item 3, 'How trades and industries used to be carried on', varied from 0·15 (technical boys) through 0·61 (grammar boys) to 0·9 (secondary modern boys), and from 0·52 (commercial girls and grammar girls) to 1·05 (secondary modern girls). Again in response to item 8 on world problems, the grammar school girls scored −0·11 while the 14+ secondary modern girls scored 1·0.

Though we need to keep in mind that Cairns's pupils were younger than those of Jones and were not drawn only from grammar schools, these two researches give each other appreciable support. They agree on the high popularity of biography and of adventurous deeds in warfare for both sexes. They find political history moderately popular, and constitutional history of low popularity, with little or no sex difference. They agree also that girls are slightly more interested than boys in social history. One apparent disagreement is that while Cairns found (surprisingly) no sex difference on 'How trades and industries used to be carried on', Jones obtained a sex difference in favour of the boys. This seeming conflict might stem partly from the population difference, but may be due to the different content of the aspect in the two enquiries, for example the inclusion by Jones of relevant scientific discoveries.

The remaining portion of the Jones research, concerned with the overall popularity of history for boys and for girls, links up naturally with the work of Pritchard (1935). Using a population of 8,000 grammar school boys and girls, of age range $12\frac{1}{2}$ to 16, to discover the relative popularity of ten subjects, he found that on a scale ranging from 200 (if a subject was placed first by all pupils) to 0 (if placed last by all pupils), history scored 114 in boys' schools, 117 in girls' schools, 115 among boys in mixed schools and 108 among girls in mixed schools. History was third in boys' schools, second in girls' schools, third among boys in mixed schools, and third among girls in mixed schools (one point behind French). Both Jones and Pritchard therefore find little difference between the sexes in the relative popularity of history in grammar schools.

Interest cannot be the sole factor which decides the historical topics which are taught in our schools, but it is an important one. The argument, therefore, that sex differences in interests create a need for a sex differentiation in curriculum and in syllabus cannot be brushed lightly on one side. Research such as that presented here will reveal the extent of the differences and similarities, so that the matter may be judged with less emotional bias. A further field which might usefully be explored is that concerned with the interaction of the different interests of the sexes in mixed classes. Does the greater interest of the boys in economic topics communicate itself to the girls, and does the interest of the girls in some of the history of religion communicate itself to the boys? Is the interest of each sex widened? Has the male sex a different approach to the subject compared with the female, and if this is so is a better understanding of history obtained by separating the sexes or by combining them in the same class? All these questions need investigation, but the wide variation within each sex in attitude to history points strongly not to the need to cater for sex differences, but to the need to cater for *individual* differences.

The averages presented here are only central points of reference. Though the character of the material studied in the classroom is normally a powerful force in determining the interest of the pupil, every teacher knows that other forces such as the popularity of the teacher, his skill in presentation, and the method he chooses for a particular topic, have their effect. Nor does the pupil's enthusiasm for the lives of conquerors remain at a constant level for all the biographies he studies. None the less these results, which should be considered as broad tendencies rather than figures taken to the second decimal place, give us a more accurate, albeit still imperfect, conception of the interest of grammar school boys and girls in the various aspects of history in school. In this subject the case for the separation of the sexes for teaching purposes is weak, but the need to make some provision for individual differences (e.g. by classwork assignments for part of the time) is clearly indicated.

Addendum

LIST OF QUESTIONNAIRE ITEMS (JONES)

In the original questionnaire examples were given for each item

A1 The history of wars, conquests and battles in British history
A2 The history of wars, conquests and battles in other countries
A3 Why the wars began, and the results of the wars
A4 The lives of the great conquerors, warriors, generals and admirals

B5 The history of religion in Britain
B6 The history of the Christian church in other countries
B7 The history of other religions
B8 The lives of the great religious leaders

C9 How people lived at different times in British history
C10 How people lived at different periods in other countries
C11 The history of customs, games, sports, pastimes in Britain and other countries
C12 The lives of the great social reformers

D13 The history of the arts (i.e. of painting, sculpture and architecture)
D14 The history of the crafts (i.e. of metal-work, weaving, carving and pottery-making)
D15 The history of literature (poetry, prose and drama), of the theatre and of music
D16 The lives of the great painters, sculptors, writers and musicians

E17 The history of agriculture and of industry
E18 The history of trade and commerce, transport and communications
E19 How scientific discoveries have helped progress in agriculture, industry and trade
E20 The great men who advanced agriculture, industry, trade and communications

F21 The history of government in Britain
F22 The history of government in other countries
F23 The history of political struggles, revolution and civil wars
F24 The lives of the great rulers and statesmen

15

R. R. Dale and J. A. Jones

Attitudes of boys and girls
to Scripture

When girls and boys are taught together, it is important for teachers to know the extent of any differences between the sexes in their attitudes towards the subject of the lesson. In this chapter the subject is Scripture, but the term covers a wide variety of topics, about which the attitudes of boys and girls might differ. If some indication of the nature and extent of these differences can be given, an appropriate allowance can be made for them, so that they may be fully utilized in building up the right attitudes and securing sufficient interest.

In order to discover and document some of the differences an investigation was conducted among girls and boys of the fourth forms of certain co-educational grammar schools. A comparison is made of the differences between the sexes in their attitudes to various sections of the subject and the hypothesis is examined that social class backgrounds would be associated with changes in response.

Previous research relating to this subject is not extensive. Lewis (1913), investigating the popularity and unpopularity of school subjects in elementary schools, found that Scripture was actually placed low in the list. Shakespeare (1936) came to the same conclusion, as did Houslop and Weeks (1948), though their enquiry was among boys in a grammar school. In the last of these researches there was a tendency for the subject to be generally disliked. On the other hand, Moreton (1944), Glassey (1945) and Daines (1949) found the attitude of adolescent boys and girls to *religion* to be moderately favourable. In Glassey's enquiry, the attitude to religion became less favourable as the child moved up the school.

Lewis found that Scripture tended to be more popular with girls than with boys. So did Shakespeare. Glassey similarly found that the attitude of grammar school girls was decidedly more favourable than that of the boys. The work of Daines produced no evidence of any clearly marked *religious* leanings in adolescent girls as opposed to boys, but he considered that possibly the girls showed a more pronounced interest. Forrester (1946) discovered only a small number of differences between the attitudes of adolescent girls and boys, and when they did occur they were seldom very great.

The investigation started with an analysis of the type of Scripture taught in the South Wales schools. On the basis of information received from thirteen co-educational grammar schools, and using also the syllabus of religious instruction for the schools of Wales, section B of the questionnaire was prepared. (See addendum at the end of the chapter.) This contained a list of twelve topics for Scripture lessons, classified under three headings: the Old Testament, the Gospels, the Acts of the Apostles. For each topic, pupils were to underline one of five responses: Like very much, Like, Undecided, Dislike, Dislike very much. The Likert scoring technique was adopted, whereby values of 1 to 5 were assigned to the five possible responses, the highest value being given to 'Like very much'.

A pre-test was carried out with one form of grammar school pupils to discover whether there were any difficulties and also to obtain an estimate of the time taken to answer these sections. Some changes were subsequently made in the wording of the questionnaire.

An attitude scale was used in section D of the questionnaire[1] (see addendum). Many of the questions in the questionnaire section were open-ended, as it was thought that the comments would increase the value of the results; this part of the work, however, is too lengthy for inclusion as it would disturb the balance of the book.

The questionnaire and attitude scale were personally administered in ten schools, with members of the staff excluded. The pupils were asked to be as frank as possible and were reassured that all answer papers would remain anonymous.

The tested population consisted of 172 girls and 108 boys, the average age being 15 years 2 months and 15 years 1 month respectively. The majority of both girls and boys were non-Welsh-speaking. The pupils were classified into four social groups, according to father's occupation. These groups were: (1) higher non-manual; (2) lower non-manual; (3) skilled manual; (4) semi-skilled and unskilled manual (Glass, 1954). In five of the schools the pupils were taught Scripture by a mistress, and in the remaining five by a master. 66·8 per cent of the girls were regular attenders at Sunday School, but only 43·9 per cent of the boys. 69·6 per cent of the girls were regular attenders at a place of worship, but only 47·2 per cent of the boys.

A comment is needed on the disproportion between boys and girls in the sample. In order to obtain the willing co-operation of the school and forestall any deliberate selection of pupils it was decided to administer the questionnaire to one entire form in each school. To secure a reasonable homogeneity of age and ability only fourth form A streams were chosen. To the surprise of the experimenters this resulted in an imbalance of the sexes, and the question arose whether the two groups were sufficiently representative. Enquiries showed that this imbalance

[1] Split-half reliability +0·973.

TABLE 15.1   *Attitude to Scripture lessons in general: mean scores of the girls and boys*[1]

Schools	No. of pupils		Section B Possible range 12–60			Section D Possible range 29–121		
	Girls	Boys	Girls	Boys	Differ-ence	Girls	Boys	Differ-ence
1	18	8	49·4	46·0	3·4	104·9	97·3	7·6
2	18	12	46·6	43·5	3·1*	90·7	72·8	17·9†
3	19	9	48·7	40·8	7·9†	99·2	91·1	8·1
4	13	6	45·9	46·8	−0·9	93·0	101·7	−8·7
5	17	15	50·7	44·1	6·6†	106·4	81·8	24·6†
6	17	12	45·9	48·3	−2·4	99·8	104·5	−4·7
7	16	10	49·7	45·2	4·5	100·7	88·1	12·6
8	16	10	48·5	43·8	4·7*	101·8	91·6	10·2*
9	22	14	44·7	41·5	3·2	88·0	72·8	15·2
10	16	12	48·2	47·0	1·2	96·0	89·7	6·3
Total	172	108	—	—	—	—	—	—
Mean			47·8	44·6	3·2†	97·9	87·6	10·3†

[1] Section B is the questionnaire, Section D the attitude scale. * indicates significance at the 5 per cent level; † at the 1 per cent level.

was mainly caused by legitimate administrative factors, such as the chance selection of science and arts streams and by the girls obtaining more places than the boys as a result of the selection at 11 plus.

Though the overall appraisal of the sample was reassuring, there remained two schools (1 and 6) in which there might have been some special selection. In the analysis of the results it was, therefore, necessary to keep this difficulty in mind; the principal corrective was that the researchers gave careful attention to the pattern produced by the results from the ten individual schools, and to the effects produced on the findings if schools 1 and 6 were excluded.

The response scores which represent the pupils' attitude to Scripture lessons in general are given in Table 15.1.

The *girls'* mean scores indicated that they liked Scripture as a school subject (section B), and gave a favourable response to it on the attitude scale (i.e. section D). The exclusion of schools 1 and 6 made no difference to the findings, even though the attitude score was thereby slightly reduced (to 96·7).

The *boys'* mean scores indicated that they had a moderate liking for Scripture (section B), and gave a moderately favourable response to it on the attitude scale. As in the case of the girls, the exclusion of schools 1 and 6 reduced the attitude score (to 84·4); their score in section B was also slightly lower. The findings are unchanged.

The difference between the girls' and the boys' mean scores (3·2 in a range of 48 for section B, and 10·3 in a range of 92 for the attitude scale) is statistically significant at the 1 per cent level of confidence in both sections. If schools 1 and 6 are omitted, the difference is increased to 12·3. It would thus appear that the girls were rather more interested than the boys in Scripture as a school subject. This result was checked by the use of a small sample statistical technique whereby the school means were used as the unit instead of the scores of individuals. This method enabled us to see whether the difference between the response of the boys and the girls was found sufficiently consistently in the different schools. The statistical outcome was the same as in the case of the previous tests. For section B and for section D the difference was in the expected direction in each of eight schools, and in the reverse direction in the two others. (The Wilcoxon sign-rank non-parametric test again confirmed these differences when the boys' and girls' means within each school were taken as the unit.)

As one would expect, there was a considerable overlap between the scores of boys and girls. In section B (questionnaire) 32 per cent of the boys had a higher score than the mean score of the girls, while 21 per cent of the girls had a lower score than the boys' mean score. Similarly, in section D (attitude scale) 35 per cent of the boys had a higher score than the mean score of the girls, and 19 per cent of the girls scored less than the boys' mean score. In both the questionnaire and the attitude scale, there was a slightly greater percentage of boys than of girls in the highest scoring group. This difference was not statistically significant and might be due to the slight element of special selection in the boys' sample.

Table 15.2 shows that neither the girls nor the boys liked each section equally well. Both the girls and the boys liked The Gospels most. (Girls had a great liking for it, boys liked it.) Next for both the girls and the boys came The Old Testament. (Girls and boys liked it.) Least liked by both the girls and the boys was The Acts of the Apostles. (Girls had a moderate liking for it, boys were undecided but tended towards having a moderate liking.)

The difference between the responses of the sexes was not the same in each section of the syllabus. For The Gospels, the difference between their mean scores (10 per cent) was statistically significant at the 1 per cent level of confidence. The direction of the difference was the same in all ten schools and the means of nine girls' groups were higher than that of any of the boys' groups. In the other two sections, the differences

TABLE 15.2 *The difference between the girls' and the boys' mean scores for the three sections of the syllabus*[1]

School	No. of Pupils		Mean scores		
			Old Testament	Gospels	Acts
1	Girls	18	15·7	18·9	14·8
	Boys	8	15·9	15·3†	14·9
2	Girls	18	15·3	17·9	13·4
	Boys	12	15·3	16·3	11·8
3	Girls	19	16·6	17·9	14·3
	Boys	9	16·1	13·4†	11·3*
4	Girls	13	15·2	18·0	12·8
	Boys	6	16·8	16·8	13·2
5	Girls	17	17·0	18·7	15·1
	Boys	15	15·2	16·5	12·5*
6	Girls	17	14·8	17·7	13·5
	Boys	12	15·8	17·4	15·2
7	Girls	16	16·8	18·3	14·6
	Boys	10	15·7	16·4	13·1
8	Girls	16	15·8	18·3	14·5
	Boys	10	16·0	15·6*	12·2
9	Girls	22	16·2	16·9	11·6
	Boys	14	14·3	14·9	12·4
10	Girls	16	15·4	18·2	14·7
	Boys	12	16·2	17·2	13·7
Total	Girls	172	—	—	—
	Boys	108			

[1] * indicates significance at the 5 per cent level; † at the 1 per cent level.

between the girls' and the boys' mean scores (1·5 per cent for The Old Testament and 4·5 per cent for The Acts) were statistically significant. In each section of the syllabus, the girls' mean score was higher than that of the boys. For The Old Testament and The Acts, the girls' mean scores were lower than those of the boys in some schools, higher in others.

It would thus appear that so far as The Old Testament and The Acts are concerned, the difference between the girls' and the boys' responses were not sufficiently great to be of practical importance in the teaching of Scripture in co-educational grammar schools. The difference between the responses to The Gospels was greater and may be of practical importance, although even here their responses were more alike than unlike, and even the boys claimed to like this section of Scripture; their 'popularity' score for it *in this section* placed it higher than the other two sections. In another part of the questionnaire, as a partial check on the above results, the girls and boys were asked to indicate their order of preference for the three sections of the syllabus. A difference between their preferences then emerged. The *girls'* order of preference was: 1 The Gospels, 2 The Old Testament, 3 The Acts. This order was the same as before. The *boys'* order of preference was: 1 The Old Testament, 2 The Gospels, 3 The Acts. This order differed from that found previously, in that the first two sections of the syllabus had changed places. This shows the value of the inclusion of check questions. One reason for the reversal of the rank order of the two sections was that in section B of the enquiry, the boys placed them close in 'popularity', averaging 15·6 for The Old Testament and 16·0 for The Gospels, out of a possible 20. The emphasis here is on similarity rather than difference. As, however, the difference became more substantial for the check question, there must be one or more additional reasons for the change in rank. The fact that 'The Old Testament' was printed on the first line, with the two other titles on successive lines below, might have increased its score slightly, but this alone would probably be too small an influence. Two other suggestions are made. First, that the thirty-two topics given in each of the relevant sections of the questionnaire as examples of the Scripture of The Old Testament and The Gospels, taught in the sample schools, might not have been quite as representative as we had hoped, in spite of the great care that was taken. Second, that some attitude or prejudice may have affected the response of the boys to either of the sections as a whole which had little effect on their response to individual topics within those sections. To keep this matter in the right perspective, if we weight these preferences 1, 2 and 3 for first, second and third preferences, the scores are 1·71 (The Old Testament) and 1·97 (The Gospels). The change in attitude score which produced the reversed rank order is not great enough to cause serious concern when placed beside the cases where there was agreement, but it is sufficient to require comment.

Certain trends were noticeable when the differences between the sexes were examined in relation to social class. Starting from fairly similar responses of boys and girls (sections B and D) in social group 1, the responses of the non-Welsh-speaking *girls* showed a tendency to become progressively *more favourable* in successive social groups, whereas the responses of the non-Welsh-speaking *boys* showed a slight tendency to become progressively *less favourable* in successive social groups. In the case of the girls, the tendency was surprisingly regular from group 1 to group 4, but in that of the boys it consisted only of a more favourable response in group 1 than in all other groups, the scores of these latter groups differing very little among themselves. The above social class differences were not due to 'between school' differences. The gap between the mean responses of the sexes, therefore, tended to become progressively greater in successive social groups.

In social group 1, the difference between the sexes was statistically insignificant. In group 2, the difference between mean scores was statistically significant in section D only. In group 3 it was statistically significant at the 1 per cent level of confidence, and at least at the 5 per cent level in group 4.

A difference in social group was therefore accompanied by a change in the responses of both the girls and the boys, and also in the size of the gap between them. This seems to support one of Forrester's conclusions (1946) that one of the chief reasons for differences in attitudes may be personality differences which go back to innate or environmental factors. She says that the question then is what kind of home life produces the most positive attitude to the topic under investigation. In this enquiry, the only indication of the kind of home life was that provided by the social group to which a pupil belonged. So far as the girls were concerned, the most positive response was given by those who belonged to social group 4, and the least positive response by those in group 1. For the boys the most positive response was given by those in group 1, the least positive by those in group 4.

The mean responses of the non-Welsh-speaking girls were more favourable than those of the non-Welsh-speaking boys, whether they were taught by mistress or master, the difference between mean scores being statistically significant at the 1 per cent level of confidence (sections B and D) when the teachers were mistresses, and at the 1 per cent level in section B and 5 per cent level in section D when the teachers were masters. Nevertheless, a difference in the sex of the teacher was accompanied by a difference in both the girls' and the boys' responses, as follows. Both the girls and the boys tended to give slightly more favourable responses when they were taught by a mistress. The difference between the responses of the girls and the boys taught by mistresses tended to be less than that of the girls and the boys taught by masters. As there were only five masters and five mistresses these particular results are not presented as findings, but await the verdict of future research.

Although the samples were small, the above tendencies were also observed within each social group. Furthermore, it appears that the observations made previously regarding social group differences applied whether the pupils were taught by mistresses or masters.

The results when scores were grouped according to attendance at Sunday School were fairly similar to those when scores were grouped according to attendance at a place of worship. The mean scores of the non-Welsh-speaking girls were higher than those of the non-Welsh-speaking boys in both cases. Certain other tendencies are observable. The responses of the girls whose attachment to a religious institution was strong (i.e. regular attendance) tended, as one would expect, to be more favourable than those of the girls whose attachment was weak or non-existent. The same was true also for the boys, for whom this tendency is more pronounced. The difference between the responses of the girls and boys whose attachment to a religious institution was strong, was less than that between the girls and boys whose attachment was weak or non-existent.

The pattern of the results indicated that these observations probably applied to each social group, though here the samples were small.

Where there was a strong attachment to a religious institution, the tendencies of the girls' and the boys' responses to vary according to their social group were not much in evidence. However, where there was a weak or non-existent attachment to a religious institution, the tendencies of the girls' and the boys' scores to vary according to their social group were pronounced.

Comment

Much of this enquiry was concerned with an examination of differences in the response of girls and boys towards Scripture. The extent of the agreement is, however, more striking and more important. In section B, where the possible score range is 48, for attitude to the subject as a whole, the boy–girl difference in score in eight out of the ten schools is 4·7 or less. Similarly, in the attitude scale, where the maximum possible score is 121, with a range of 92, the girls' score is 98, while that of the boys is 88. In no overall or section score does one sex record liking and the other sex dislike. The study brings out clearly the difference between something which is statistically significant and something which is of practical significance. A number of the differences reported in the study have statistical significance, but none of them would appear to be of serious practical significance for class organization, though a knowledge of them might well be of value to a teacher of Scripture. As with history, this chapter provides little support for the argument that the sexes should be separated for the study of this subject on account of their divergent interests. Another point made in the chapter on history is also applicable here, namely that some difference in interests might be good because of its educative and broadening effect.

The size of the sample, ten schools and 280 pupils, was limited by practical considerations, as was its restriction to one area. For this reason, these findings are presented tentatively, in the hope that they will form a useful guide for future hypotheses and research. Of particular interest in this respect are the results with regard to social class.

Addendum

SCRIPTURE QUESTIONNAIRE, ABBREVIATED

SECTION B TOPICS FOR SCRIPTURE LESSONS

THE OLD TESTAMENT: THE HISTORY AND RELIGION OF ISRAEL
1 *The history of the Israelites from Abram to Joseph.*
   e.g., God's covenant with Abram, Isaac blessing Jacob, Jacob's dreams, Joseph's dreams, Joseph sold into slavery by his brothers, Joseph in Egypt.
   Like very much/Like/Undecided/Dislike/Dislike very much.
2 *The history of the Israelites in Egypt, the Exodus and Wanderings.* (Examples omitted.)
3 *The history of the conquest and settlement of Canaan.*
4 *The history of the United Monarchy.*

THE GOSPELS: THE LIFE AND TEACHING OF JESUS CHRIST
5 *Stories of the birth of John the Baptist, and of the birth and childhood of Jesus.*
6 *The teaching of Jesus.*
7 *The Miracles of Jesus.*
8 *The events of the last week of Jesus's life.*

THE ACTS OF THE APOSTLES: THE BEGINNING OF THE CHRISTIAN CHURCH
9 *The promise and the coming of the Holy Spirit.*
10 *The Church in Jerusalem.*
11 *The Church in Samaria.*
13 *The Church among the Gentiles.*

SECTION C
1 What do you think of Scripture as a school subject?
   Like very much/Like/Undecided/Dislike/Dislike very much.
   Give a short reason for your answer.
2 Number the following sections of Scripture lessons in your order of preference:
   The Old Testament
   The Gospels
   The Acts of the Apostles
3 Give a short reason why in question 2 you like your first choice best and your last choice least.
   Reason for my first choice is
   Reason for my last choice is
4 Where would you place Scripture in a list of your subjects in order of preference? Underline your answer.
   Very high/High/Middle/Low/Very low.
5 What do you like most in Scripture lessons?

6   What do you dislike most in Scripture lessons?
7   Do you intend taking Scripture as one of your examination subjects at the Ordinary level?
    Yes/Undecided/No.

SECTION D (attitude scale)

1   We ought to study Scripture carefully and thoroughly.
    Strongly agree/Agree/Undecided/Disagree/Strongly disagree.
2   Scripture lessons do not deserve the praise that some pupils give them.
    Strongly agree, etc.
3   Scripture lessons are important for all pupils.
4   I have no desire at all to learn Scripture.
5   I would not encourage anyone to study Scripture seriously.
6   Without Scripture lessons our education would be incomplete.
7   I would never study Scripture in school unless I had to.
8   Scripture is a very interesting subject.
9   Scripture lessons are a waste of time.
10 I think that when pupils speak ill of Scripture lessons they are right.
11 Scripture lessons are a necessary basis for the best way of life.
12 What I learn in Scripture lessons is usually worthwhile.
13 School would be better off without Scripture lessons.
14 More time should be given to Scripture lessons.
15 I should like to stop Scripture from being taught in schools.

Part III

A follow-up research

R. R. Dale and P. McC. Miller   **16**

Comparative attitudes of university students from co-educational and single-sex schools towards school, university and the opposite sex[1]

Introduction

Research described in the previous volumes has demonstrated that there are important differences in atmosphere between co-educational and single-sex secondary schools. For example, single-sex schools—especially those for girls—seem, on average, to place greater emphasis on conformity to rules and regulations, to be stricter in discipline, to be less happy, and tend to have less pleasant relationships amongst the staff, amongst the pupils and between staff and pupils. The question arises as to whether these differences in atmosphere and hence in attitude to school give rise to differences of attitude towards institutions of further education such as the university. The chapter describes work which explores some evidence on this matter but at the same time, by the use of an indirect technique on the attitude of a new sample of students towards their schools, examines whether the tenor of previous findings is confirmed. It is also hypothesized that such differences in the evaluation of school concepts may well be greater between the women's groups than between the men's.

To explore these points the semantic differential technique developed by Osgood, Suci and Tannenbaum (1957) and recently reviewed by Heise (1969) was employed. This represents a somewhat more indirect approach than the questionnaire methods previously used, in that it is rather less obvious to the subjects just what is being measured. They rated *concepts*, such as 'my school', on a series of seven-point scales the extremes of which were defined by pairs of adjectives such as 'good—bad', 'hard—soft' etc. Combinations of certain of these scales provide measurements on three different and independent *factors* labelled by Osgood *et al.* (1957) 'evaluation', 'potency' and 'activity'. 'Evaluation' is a combination of ratings on Pleasant/Unpleasant, Trivial/Important, Negative/Positive, Valuable/Worthless and Good/Bad. 'Potency' similarly combines scores on Severe/Lenient, Weak/Strong and Hard/

[1]This chapter is based on the results of part of a research project financed by the Social Science Research Council.

Soft. 'Activity' is made from Passive/Active, Sharp/Dull and Slow/
Fast.

The sample

The sample consisted of 145 men and 129 women from the 1968-9 and
1969-70 first-year classes at the University College of Swansea. It was
limited to those students in the faculties of arts and pure science who
had sat the WJEC[1] A-level examination and were taking at least one of
the following subjects: French, history, geography, applied mathematics,
pure mathematics, physics, chemistry, botany, but there were 24 non-
co-operators and 18 who had attended both types of school were
eliminated.

The semantic differential concepts

Nine concepts were chosen, of which four related to school. These were
'my school', 'schoolteacher', 'my class at school', and 'classroom'. Four
others were concerned with university and were intended to be closely
analogous to the school concepts, namely 'this university college',
'university lecturer', 'student', and 'lecture theatre'. 'Student' and 'my
class at school' are however not as closely analogous as might be
desirable. The remaining concept was 'the opposite sex'. An example of
a concept and its rating scales is given in the addendum to this chapter.

Procedure

In the second and third weeks of the winter term the students were
asked to co-operate in a large survey, of which the semantic differential
test formed a part. They were usually tested in large groups but
occasionally individually.

Before calculating the mean differences between the principal groups,
the A-level attainment, faculty and social class variables were controlled
by choosing from the main group a special 'balanced' sample. All the
subcells of this sample had nearly equal proportions of students from
the two faculties who were also of comparable categories of A-level
attainment and of social class. To preserve correct proportionality the
sample had to be drawn from the top three A-level categories only (out
of four) reducing this balanced sample to 104 students. The remaining
170, however,[2] were used as a cross validation sample (termed the
'remainder sample'); results for both samples are reported. Those
variables which could not be balanced out from either sample, notably

[1] Welsh Joint Education Committee.
[2] Except for eighteen randomly eliminated for procedure by analysis of variance.

the urban/rural variable, were also examined to determine whether they could account for the significant differences found.

Results and discussion

The means for 'evaluation', 'potency' and 'activity' are set out in Tables 16.1 to 16.3.

School concepts

A principal feature of the tables is the higher ratings given by women than men (cf. Heise, 1969). This occurred in 45 out of the 54 possible comparisons of the type co-educated women against co-educated men, and when the co-educated and single-sex educated groups are combined the difference between men and women reaches significance in 13 cases out of 27. This effect is examined more fully elsewhere (Miller, forthcoming) but is pertinent here because two exceptions to this trend are of considerable interest; they arise from the 'evaluation ratings' of 'my school' and 'schoolteacher'. Close examination of the data for these two concepts reveals that the *co-educated women* conform to the usual trend by giving higher evaluations than the men, but there is a reverse effect among those educated in single-sex schools, the women giving lower evaluations than the men especially in the more dependable balanced sample. Furthermore the evaluations of 'my school' and 'schoolteacher' are somewhat lower for the women from girls' schools than for the corresponding co-educated women.[1] These evaluations by the former group are therefore lower than one would expect from a general appraisal of the data and are in line with the findings in the two earlier volumes about the less happy atmosphere in some single-sex schools compared with co-educational.

For the men's groups there is virtual equality between the co-educated and the single-sex educated on the evaluation of 'my school', and for 'schoolteacher' a non-significantly higher evaluation among those from boys' schools. The present 'evaluation' score, however, for both men and women contains elements not included in the earlier research on happiness and school atmosphere. For example, 'my school' is here evaluated on an amalgam of scores from the scales Pleasant/Unpleasant, Trivial/Important, Negative/Positive, Valuable/Worthless and Good/Bad, and it is quite possible for a school to be evaluated highly because owing to its age and tradition it is an 'important' and maybe 'valuable' school, though its score on 'pleasantness' may be only average.

When the two scales Pleasant/Unpleasant and Important/Trivial

[1] $P < 0.1$ and $P < 0.2$ respectively.

TABLE 16.1 *Semantic differential—mean evaluation ratings for the concepts: first-year university students (range 5-35)*

Concept	Balanced sample (N = 104)				Remainder sample (N = 152)				Combined samples (N = 256)			
	Men (N = 52)		Women (N = 52)		Men (N = 76)		Women (N = 76)		Men (N = 128)		Women (N = 128)	
	Co-ed (N=26)	Single-sex (N=26)	Co-ed (N=26)	Single-sex (N=26)	Co-ed (N=42)	Single-sex (N=34)	Co-ed (N=42)	Single-sex (N=34)	Co-ed (N=68)	Single-sex (N=60)	Co-ed (N=68)	Single-sex (N=60)
My school	28·19	29·19	29·46	27·69	27·52 (28·37)	26·79	29·36	27·53 (27·49)	27·78 (28·32)	27·83	29·40	27·60 (27·57)
This university college	28·92	31·00	30·85	32·62	29·43 (29·81)	30·06	31·00	30·85 (30·97)	29·24 (29·54)	30·47	30·94	31·62 (31·67)
School-teacher	28·46	29·46	29·35	28·15	27·21 (27·88)	28·21	29·45	27·85 (28·03)	27·69 (28·06)	28·75	29·41	27·98 (28·08)
University lecturer	27·46	28·77	28·00	28·88	26·79 (26·68)	27·76	28·55	27·62 (27·74)	27·04 (26·92)	28·20	28·34	28·17 (28·23)
My class at school	28·19	28·38	29·65	29·73	27·81 (28·32)	26·62	29·71	29·82 (29·86)	27·96 (28·28)	27·38	29·69	29·78 (29·80)
Student	27·27	29·00	28·88	30·23	26·93 (27·22)	28·24	28·88	29·53 (29·69)	27·06 (27·24)	28·57	28·88	29·83 (29·92)
Classroom	24·23	25·19	25·00	25·50	23·69 (24·71)	23·97	25·86	27·18 (27·06)	23·90 (24·56)	24·50	25·53	26·45 (26·39)
Lecture theatre	24·77	23·15	24·73	26·50	25·26 (25·19)	25·76	26·14	27·03 (27·14)	25·07 (25·06)	24·63	25·60	26·80 (26·87)
The opposite sex	30·77	31·31	31·77	31·50	31·07 (31·27)	29·50	30·60	30·41 (30·54)	30·96 (31·12)	30·28	31·04	30·88 (30·95)

NOTE: Figures in brackets are the means before the random elimination of eighteen students mentioned earlier in the text.

TABLE 16.2 *Semantic differential—mean potency ratings for the concepts: first-year university students (range 3–21)*

Concept	Balanced sample (N = 104)				Remainder sample (N = 152)				Combined samples (N = 256)			
	Men (N = 52)		Women (N = 52)		Men (N = 76)		Women (N = 76)		Men (N = 128)		Women (N = 128)	
	Co-ed (N=26)	Single-sex (N=26)	Co-ed (N=26)	Single-sex (N=26)	Co-ed (N=42)	Single-sex (N=34)	Co-ed (N=42)	Single-sex (N=34)	Co-ed (N=68)	Single-sex N(=60)	Co-ed (N=68)	Single-sex (N=60)
My school	11·88	14·35	13·23	13·96	11·17 (11·70)	12·50	12·02	13·44 (13·20)	11·44 (11·75)	13·30	12·49	13·67 (13·52)
This university college	12·12	12·00	12·85	13·00	12·02 (12·20)	11·60	13·40	12·97 (13·00)	12·06 (12·18)	11·77	13·19	12·98 (13·00)
School-teacher	12·81	14·27	13·58	14·19	12·14 (12·69)	13·32	13·40	13·53 (13·57)	12·40 (12·73)	13·73	13·47	13·82 (13·84)
University lecturer	11·62	11·85	12·04	12·85	11·29 (11·41)	10·79	12·40	12·79 (12·83)	11·41 (11·47)	11·25	12·26	12·82 (12·84)
My class at school	12·69	13·58	12·50	13·46	12·48 (12·64)	12·50	12·69	12·47 (12·49)	12·56 (12·66)	12·97	12·62	12·90 (12·90)
Student	12·50	13·15	13·12	14·38	12·21 (12·44)	12·09	13·10	12·97 (13·06)	12·32 (12·46)	12·55	13·10	13·58 (13·62)
Classroom	12·15	13·35	13·23	13·31	12·21 (12·39)	12·94	12·57	13·41 (13·31)	12·19 (12·32)	13·12	12·82	13·37 (13·31)
Lecture theatre	12·31	11·31	12·08	12·69	12·64 (12·80)	11·65	12·95	12·47 (12·43)	(12·51) (12·65)	11·50	12·62	12·57 (12·54)
The opposite sex	11·27	9·58	13·62	13·85	9·67 (9·95)	9·68	13·67	14·59 (14·66)	10·28 (10·35)	9·63	13·65	14·27 (14·31)

NOTE: Figures in brackets are the means before the random elimination of eighteen students mentioned earlier in the text.

TABLE 16.3 Semantic differential—mean activity ratings for the concepts: first-year university students (range 3–21)

| | Balanced sample (N = 104) | | | | Remainder sample (N = 152) | | | | Combined samples (N = 256) | | | |
| | Men (N = 52) | | Women (N = 52) | | Men (N = 76) | | Women (N = 76) | | Men (N = 128) | | Women (N = 128) | |
Concept	Co-ed (N=26)	Single-sex (N=26)	Co-ed (N=26)	Single-sex (N=26)	Co-ed (N=42)	Single-sex (N=34)	Co-ed (N=42)	Single-sex (N=34)	Co-ed (N=68)	Single-sex (N=60)	Co-ed (N=68)	Single-sex (N=60)
My school	12·27	15·15	14·92	13·04	13·31 (13·8●)	12·62	13·76	13·97 (13·74)	12·91 (13·38)	13·72	14·21	13·57 (13·44)
This university college	15·58	16·42	16·88	17·31	15·31 (15·6○)	15·59	17·24	16·21 (16·29)	15·41 (15·64)	15·95	17·10	16·68 (16·72)
School-teacher	14·35	15·19	14·15	15·00	13·6● (14·c5)	14·12	14·64	14·15 (14·31)	13·88 (14·14)	14·58	14·46	14·52 (14·61)
University lecturer	15·08	14·58	15·50	15·15	14·17 (14·15)	15·21	15·19	15·09 (15·09)	14·51 (14·44)	14·93	15·31	15·12 (15·11)
My class at school	14·46	15·31	15·92	16·08	15·31 (15·64)	14·82	15·93	16·26 (16·31)	14·99 (15·28)	15·03	15·93	16·18 (16·21)
Student	15·92	16·85	17·69	17·69	16·7 (16·5)	16·21	17·48	17·24 (17·34)	16·07 (16·08)	16·48	17·56	17·43 (17·49)
Classroom	11·46	12·12	12·96	12·12	11·50 (12·12)	11·06	13·21	12·38 (12·26)	11·49 (11·92)	11·52	13·12	12·27 (12·20)
Lecture theatre	12·73	11·38	11·81	12·50	12·45 (12 39)	12·68	13·17	12·91 (13·00)	12·56 (12·49)	12·12	12·65	12·73 (12·79)
The opposite sex	15·46	14·35	17·27	16·77	14·74 (15·25)	14·68	16·69	17·15 (17·23)	15·01 (15·32)	14·53	16·91	16·98 (17·03)

NOTE: Figures in brackets are the means before the random elimination of eighteen students mentioned earlier in the text.

were analysed separately it was found, as anticipated, that on 'pleasant-ness of school' the co-educated men gave the higher scores in both balanced and remainder samples. The same holds for the women, the differences between the co-educated and single-sex educated students being significant when men and women were combined.[1] On Import-ant/Trivial there were no significant differences.

The same type of procedure was used for 'schoolteacher', again producing higher scores on Pleasant/Unpleasant for the co-educated men (slight) and co-educated women[2] as against the same groups from single-sex schools, while on Important/Trivial the co-educated men tended to rate 'schoolteacher' lower than did men from boys' schools and the co-educated women vice versa (both not significantly).

It is on the 'potency' factor that the most striking results are to be seen and here there is strong indirect support for previous findings relating to the stricter discipline in single-sex schools. It would be expected that students from such schools would tend to rate them as more 'potent', i.e. more severe, hard and strong than the co-educated students would rate their schools. This is in fact what we find. On three of the four school concepts the single-sex educated gave higher 'potency' ratings than the co-educated and, particularly on 'my school', the effects reach a high level of significance.[3] The difference is in the same direction for the fourth concept 'my class at school' but is not statistically significant.

The ratings for 'activity' produce no consistent and significant differences between the co-educated students and those from single-sex schools. This aspect is not as straightforward as it might seem because many co-educational schools are situated in rural areas and have problems with out-of-school activities owing to the fixed times of school buses and the lack of alternative transport.

It is of some interest that the higher ratings of school on 'potency' by the single-sex educated do not extend to the 'activity', or to the 'evalua-tion' of school. It may be that an essential difference between the two types of school lies in the greater strictness that appears to obtain in single-sex schools. This need not, and apparently does not, lead to lesser 'evaluations' by the single-sex educated, although, as we have seen, the single-sex educated pupil does appear to regard his school as less *pleasant* than does his counterpart in the co-educational institution.

As hypothesized at the start of the research the differences in the evaluation of the school concepts do indeed tend to be larger between the co-educated women and those from girls' schools than between the two corresponding groups of men.

[1] $P < 0.05$.
[2] $P < 0.05$.
[3] $P < 0.001$.

The university

The differences between the co-educated students and those from single-sex schools are smaller for the university concepts than for the school concepts. Taking evaluation first we find that in the balanced sample the students from single-sex schools evaluate university higher than do the co-educated students,[1] but in the remainder sample for both men and women there is a near equality. However, the difference due to school type may be a little greater than that found, since students from rural schools, in general, tend to rate university higher than do those from urban schools, and proportionately more of the co-educated students come from rural areas.

The students from single-sex schools also tend in both samples[2] to evaluate 'student' higher than do the co-educated students; the former also evaluate 'student' higher than 'my class at school', while the co-educated students have a contrary tendency.[3]

A possible explanation of the differences in the ratings given by the students from the two types of school is that those from the single-sex schools welcome the relaxation from the undeniably stricter discipline of their schools (compared with co-educational schools) and also evaluate 'student' more highly because they welcome the opportunity to mingle with the opposite sex at the university. A relevant point is that an important reason why pupils tend to be happier in co-educational than in single-sex schools is that they like the presence of both sexes in the school. However, this hypothesis about attitude at the university is tentative. Nor, of course, is high evaluation entirely synonymous with happiness or liking.

Results on 'potency' are again more pronounced on the school than on the university concepts, where there is no consistent difference between the two types of student. Yet, whereas the students from single-sex schools saw 'this university college' and 'lecture theatre' as less 'potent' than 'my school'[4] and 'classroom',[5] the co-educated did not, due largely to their lower ratings of the school concepts.

Similarly the ratings for 'activity' did not reveal any consistent differences between the students from the two types of school.

To sum up, the only differences of note are those on the evaluation of 'student' and 'this university college', where the single-sex educated have the higher score. As mentioned before, this would seem to be a reaction by such students against the artificial segregation of the sexes at school, though this is only an hypothesis. On the other hand, several

[1] $P < 0.05$.
[2] $P < 0.05$ for combined samples.
[3] $P < 0.1$ only.
[4] $P < 0.01$.
[5] $P < 0.05$.

wardens of women's hostels have commented in free responses to questionnaires that women from girls' schools behave as if they were 'let loose' when first at a co-educational university, which might well increase their evaluation both of university and of students. We do not know, however, how long this higher evaluation lasts, as the students were in their first few weeks at the university.

The opposite sex

Comparing first the mean scores of the co-educated men and women, taken separately, with those from single-sex schools we find no consistent tendency in the 'evaluation' of the opposite sex, the only points of interest being the similarity between the average scores of the co-educated and single-sex educated women, and the higher overall rating of women by the co-educated men, though this is a little way from statistical significance. The results were more consistent on the 'potency' factor. The co-educated men rated the women as more 'potent', i.e. severe, strong and hard, than the men from boys' schools rated them,[1] and the co-educated women rated the men as less 'potent' than the women from girls' schools rated them.[2] On the activity factor there was a tendency for the co-educated men to assess women as more 'active' than did the men from boys' schools (not statistically significant) but there was no consistent difference between the average scores of the women's groups and overall a virtual equality for them.

By far the most definite result is that females see men as more 'potent' and more 'active' than men see women (P < 0·001 in both cases), but the difference between the ratings given by men and by women is smaller within the co-educated group of students than it is between the ratings given by men and women from boys' and girls' schools, though only on the potency scale does this last difference reach the 0·05 level of significance.[3] Throughout research on co-education there are frequent hints that experience in a co-educational secondary school modifies the concept that each sex has of the other; here the tendency appears to be for the co-educated men to view the women as less lenient, soft and weak and perhaps less passive, dull and slow than do men from boys' schools, while there appears to be a comparable tendency for women from girls' schools to have an exaggerated view of the 'manly' qualities of men, viewing them as more severe, strong and hard than do women from co-educational schools.

The differences between the products of the two types of school might

[1] Almost statistically significant at the 0·05 level.
[2] P < 0·1.
[3] Assessing the whole sample and using the *t* test of the difference between differences.

well be due to the lack of contact between the sexes in single-sex schools, cultural stereotypes suggesting to the men educated in boys' schools that women are weaker than they really are, and to the women from girls' schools that men are all good imitations of their heroes on the television screen. This effect will be different for individual pupils and one would expect it to be strongest in single-sex boarding schools, for those who have no siblings of the opposite sex and for those who are otherwise unable to meet the opposite sex socially in the evenings and in the holidays. In one extreme case a girl reported that she did not think she had spoken to a boy for several years.

Another interesting problem concerns the stability of the differences found. In general, this is an open question. Work reported in this chapter and in chapter 7 has tended to show that the effects on attitudes to university and on first-year university academic performance are relatively slight. On the other hand there are Atherton's (1971) findings on the better adjustment in marriage of co-educated adults. Perhaps, if long-term effects are confirmed, they will be found predominantly in areas of the understanding of the opposite sex, where experience at school, while growing up, might be helpful.

Addendum

Code number _____

CONCEPT   (e.g.) My school _____

PLEASANT	:	:	:	:	:	:	UNPLEASANT	(E)
PASSIVE	:	:	:	:	:	:	ACTIVE	(A)
TRIVIAL	:	:	:	:	:	:	IMPORTANT	(E)
SEVERE	:	:	:	:	:	:	LENIENT	(P)
SHARP	:	:	:	:	:	:	DULL	(A)
WEAK	:	:	:	:	:	:	STRONG	(P)
NEGATIVE	:	:	:	:	:	:	POSITIVE	(E)
HARD	:	:	:	:	:	:	SOFT	(P)
VALUABLE	:	:	:	:	:	:	WORTHLESS	(E)

SLOW ____ : ____ : ____ : ____ : ____ : ____ : ____ FAST (A)

GOOD ____ : ____ : ____ : ____ : ____ : ____ : ____ BAD (E)

Ratings were made on each scale by the putting of a cross in one of the seven spaces.

The scoring on each side is weighted from 1 to 7 according to the adjectives constituting its extremes.

The score on the *Evaluation* factor is the sum of the scores on the items marked (E) above. Similarly for *Potency*, where items are marked (P) and *Activity*, where items are marked (A).

Part IV

Overview

Preamble

1 Extract from a lecture by James Simpson, Esq., Advocate, Edinburgh 1844[1]

A refreshing and at times amusing advocacy of co-education by an almost forgotten pioneer.

The learned lecturer said he was a zealous advocate for another new-fangled notion, which on its first announcement absolutely horrified the old school, especially the good ladies of it, and that was that the boys and girls, who are together in the infant school, shall go up stairs to the juvenile (junior) school together, and never lose sight of each other till they both leave school for good and all. How indelicate! how improper! He would ask why? wherefore? how? and pause for a reply. Under the old system, where character was deformed, there might be indelicacy and danger, and where there were, it was not separating the sexes that would put an end to them. But the better manners and purer thoughts of the new system, and, above all, the ceaseless occupation in school, will give to the joint schooling of the sexes the good of a legitimate and innocent rivalry, and the refinement which their regulated intercourse never fails to produce. The two sexes can never be more safely together than engaged in the duties of a well-regulated school. They are together round the domestic hearth, together when they worship in the house of God, together in their holiday meetings, at the festive board, and in the merry dance; and that they should only meet for mutual corruption when, under the guidance of a kind and enlightened teacher, they are exercising the noblest feelings, and reaping knowledge from the wonder of God's works, is a notion more preposterous than any that has lingered in the same prejudiced and ignorant quarter. Mr. Simpson added that he did not depend entirely upon *a priori* argument for this his conclusion. He had been one who had fought this very battle in one of the largest seminaries in Edinburgh, the Lancasterian school in Davy Street, of which he has long been a director. After

[1] Simpson, James, 'Lecture delivered to the Working Class of Edinburgh, on Joint Education of the Sexes', *Edinburgh Weekly Chronicle*, 9 March 1844.

much opposition the point was conceded to the extent of a trial. The results were so satisfactory of an occasional re-union, that prejudice gave way; the girls, above 300 in number, were put under the superintending tuition of the excellent teacher of the boys, Mr. Dun; the two sexes met daily—not promiscuously, which was never meant, but in classes. The improvement on the girls was great and well-marked, while the zeal of the boys was much increased, to the effect of a decided improvement on the general character of the school. . . . He, Mr. Simpson, would only add that the meeting of the sexes, which he advocates, should be during the well-regulated decorous hours of the school-room alone. The playground of the girls should be scrupulously separated from that of the boys, with distinct entrance and exit to it, and to the school-room above.

2   Extract from a lecture by Esther Higgs, 1897[1]

So long as men and women are on this earth, there will always be a profound difference in the essential nature of each. But to accentuate that difference artificially is both foolish and wrong, and for this reason I advocate co-education. . . . But with regard to co-education, I urge it chiefly on account of the advantages to be attained by the mutually beneficial influence which would be exercised upon the characters of both; the boys would impart a certain robustness of mind to the girls, and they, in their turn, would elevate and refine the boys.

[1] Higgs, Esther, *Woman, the Individual.* Paper read before Fowler Institute 1897 and Women's International Progressive Union in 1898.

17

Overview

It is now time to summarize and survey the contents of the three volumes. In them the writer was concerned first, to give the reader sufficient data for him to make his own judgments, second, to demonstrate how the numerous unwanted and sometimes hidden factors have influenced the data. The primary objective was the furtherance of knowledge and compilation of a reliable centre of reference on which future researchers might base their efforts, whether their work pursued the same or other educational topics concerned with the characteristics and functioning of schools. This entailed the inclusion of numerous tables of statistics and of detailed discussion which at times did not make for easy readability. Here in this chapter an attempt is made to present a simplified summation and survey of the results, illustrated by histograms rather than statistical tables. Simplification, however, brings its dangers, and those busy readers who rely on this chapter alone will lose not only the vivid and at times humorous life contributed to the body of the work by the quotations from teachers, pupils and ex-pupils, but may also fail to appreciate the complexity of some of the problems, and even lose something of the balance provided by the detailed discussion.

These books are a study of three types of communities: girls' schools, boys' schools and co-educational schools. It has been shown that the communities differ considerably from each other in tone or atmosphere, and it follows that each must be exerting a different influence on the attitudes, emotional well-being and temperamental development of its constituent pupils and staff. How strange it is, therefore, that the study of these differences has in the past been so much neglected, leaving the protagonists on each side to debate the matter with few facts and much prejudice, with the public in general and educationists in particular regarding the contest as a little side-show, like a match on the outer courts at Wimbledon, while what seemed to be considered as more important affairs, such as 'comprehensivization', were being decided elsewhere, as on the Centre Court. Even the educational philosophers, who should have been leading our thinking, confined themselves to the programme on the Centre Court, apparently oblivious of the importance of the contest between co-educational and single-sex schools.

Yet in this work there is the contrary danger—that factors other than co-education might be ignored, thus giving a misleading impression. There are many forces which help to determine whether a school is good or bad—or merely mediocre—and although this is not the place for a comprehensive review of them, their mention, even if in elementary outline, should help to keep matters in perspective.

The well-being of a school naturally depends to a great extent on the personality of the head, or, in a large comprehensive school, the personality of four or five key people. The extent of this influence will in turn depend partly on the interaction of the personalities of these leaders with the personalities of the rest of the staff, and the interaction of both leaders and staff with the type of pupil at the school. Parents' associations also are already influential in some schools and they are increasing rapidly in number. Most other factors, such as the influence of external examinations, the school neighbourhood, the building and equipment, though not without their importance, are usually minor in nature. In a co-educational school, however, several major factors are added—the interactive influence of boys and girls, of masters and mistresses, and even of boys and mistresses, girls and masters. These add a new dimension to the school community, a dimension which springs from the roots of human nature and is perpetually at work in the world—the influence of one sex on the other. This chapter demonstrates some of the differences between school communities which spring from the presence or absence of this force.

An appropriate start to the summing up would seem to be school preference, i.e. which type of school did teachers and pupils prefer? Some would devalue this approach by calling it 'subjective', others would decry it, saying 'they might prefer co-education because they merely found it pleasanter', or 'because they liked an easier life'. To the first the reply is that this collective judgment is based on experience—which is how we judge many things; to the second, that if teachers or pupils find co-educational schools 'pleasanter' surely this is a desirable quality in a school, especially when coupled with the third reply, namely, that the early part of this book shows clearly enough that co-educational schools are—at the least—not inferior to single-sex schools in the *progress* they secure from their pupils.

The verdict of the teachers, especially of those who had taught in both types of school, was emphatically in favour of the fully co-educational school.[1] Teachers in co-educational schools were not far from being

[1] Eighty per cent of the 72 heads of co-educational schools who replied to Clark's questionnaire said that co-educational schools had marked advantages over single-sex schools. Ninety per cent of these heads had taught in a boys' school. Two replies were: 'I was a house master in a public school, and I want no more of it.' 'For 17 years, then I became the head of a mixed school and saw the folly of segregation.' See also the small survey by Breuse (1970), pp. 62-4.

unanimously in favour of them, while opposition came mainly from teachers who had never taught in such schools, i.e. much of it came from ignorance. In a sample of lecturers in departments of education some three-quarters preferred co-educational schools and only 11 per cent single-sex or 'dual' schools. The reasons given in favour were mainly concerned with social education and the preparation of pupils for life in the adult world. Children 'grow up in a natural way as in a family', and 'it enables each sex to know and learn from the points of view of the other, contributing to better mutual understanding between the sexes and avoiding the rather immature attitude of one sex to the other which is often found in the products of single-sex schools'. Again, 'Life at home is the living together of father and mother, sons and daughters. A co-ed school is an extension of life at home and can serve as an apprenticeship to becoming an understanding member of society.' Similar in theme and well expressed is 'The best type of school is that which is a microcosm incorporating within it the essential features of life in the world outside. Segregation of the sexes is purely artificial. Education cannot claim to be a training for life unless it prepares the child to take his place naturally in the community of men and women.' Linking with these themes is the judgment that the two sexes have an ameliorating effect on the conduct of each other, restraining the extremes of conduct, the boys losing some of their boisterous rudeness and the girls becoming less 'giggly, simpering and catty', e.g. 'The girls tend to make the boys less "barbarous", the boys tend to make the girls less "gushing".'

Other noteworthy aspects were, first, the use of the word 'atmosphere' in expressing preference for co-educational schools—rarely used in this sense about single-sex schools—and the occurrence of such terms as 'gaiety' and '*joie de vivre*', which were never used in the comments about single-sex schools,[1] e.g. 'There was a lightness which took away much of the drudgery from teaching', 'The community life of my youth in a mixed school gave me a joy which I find lacking in a boys' grammar school.'

Also stressed is the effect of the friendly rivalry between the two sexes on the standard of work. This last aspect is illustrated by:

'Boys tend to raise the standard of girls in certain subjects, e.g. maths and science.'

Competition between the sexes produces better work. The girls up to fifteen are more conscientious workers and lead the boys to a higher standard of achievement.'

'As a maths teacher, I find boys are naturally quicker at working out mathematical problems and they help to create an enthusiasm for the

[1] See also Breuse, p. 84.

subject. On the other hand, girls are more conscientious in working out the longer but easier questions and set a good example of neatness and perseverance.'

The comments against co-education were much less numerous but more widely ranging, with an emphasis on academic work. The objections included the different rates of intellectual development of the sexes, the different interests, work suffering from distractions, the bad effect of competition on the girls and lack of opportunity for promotion for women. Some of these are discussed later in the chapter, but a few quotations are given. The first will at first seem innocent enough to most readers as it rests on a widely accepted though unfair stereotyping of co-educational schools. It was written by a man who had no experience of co-education.

'The scholastic standards of single-sex schools are higher generally than those of the mixed school.'

If the teacher means that a pupil will make better *progress* in a single-sex school because of the separation of the sexes the statement is not true, as demonstrated early in this book; if, on the other hand, the teacher means that he prefers single-sex schools because he believes *attainment* is higher (e.g. because the standard of entry is higher) then this does not represent opposition to the theory of co-education. A similar misconception is:

'For girls co-education is a disadvantage as they would be superseded in class by the boys.'

Anyone with experience in co-educational schools knows this is not true, but its untruth has been demonstrated by Mathews (1925). The following quotation, 'The social graces allegedly acquired in a co-ed school by boys seem to be acquired at the expense of their work', may originate in a similar confusion between the effects of a lower social class entry to a co-educational school and the effect of co-education itself.

A small section of the observations made against co-education are highly emotional, e.g. a headmistress herself wrote, rather amusingly, 'I have had considerable experience as a teacher and pupil in co-educational schools. My objection to the system is based on the indubitable fact that only the poorest type of staff can be recruited for these schools.'

Other objections rest on a more solid basis, e.g.:

'The girl develops emotionally (biologically) earlier than the boy—the outlook and interests of the two sexes from 11 to 16 years are very different.'

'Co-education provides distraction during the day.'

'One aspect of co-education that seems to me unfair is that in such a school there is less prospect of promotion for women teachers.'

'My experience of co-education suggests that the boys are well catered for at the expense of the girls. In the school I attended Botany was the only science subject available to girls.'

The first quotation is broadly true, but teachers often say that this very difference of interest enriches the lessons, and as education is concerned with social development it would seem wise to enable the two sexes to grow up together so that they might get to know each other's outlook. Also, though girls do tend to develop earlier than boys, they actually took the O-level examination or its equivalent at a slightly *later* age (from girls' schools) during the time of the researches analysed in chapter 1 so their earlier development seems to be no valid reason for keeping the two sexes apart in classes; they have been together in schools in Great Britain and the USA for many years, without any apparent ill effects.

The arguments put forward in most of the other comments have been answered elsewhere but in the last the head does appear to be at fault, and although such unfortunate organization must be rare the incident supports a plea made previously by the writer for the up-grading of the post of senior mistress in co-educational schools. This move would also help to allay the justifiable anxieties of the women about promotion prospects.

In three other large-scale surveys those ex-pupils of secondary schools (excluding secondary modern) who were training to be teachers were also asked their preference. The most important of these samples consisted of 620 women and 175 men who had attended both a co-educational and a single-sex school; a large majority of them preferred their mixed school, most of them 'very much' (Figure 17.1).[1]

Figure 17.1 shows the influence of the order in which the schools were attended, the last one exerting an extra pull, so that if the boys' school was attended last the majority preferring the mixed school was much smaller than if the boys' school was attended first. Among the reasons given by both men and women students for this preference were the natural relationship between the sexes, the educative effect of the presence of the opposite sex, the relaxed and friendly atmosphere, the social life and enjoyable school activities, the friendliness of staff–pupil

---

[1] Cf. Hare (1969). Of 230 male students, 94 per cent from mixed and 56 per cent from boys' schools preferred co-education; 64 per cent preferred to teach in mixed schools and 19 per cent in boys' schools. Also Collins (1964). Of 478 student teachers 55 per cent preferred to teach in a co-educational school, rising to 65 per cent for students for whom teaching was second choice; only 25 per cent had themselves attended a co-educational school (p. 29).

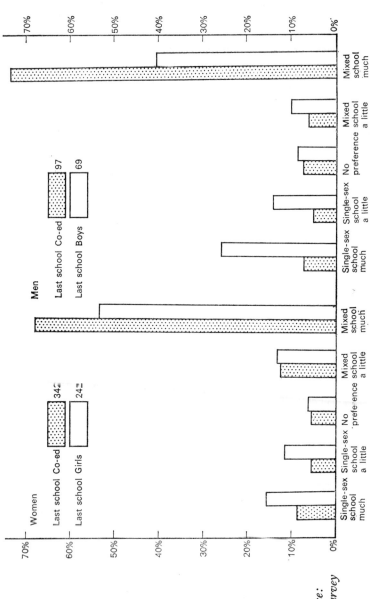

FIGURE 17.1
School preference:
'Both schools' survey

relationships and of relationships within the staff, the broad, balanced outlook on life and the preparation for life in the outside world. Also stressed was that work was more enjoyable, lessons more interesting, and that there was greater freedom, with fewer unnecessary rules. Readers who would like to read these comments fully should turn to volume II, but a few illustrations are given here:

'Very happy at co-educational and first single-sex school but cattiness and sex obsession at the second single-sex school left me uncertain as to its merits.' (F)[1]

'Life in a mixed society is decidedly more colourful and helps to bridge the conscious gap between the male and female adolescent.' (F)

'The narrowness and staid atmosphere of the single-sex school seemed to be crushing my personality.' (F)

'More robust atmosphere, livelier, happier.' (F)

'In classes the boys were far livelier and amusing at times.' (F)

'In the single-sex school the behaviour of the girls was much less mature than in the mixed school.' (F)

'It meant an opening-out whereby a whole new social horizon was established.' (M)

'Women and girls' influence calms down excess of lots of things.' (M)

'Much more friendly attitude which is more conducive to work.' (M)

Those comments favouring the single-sex school were mainly about academic work, e.g.:

'One was much more able to concentrate on one's work and the work was of much higher standard in consequence.' (F)

'The good atmosphere of boys enjoying life together. Girl friends were always out of school and much more forgotten during working hours. There is a tendency for shyness to arise, however.' (M)

'A delay or rest period before being exposed to the human female.' (M)

The number of the comments classified as opposing co-education contained, however, some which either opposed it for what were in reality extraneous reasons or had important limiting clauses, whereas there were distinctly fewer of this kind of comment among those favourable to co-education. Examples of those against co-education are:

'There was more of a feeling of being an individual rather than being

[1] F indicates female, and M, male.

one of a huge institution,' where the objection is not to co-education but to the largeness of the school (F). Similar comments came from the men.

'The boys were resented and rather destructive to the building' (F Am).[1] This is in part an objection to the problems created by a sudden amalgamation of schools.

'I preferred the attitude of the single-sex school but if it could have been run on the same lines as a co-educational school I feel that it could have been even better.' (F)

'I concentrated far more on my work. On the other hand I think girls who do not meet boys at home *definitely* need a co-educational school.' (F)

'It was a "better" school, the pupils were "nicer".' This remark probably indicates a school of higher prestige, taking pupils from the higher social classes! (F)

'Enjoyed the tradition and pride in belonging to the school.' (M)

'I approve strongly of co-educational schools. Academically o.k. They don't put this bullying business into everything.' But he strongly preferred the boys' school he attended, 'Keep up the tradition and all that (Dad went there).' (M-boarding)

One is reminded by these comments that there will be a large overlap between single-sex and co-educational schools in academic standard, and some pupils will experience this in one direction and others in the reverse. A curious phenomenon, which astonished the writer and may surprise the reader, is that when these young men and women were seeking a word with which to pinpoint the difference between life in a co-educational and in a single-sex school the thoughts of a large section of those who preferred the co-educational school arrived, as the teachers did, at the word 'atmosphere'. (This word was not part of the question itself.) Among the 163 men who gave a free response rather more than one-quarter (43) actually used this word for praising their co-educational school, and about the same proportion among the women (152 out of 572 free responses). (Ten of the men and twenty of the women used the word when preferring their single-sex school!) This may be called 'subjective judgment' but it signifies an experience which made a deep impression on those who participated in it.

Nor do the figures include the whole of the story, because many of the other free responses favouring the co-educational school used some phrase meaning 'atmosphere' even though the precise word was missing. Such phrases were, 'community spirit', 'all-round pleasantness', 'camaraderie', 'the whole school was alive'.

[1] Amalgamated.

Lack of time prevented the making of a similar large-scale survey among present pupils, but the writer administered to the pupils of ten sixth forms a questionnaire which included a question on the type of school they would prefer if they had the choice. It might be thought that there would be some joking and leg-pulling. Not a bit of it. The pupils completed the questionnaire under examination conditions, with an occasional smile at some questions but with a seriousness of purpose that was impressive. A truly astonishing result was that of 105 pupils from five co-educational grammar schools only one—a boy—preferred single-sex schools. Three girls' schools had percentages of 92, 67 and 63 for co-educational schools and the two boys' schools 88 and 85 per cent. A sketchy survey, but not without value.[1] Chapter 11 of volume II also includes a survey of preference among pupils of the whole grammar school range, which, as anticipated, showed a dip to 75 per cent preference for co-education at the age of 13, for both sexes, and a rapid climb afterwards. There is little comfort there, however, for those schoolmasters and others who advocate separation for the young teen-age boys 'because they like to play apart from girls'. It is difficult to brush aside the opinion of the 75 per cent or to make any provision for what appears to be a short-lived hiatus in the preference of the other 25 per cent for co-educational schooling.[2]

Linking up with the school preference data are the results from a direct question on atmosphere: 'Do you think the school atmosphere was Very pleasant/Pleasant/Neutral/Rather unpleasant/Very unpleasant?' Few pupils from either type of school considered the atmosphere very unpleasant, but a greater proportion of both co-educated boys and girls endorsed the 'very pleasant' reply, while there tended to be more pupils from the single-sex schools in the 'rather unpleasant' section. As we are principally concerned with such differences they are epitomized in the following quotations, taking first those about the 'very pleasant' atmosphere in co-educational schools:

'The atmosphere—marvellous school spirit and unity.' (F)

'Discipline was observed by all but not drilled into you. We were not aware we were under rules and regulations.' (F)

'Boys and girls were learning side by side, as a family almost. This was considered to be perfectly natural and from this stemmed the very pleasant atmosphere.' (F)

[1] A similar result was obtained in a survey conducted by *Sixth Form Opinion*, published in their second issue (March 1968).
[2] Clark (1937) maintains, 'It is the mixed school which gives them freedom; the separated school which brings them under restraint' (p. 71). See also Breuse (1970). Of 343 pupils in a co-educational school 330 approved of co-education, giving good educational reasons; the others were new arrivals with difficulties of adjustment.

'An all-female community leads to bad feeling arising. Men seem to introduce a practical, logical element which keeps things in perspective.' (F)

'Everything seemed natural, relaxed, complete. The staff and pupil morale was very high indeed.' (M)

'Pupils and teachers mixed on the same level and pupils admired the teachers for this.' (M)

'The different sexes treated each other with respect and there was a pleasing atmosphere of co-operation.' (M)

In order to underline the differences, quotations are now given in which pupils found the atmosphere in the single-sex schools 'rather unpleasant' or worse:

'Tendency for an all-female community to become extremely spiteful and callous.' (F)

'Fear was the key word in all discipline.' (F)

'An unhealthy attitude towards and preoccupation with the opposite sex. They were sex-mad and frequently coarse. When I first went there this revolted me.' (F)

'I was scared stiff; glad to get home. Staff seemed hard, demanding, and bossy.' (M)

'There always seemed to be violence of one sort or another in the school.' (M)

'Life was so formal that school resembled the army.' (M)

'A boy of 10 is likely to be affected by very harsh treatment. I've never forgotten this and it seems to have shown itself in stronger forms than it perhaps ought.' (M-boarding)

The contrast between the schools is not as stark as this, as no quotations have been taken from the large groups in both schools who found the atmosphere 'pleasant' rather than 'very pleasant'. Chapter 4 in volume II gives the balanced appraisal, but it should be said that very few of the comments described the atmosphere of the co-educational school as bad in any way, and most of these were concerned with some aspect of school organization other than co-education. Fifteen female ex-pupils said the headmaster was poor, nine found the discipline too lax, and nine found the school too impersonal (some of the co-educational grammar schools had become comprehensive schools which a few pupils thought to be too large) while several others thought the new lower social class pupils too rough. These numbers compare with 175 who praised the atmosphere and 145 who referred to the good teacher–pupil relationship.

Using a different sample—one of 274 first-year university students—and a somewhat more indirect technique (Semantic Differential Test), the above results on 'pleasantness of school' were replicated, both men and women from co-educational schools rating them as 'more pleasant' than did those from single-sex schools. For the wider concept 'evaluation' there was also a tendency for the co-educated women to give higher ratings for 'school' and 'schoolteacher' than the women educated in single-sex schools gave them.

One of the factors forming the atmosphere of a school is the nature of the inter-pupil relationship. In a co-educational school one would expect a difference to be created by the existence of two sub-communities—that of each sex—within the whole. Both male and female ex-pupils found it easier to make friends in the co-educational schools and the women considered the pupils friendlier there than in the girls' schools, while present pupils found them less spiteful (Check questionnaire).[1] On the whole the presence of the boys seemed to improve the conduct of the girls:

'Some girls could be very spiteful indeed. I found this only seemed to happen in all-girls' schools.' (F)

'Some were spiteful but the boys in the class laughed at them, so they were not spiteful in public.' (F)

The difference in relationships between pupils was also strongly marked by the reduced incidence of bullying, and of related conduct for girls, in the co-educational schools.

Figure 17.2 is composed from the replies of boys who had attended at least one co-educational and one boys' school, and its message is clear—there was far less bullying in the co-educational school whether the comparison concerned schools attended first or attended last. The reasons given were predominantly the restraint created by the presence of girls and the friendly atmosphere of the school. In the worst comments about boys' schools the results were decidedly undesirable:

'A kind of outlet for tension built up in the classroom—and this was *real* bullying.'

'This was the dominant feature of the school social life.'

'You were put in the coal hole and thumped.'

'I never recall any large amount of bullying as I experienced it in a single-sex school.'

[1] Cf. Rowland (1955). 'Co-education does . . . encourage the socialization of the individual.' (Research study.)

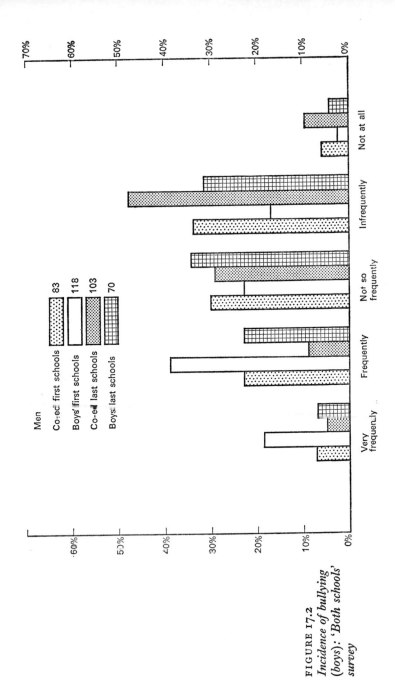

FIGURE 17.2
Incidence of bullying (boys): 'Both schools' survey

Female ex-pupils also experienced more bullying—systematized unpleasantness—in their girls' than in their co-educational schools, a difference they characterized as:

'This often happens among girls, and more so in single-sex school than co-educational.'

'There is not the same sense of "fair play" as in schools with mixed staff.'

'There seemed to be more "ganging up" when the school split up than before it did.'

There was a strong consensus that girls were less 'catty' and ganged together against individuals less often if boys were about.

Both sexes were also of the opinion that prefects in the single-sex schools were 'more officious' than they were in the co-educational schools.

In line with these results, both boys and girls experienced more kindness, found more enthusiasm, more liveliness, and the boys thought there was more variety as opposed to monotony, in the co-educational schools. At the opposite end, those girls who disliked their girls' school expressed themselves far more forcibly than did those from co-educational schools, e.g.:

'School stinks.'

'School's a drag.'

'As I have said before, I *hate* school.'

'I am always tired and the thought of school is awful.'

The factors which have been examined contributed to the greater happiness of both girls and boys in the co-educational schools. The results from the ex-pupils of the important 'Both schools' survey in answer to a direct question on happiness in school are given in Figures 17.3 and 17.4.

In giving these estimates the ex-pupils have compared the co-educational and single-sex schools they attended, and they leave no doubt about the result; similarly for the girls in the 'Check' survey, and women ex-pupils of the Second College survey. The greater happiness is mainly due to more satisfactory relationships and the ensuing friendly atmosphere, e.g.:

'Very happy—mixed; rather unhappy—single-sex. Less happy because it was more formal.' (F)

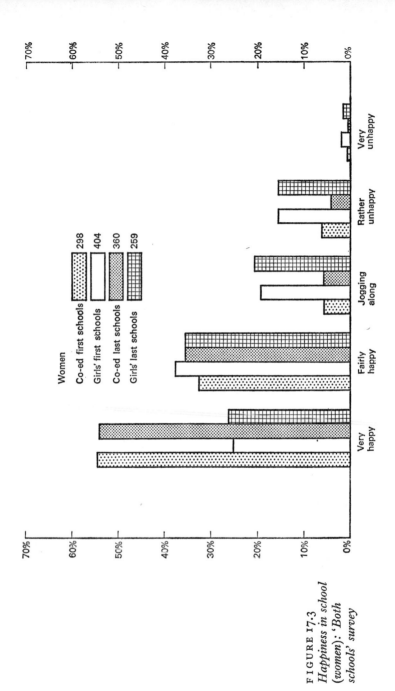

FIGURE 17.3
Happiness in school (women): 'Both schools' survey

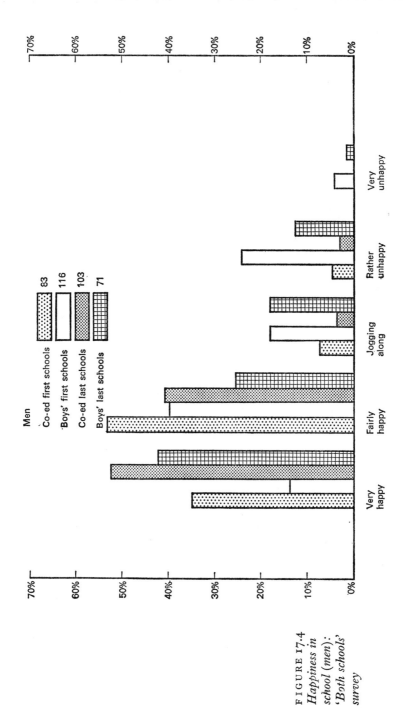

FIGURE 17.4
*Happiness in
school (men):
'Both schools'
survey*

243

'Happy in the single-sex school, but very happy in the co-educational school where there were no barriers between staff and pupils.' (F)

'A very friendly atmosphere in the co-educational school between all pupils and teachers and pupils.' (F)

'It was only towards the later stages of co-educational school life that I realized how happy school could be.' (M)

'Happy co-educational; very unhappy single-sex. Complete change of atmosphere in single-sex schools, unable to re-orientate myself. Lost in the artificial segregation I think.' (M)

To be unhappy or merely 'rather unhappy' at school is, putting it mildly, a very undesirable fate for a child. Fortunately there were few among the girls in the Schools project—17 out of 511 from co-educational schools and 27 out of 517 from girls' schools. A detailed examination of each of these cases showed that the unhappiness of the girls in the co-educational schools was largely due to 'out of school' or home difficulties and trouble with academic work (they were of low intelligence compared with their opposite numbers), whereas the girls from girls' schools placed general dislike of the school first, with teachers' discipline second.[1] An interesting trend is the tendency for the unhappy girls from girls' schools to be more extraverted than those from co-educational schools. Unfortunately these last results could not be followed up, but if they are replicated a possible explanation might be a greater tendency for an extravert to feel 'out of place' or unduly restricted in a single-sex community.

Characteristic quotations from the unhappy pupils are:

Co-educational

'My mother had a nervous breakdown last year and had to give up work. Now she misses this and doesn't eat anything. She seems to get terribly irritated with myself, father, etc.'

'Often ill at ease with friends, not knowing if they really like me (especially boys). I lack self-confidence. We [family] worry too much about friendship, money, everything.'

'School average marks not encouraging. Not allowed to go out except at week-ends. Exams and not enough pocket-money.'

[1] Cf. Campbell (1968). Reports significant tendency for segregated girls to regard school in more hostile light than those in co-educational schools.

Girls' schools

'School atmosphere rather unpleasant. Getting into trouble with the teachers for no reason.'

'I hate school and want to start work. At school you are treated much younger than you really are. I am always having arguments with my parents about boys I go out with.'

'I hate school and will be glad when I leave. Teachers expect you to know too much and if you don't know they get mad. A lot of teachers at our school are grumpy. Before German lessons I always get butterflies in my stomach.'

Several paper-and-pencil tests of anxiety were also given to all pupils in the Schools project, and though results were not dramatic they showed one interesting feature—that among all the seven areas of anxiety examined—home, people in general, school etc—it was in relation to school that the co-educational pupils did best; within the school itself the co-educated girls tended to be less anxious in 'personal relationships' than were those in girls' schools.

The chapter on anxiety about school sets out in detail the reasons why the difference in this type of anxiety, between the opposing groups of pupils, is not as great as might have been expected, and emphasizes the need for a research project which would concentrate on this aspect. The anxious child is a hostage to fortune, liable to physical illness as well as to nervous complaints. No matter how able the child or how high the academic attainment the future is not bright unless the anxieties can be removed or the anxiety habit modified. In this task the school can exert a strong influence for good or ill, and the nature of this influence may be profoundly affected by the alternatives of single-sex or co-educational schooling.

In paper-and-pencil tests of neuroticism the co-educated boys consistently had lower scores,[1] but for the girls a similar trend was unreliable and also inconsistent between social class groups. Theoretically the lower scores of the co-educated boys might be linked to their greater happiness and the milder discipline; the reduction in the difference for the girls' groups might be the effect of the rather lower intelligence of the co-educated girls (as against those in the girls' schools) which would increase their anxieties about academic work, as was found for the unhappy girls.

For the introversion–extraversion personality trait the picture is less clear, the only consistent tendency being for girls from girls' schools to be slightly more extraverted than their counterparts, though this is not

[1] Furneaux (1961) had opposite findings but his boys were older and a more selective sample (pp. 80–1).

statistically significant. Further questions on shyness and 'taking the lead in group activities' gave no clear differences but hinted at the possibility that co-educated girls of social classes 3, 4 and 5 were more reluctant to take the lead than were similar girls in girls' schools (though there was an opposite tendency for social classes 1 and 2).

Central to most of these questions is the nature of the influence of boys and girls on each other in the co-educational schools. A great majority of the ex-pupils believed this influence to be good. Only 5 per cent of the boys in 'first schools' and 3 per cent in 'last schools' estimated that it was bad, with few endorsing 'no effect', while for female ex-pupils judging their own sex some 18 and 10 per cent thought it bad, while three-quarters thought it to be good ('Both schools' survey).[1] This influence has many facets, e.g.:

'Tended to calm the boys down and gave an incentive to work.' (M)

'Seemed to keep the boys more in discipline than the school rules.' (M)

'Much of the roughness of an all-boys' school was removed on the change to a new co-educational school.' (M)

'We have an insight into their life. Therefore our outlook became broader. Social events were more natural. Culture varied—more like life.' (M)

'The girls had an extra competitive effect on the boys in both the classroom and in other school activities. I had never felt this before, but I am sure it did nothing but good.' (M)

'Girls did help the boys to be more considerate towards them so in fact they acquired a sense of respect.' (F)

'Boys accepted girls, girls accepted boys. There was no shyness or restraint. We learnt together in an easy atmosphere.' (F)

Of those female ex-pupils who considered the influence of their own sex was bad most gave a reason resembling the following:

'The girls often encouraged the boys to bad behaviour and showing off.'

No doubt this sometimes occurred but a big majority of both ex-pupils and teachers believed that the presence of girls improved the behaviour of boys.

Similarly a large majority of both male and female ex-pupils believed that the influence of the boys on the girls was good. The girls became more stable emotionally, had an improved appearance and a better social development. They were less petty-minded and 'catty' and friendly rivalry with boys had a good effect on their work.

[1] Clark's enquiry (1937) gives strong support (p. 65). See also Breuse, pp. 61–2.

'It taught us to get along with the opposite sex, which is important for future life.' (F)

'Boys made life less petty and catty. Made girls conscious of having good table manners etc, because theirs were very poor. Sense of humour from boys infected school.' (F)

'There was a good atmosphere, problems on both sides were discussed freely, seriously and intelligently. The atmosphere was very natural.' (M)

Springing naturally from this interaction come the results of the research on the comparative effect of co-educational and single-sex schooling on the attitude of pupils and ex-pupils towards the opposite sex in general. The male student teachers who had attended co-educational schools had a rather stronger belief in the equality of the sexes and were a little less inclined to extremes of opinion about women than were their counterparts from boys' schools. Though this difference did not quite reach the conventional level of statistical significance it is unlikely to have occurred by chance, and some of the students from single-sex schools stated that their views had been modified since they left school, e.g.:

'After two years in a mixed training college I have grown out of regarding girls as inferior.'

As a substantial part of the sample had been away from school for four years there is little doubt that experience in the world would have modified the more extreme opinions held by some of the ex-pupils from boys' schools.

It is of interest that the two groups of female ex-pupils showed an almost identical pattern in their estimates of men. Perhaps the women from single-sex schools modified their views more quickly when they came fully into contact with the adult world, or girls' earlier maturity may have resulted in their introduction to adult life while they were still at school. Alternatively the *average tendency* for women, in our society, to regard men as rather superior may have been too strong to be overcome or even modified by co-educational schooling. Whatever the reason, some two-thirds of both groups believed the male to be equal to the female and one-third believed the male to be 'superior'. None out of more than a thousand women thought men were 'very inferior' and only three of them thought men 'very superior'. (When one looks at the sad mess man has made of the world one begins to have an uneasy feeling that this superiority belief may not be justified; the male of the species may throw up its geniuses in art, music and literature, but it has also placed some queerly dangerous types in control of nations; while one acknowledges with awe the achievements of the—mainly male—leaders of science, with the benefits their achievements have brought, one contemplates with a more powerful alarm the several precipices to which their genius has conducted us. The scientist may claim that he only shows how the goods may be produced, while it is others who misuse them, but does one produce for a child a toy which enables him to kill himself? Genius is a two-edged sword.) However, to return to the research, this third of the women who believed in the superiority of men gave replies such as:

'More original. Women on the whole mediocre and less interesting', and, with resignation, 'Women will never be men's equals.'

To add insult to the injury already felt by female readers, some 13 to 14 per cent of women from both types of school actually *wanted* men to be superior, though a few said only if the man was their husband!

As the presence of the opposite sex is, by definition, an essential feature of a co-educational school an attempt was made, by direct question, to ascertain whether they liked each other's presence in a school. Those ex-pupils replying had attended at least one co-educational and one single-sex secondary school. Of 186 replies from men, only two thought the presence of girls to be bad and only one estimated 'very bad', while of 657 replies from women, only four thought the presence of boys bad and two 'very bad'. Whether the schools were attended first or last, between 80 and 90 per cent of both men and women said they 'liked very much' or 'liked' the presence of the opposite sex.

Also a key item was the question put to the ex-pupils of the 'Both schools' survey: 'In your single-sex [or co-educational] school was the general attitude of most of the pupils towards the opposite sex Pleasant/ Fairly pleasant/Neutral/A little unpleasant/Unpleasant?' Some difficulty occurred here over the interpretation of the word 'pleasant', but an analysis of the free responses demonstrated that the interpretation 'pleasant because they wanted to date girls' was much more characteristic of the single-sex than of the co-educational schools.

The male ex-pupils judged the attitude to be much pleasanter—and much less unpleasant in their co-educational than in their boys' schools. For example, in co-educational schools attended as seniors not one of the 104 replies estimated that this attitude was 'a little unpleasant' or 'unpleasant' in their co-educational school, but this proportion in the corresponding boys' school was over a fifth. The replies about the co-educational schools spoke mostly of a good friendly relationship, with girls treated as equals, or that there was normal interest, e.g.:

'The general attitude was that the girls were an asset to the school.'

'As regards members of the opposite sex relations could not have been better.'

'The opposite sex was there and as we grew up in the school that was all there was to it, they were just accepted as being there.'

In the replies about the boys' schools there was a more varied content, though the largest category was accompanied by the estimate 'a little unpleasant', and the replies 'sex mad' or 'attitude unpleasant sexually' were strikingly more frequent than among those about co-educational schools:

'The boys tended to look upon girls as things to be enjoyed sexually.'

'Some were anti-feminist, some sexually unhealthy in their attitudes, many immature.'

'Unbalanced; myself a tendency to fantasies.'

'They showed no consideration for girls as people, but rather treated them as animals.'

There were also those who were very cut off from the society of girls:

'I don't think I spoke to a single girl for five years.'

It may be important to remind the reader that this chapter is deliberately selecting the important differences discovered, and that only a minority of the respondents found the attitude in boys' schools to be a 'little unpleasant' or 'unpleasant'. On the other hand all or almost all these men did not find this unpleasantness in the co-educational school they attended. It would seem that a 'deprivation effect' is at work in the boys' schools.

The same kind of difference between the opposing groups is to be seen in the answers given to supplementary questions such as, 'In your co-educational [or boys'] school, was the general attitude of most of the pupils (of your own sex) towards the opposite sex, "Rather preoccupied with the opposite sex?"', and, with the same preamble, 'Boy–girl crazy?'; another item used the phrase 'normal interest'. Also segregation in a boys' school seemed to produce a greater timidity towards the opposite sex.

Like the boys, the girls seemed to suffer from a similar 'deprivation effect'. Their attitude to boys was therefore appreciably less unpleasant in the co-educational than in the girls' schools, the emphasis in the former being decidedly on normality,[1] with boys and girls growing up

[1] Cf. Clark's (1937) headmasters: 'Friendships between boys and girls are open, healthy and unsentimental' (p. 59).

together in a family-like atmosphere. Typical quotations about the co-ed schools are:

'We all seemed to be on brother and sister terms, very friendly and pleasant towards each other.'

'Enjoyed their company. Felt the boys really added to the lessons by comments and discussions.'

'We were all good friends, but we thought of them as if we were all one sex, and not as the object of the next date as we probably thought of other boys.'

A few comments remind one of the temporary effects of the sudden amalgamation of two single-sex schools:

'Some went mad the minute we amalgamated, however those mixed lower down the school regard the school as a mixed sexes school.'

The tone of the comments about the girls' schools is completely different, though the same women wrote them;[1] it is self-evident that if you starve a person he will become hungry, and it should have been like-wise evident that if a person is deprived of the company of the opposite sex the desire for that company will become keener. As the female ex-pupils themselves said:

'Most girls regarded boys as a "must" due to not seeing or being with them all day.'

'Absolutely "nuts" about the opposite sex.'

'Man-mad more like it.'

'General tendency to great excitement the moment almost anyone in trousers appeared.'

'Most of the girls had an obsessively morbid interest in boys—as I had grown up with them I could not understand this.'

'Kept away from boys—no attitude could grow healthily.'

'Ridiculous—some were boy crazy and ignorant; some were priggish, prudish and ignorant. The birth-rate was higher than *every* other school in town, secondary modern included.'

In answer to the question, 'In your co-educational [or girls'] school was the general attitude of most of the pupils (of your own sex) towards the opposite sex, "Rather preoccupied with the opposite sex?"', only 9 per cent of these women replied 'True' about their co-educational

[1] That is, allowing for their attendance at one type of school first and at the other last.

schools but 38 per cent with reference to their girls' schools. Similarly 5 per cent of them said that the girls were 'boy crazy' in their co-educational schools and 29 per cent in their girls' schools. On 'timidity' towards boys some 27 per cent said this was true or partly true of their co-educational schools but 59 per cent in the girls' schools.

There is again a logical progression to the next question: 'In which school do you consider the pupils had the healthier attitude towards sex?' ('Both schools' survey). Although rarely expressed openly, there appears to be a deep-seated fear among some people that co-educational schools might lead to an undue interest in sex at too early an age, and even to sexual misbehaviour. It might have been possible to have examined the truth or falsehood of this belief by the compilation of statistical evidence on the comparative incidence of unmarried mothers, confirmed sexual deviants, sexual crimes and prostitutes among the pupils and ex-pupils of both types of schools, but such an investigation would have needed financial aid and the assistance of a multi-disciplinary team of researchers, and these were not available. (Such an investigation would have been further complicated by the changing norms of society.) The writer therefore turned to a less objective method in order to obtain a preliminary survey of the field. Surprisingly this yielded such a conclusive verdict that the research was of much more value than was at first thought possible.

In answer to the question given in the preceding paragraph the ex-pupils were able to choose their answer from, 'Doubtful/Don't know/Single-sex school/Co-educational school' and to add their comments. In their replies they were patently sincere, and though there may be quibbles about the exact meaning of 'healthy' there is no doubt that an 'unhealthy' attitude towards sex is undesirable in any school. Readers will see that the estimates merely tell us which type of school had, in the opinion of the respondents, the healthier attitude to sex, but from the free responses it is possible to see whether either of the atmospheres is actually unhealthy.

The results are given in Figure 17.5.

In Figure 17.5 some 76 per cent of the women considered, from their experience in both types of school, that the attitude towards sex was healthier in their co-educational school than in their girls' school, while only 7 per cent were of the opposite opinion. It may be that the more rural situation of many co-educational schools is exerting some influence here in their favour, but it is unlikely in the extreme that this could account for a difference of such magnitude. This result should allay the fears of those who are afraid that co-educational schools might increase sexual misbehaviour among school pupils.

The principal reasons given for the healthier attitude in co-educational schools were the lack of preoccupation with boys, normal behaviour

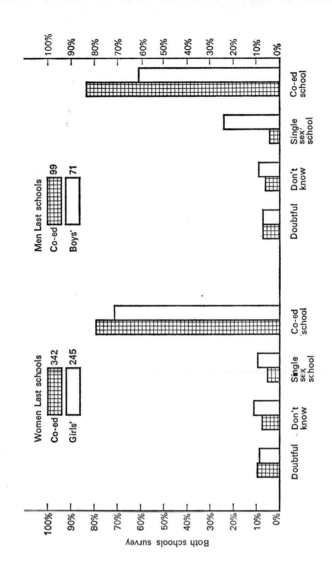

FIGURE 17.5
Healthier attitude to sex: 'Both schools' survey

towards them, the broadened outlook, open discussion and greater understanding of boys as people. Out of 209 comments only 12 said the attitude to sex was healthier in the girls' school they attended than in the co-educational. The dominant view is typified by:

'When you see boys every day the novelty wears off.'

'Boys were part of everyday life in the co-educational school, and at times were completely forgotten about.'

'Mixing with the opposite sex every day one comes into closer contact than in the single-sex school—it changes one's ideas completely—found I had more respect towards them and a healthier attitude to sex.'

A fourth quotation enlarges this concept:

'Greater maturity together, therefore far less mystery and intrigue. Accepted each other as personalities and not so much men and women.'

In order to be fair to the staffs of single-sex schools the writer stresses that this difference in attitude is something that springs automatically from the segregation of the sexes and could not be prevented by any staff, no matter how devoted and well-intentioned.

The results for the male ex-pupils were almost as overwhelmingly favourable to the co-educational schools as were those of the females (see Figure 17.5), though there was some reduction of this difference when the appraisal was limited to schools attended last. The healthier attitude in the co-educational schools was attributed broadly to the same factors as those put forward by the female ex-pupils, e.g.:

'There is less depraved sex-talk among the boys—fewer jokes, etc. The attitude is far healthier altogether.'[1]

'They grew up with it, having a respect rather than a desire for one another.'

'Close relationship with members of the opposite sex leads to a better understanding of each other's roles in society. A balanced adjustment ensues.'

Eight replies—one-ninth of the small total of comments—said there was less depravity or homosexual tendency in the co-educational schools, e.g.:

'Homosexual tendencies in single-sex schools were obvious and often quite open.'

[1] Cf. similar findings in Report of Commissioner of Education for the USA (1906).

'The attitude in the single-sex was at least 75 per cent homosexual inside school and girl-mad outside school.'

The last two comments should not be taken to represent the majority of the replies about boys' schools.[1]

The theme of the chapter now broadens somewhat and considers the impressions of pupils and ex-pupils about whether their school prepared them sufficiently well for life in the adult world. This aspect of the research was limited to the Second College survey and the Schools project. To the question 'Did your school life help or hinder you in your relations with the opposite sex?', the ex-pupils gave a decisive reply. Whereas only some 10 per cent of the ex-pupils of girls' schools said their school life was helpful, the proportion from co-educational schools was three-quarters. The difference between the men's groups was not as great but was considerable, some 40 per cent of men from boys' schools thinking they were hindered, as against three-quarters from co-educational schools who believed they were helped.

In the Schools project over 400 pupils aged 17 plus were asked, 'Apart from employment do you think your school prepared you sufficiently for the adult world?' The results, given in Figure 17.6, show that more of the pupils in single-sex schools than in the co-educational thought their education did not prepare them for the adult world.

The free comments had a wide range and many were of general educational interest rather than serving to distinguish between the two types of school, but there were a few differentiating points. Naturally some pupils in the single-sex schools pointed out the handicap of being educated away from the opposite sex, e.g.:

'Being in a girls' school—absolutely hopeless.'

'An all-girls school is always a set-back.'

'We are confined more or less to our subjects.' (F)

'Probably not, because this is a single-sex school.' (M)

'In the adult world the sexes are not kept apart.' (M)

Boys from boys' schools also stressed that they had no preparation for life's responsibilities and problems and others said they were 'treated like children' and not taught independence. One of the extreme comments was:

'Prepares you for sadism perhaps. No attempt (except by fear) to instil citizenship.'

[1] But long ago Quintilian in *Institutiones Oratoriae* admitted the dangers of herding boys together at an age 'when they are prone to vice', and Erasmus denounced monastic boarding schools partly for the same reason.

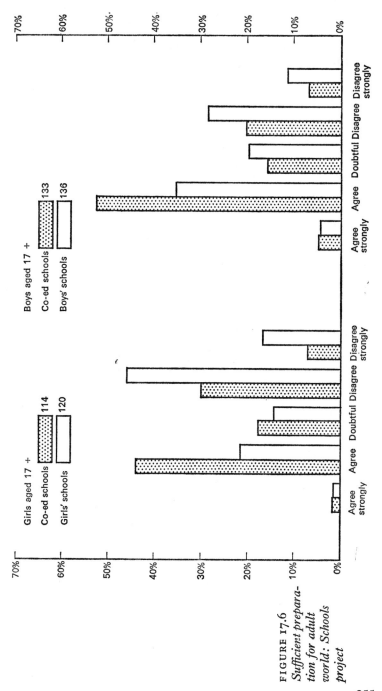

FIGURE 17.6
Sufficient prepara-
tion for adult
world: Schools
project

255

The results from this question are given support in the findings of one of the writer's research students (Atherton, 1971), whose work is described in a chapter in volume II on happiness in marriage. He put a similar question to a very large sample of adults, selected by doctors from all over England, Wales and Scotland. The wording was, 'Do you think that the type of school (mixed or single-sex) helped or hindered you in everyday relations with the opposite sex?' Respondents could choose their reply from, 'Helped/Hindered/Neither or Don't know.' For both men and women about 70 per cent of the co-educated adults thought their schooling had helped them, 2 per cent thought it had hindered and 25 per cent endorsed 'neither' or 'don't know'. Of those educated in single-sex schools the percentage of both men and women who said their schooling had helped them fell to 10, while the 'hindered' replies rose to 30 per cent, with the 'neutral' group over 50 per cent.

In the Second College survey two questions of a more precise nature were asked: 'Do you find it easy to work with the opposite sex?' and 'Do you think you would find it easy, in general, to work under the direction of a member of the opposite sex?' A seven-point scale was used for the answers, ranging from 'very easy' to 'very difficult'. The women educated in co-educational schools naturally found it easier to work with men than did women educated in girls' schools. The second question, however, produced a near equality between the two groups, probably because it is still traditional and normal in Britain for women to work *under the direction* of a man. Here again the difference might have been greater if the question had been put just after the pupil had left school rather than—in some cases—four years later, as a few women from girls' schools said:

'Had this been filled in on just leaving school I would have said "very difficult" but four years in mixed colleges have now overcome the set-backs, but I have taken four years to do so.'

The women in these studies who had attended girls' schools regarded themselves, on the average, as decidedly handicapped in their social life with the opposite sex, and, to a lesser extent, in working with the opposite sex. This is what might have been expected, but it has now been confirmed. It might be argued that girls who are shy of or averse to boys would tend to go to girls' schools and those liking boys would go to mixed schools, but in view of the usual restricted parental choice in these past years this could scarcely account for the differences found. Moreover the replies given in the 'Both schools' survey by no means indicate that averseness to boys is a characteristic of girls' schools.

The results for the men were similarly favourable to co-educational schools. In the Second College survey almost 40 per cent of the men educated in boys' schools thought their school life hindered them in their relationships with women, while nearly three-quarters of those from mixed schools believed that their school social life had helped them in this respect. Working *with* women was considered difficult by 9 per cent of the men from boys' schools but only 3 per cent of those from mixed schools. The question about working under the direction of women differentiated the two groups in the same way, 27 per cent of men from boys' schools finding it difficult, compared with 15 per cent from co-educational schools. A few of the more interesting comments from ex-pupils of boys' grammar schools were:

'Women possess an inherent quality of orderliness and method, and love of detail which is unbearable over long periods and eventually terminates in the realm of "hair splitting".'

'Women were created to be in subjection, not to rule.'

'The artificial atmosphere of the single-sex grammar school at first made my present situation [Mixed College of Education] intolerable.'

(Almost half of all comments said sex made no difference or that the answer depended on the individual's competence or age.)

Unfortunately there is little evidence on whether the effects are long-lasting or not, except for some tentative findings on marriage, of which a part has already been outlined, but the question is of some importance to the world of industry and commerce and deserves investigation. In the above researches the effects had persisted for several years after the respondents had left school.

In following the pupils, their happiness, their attitude to each other, various of their attitudes to school, their anxieties and social development, an important factor has been set on one side—the teachers. They, with the pupils, make the school, and the inter-relationship of these two ingredients has a crucial effect on the well-being of both pupils and teachers. One of the principal tests of this interaction is to be found in the nature of the school discipline. In spite of the views of some extremists the school which has a free-for-all state of indiscipline is usually a bad school, as is the school where the pupils live their lives in fear of the staff, or—in these days—the staff in fear of the pupils! Such schools are rare—or at least we would hope so—and the problem was to discover whether co-educational or single-sex schools differ appreciably from each other in inclining to one of these extremes.

The observations on discipline, made by teachers who had taught in both a co-educational and a single-sex secondary school, were strongly in favour of the type of discipline found in the co-educational school. They were almost unanimous in believing that the conduct of boys was better, and that the girls had a refining influence on the boys, though some women thought the problem of discipline more difficult. A proportion of these women, in spite of their difficulty, preferred co-education. Characteristic of the arguments, taking first those favourable to co-education, were:

'By easing the disciplinary atmosphere it leaves a free scope for interchange of ideas not seemingly possible in a boys' school.' (M)

'Discipline is easier in a mixed school because neither sex likes to look foolish in the eyes of the other.' (M)

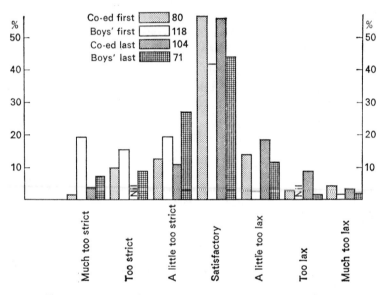

NOTE: The totals for the 'first' and 'last' schools are not equal because some individuals attended three schools and to prevent the discarding of valuable information were allowed three estimates.

The differences between co-educational and boys' groups, both for first and last schools, are highly significant; chi-square = 28·9 and 22·6 for 5 D.F.

FIGURE 17.7   *Strictness of discipline (male): 'Both schools' survey*

'Co-education has a refining influence on both sexes, particularly in the senior forms.' (F)

'Girls in a class subdue to some extent the innate wildness of boys in a mass.' (M)

'The behaviour and work of both boys and girls in mixed classes is better, in my experience, than in single-sex classes.' (F)

The few that were unfavourable are well illustrated by:

'I strongly disapprove of girls being taught by men. The girls play up to them. On the other hand I think women teachers have little bad effect on boys, though they are better handled by men.' (F)

'Proceeding to teach in a boys' school after a mixed school boys seem to be under a disadvantage in a mixed school. Girls also "get away with" a great deal under cover of the boys—but they stand to gain most in the end.' (F)

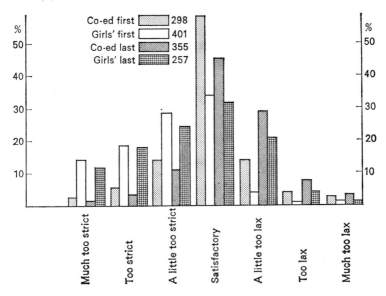

NOTE: The differences between co-educational and girls' school groups, for both 'first' and 'last' schools, are highly significant; chi-square = 120·2 and 114·0 for 5 D.F.

FIGURE 17.8 *Strictness of discipline (female): 'Both schools' survey*

The freshness of one woman's comment demands inclusion:

'When boys and girls are educated together there is a resultant vivacity which soon becomes an attitude to life. Its results are threefold: (i) alertness in the classroom, (ii) liveliness on the playing-fields, and (iii) a general "joie de vivre".'

The comments of the teachers correspond closely to the estimates and free responses about discipline made by the ex-pupils of the 'Both schools' survey (Figures 17.7 and 17.8). Fifty-seven per cent of the men thought the discipline of their co-educational schools 'satisfactory', but only some 43 per cent said the same about their boys' schools. There was a strong tendency for the remainder to find their boys' school too strict or much too strict and a slight tendency for them to classify their co-educational schools as 'a little too lax' or 'too lax'. Some of the co-educational 'too lax' estimates are due to the presence of some ex-pupils of 'amalgamated' schools in the sample. Although these free responses are the judgments of former pupils they were written by men and women who were training to teach and should have been good pupils.

Leaving on one side regretfully, but of necessity, the large group of good comments about each type of school, the following highlight the differences:

'Co-ed too lax, especially in comparison with the school when it was single-sex.' (Am.) (This latter school was judged 'much too strict'.)

'Head was one of the people who regarded being found out as sufficient punishment and he did not back his staff up on the matters of discipline.' (Co-ed)

'Arbitrary justice, army discipline. Utterly ridiculous.' (Boys' school)

'Headmaster ex-air-force, many staff similar. Strictly warped minds.' (Boys' school)

'As soon as the school changed (to boys') the discipline in the school increased considerably.' (Too strict)

'A more pathetic contemporary example of the Hitler Youth movement in England one could not wish to find.' (Boys' school)

The picture for the girls resembles that of the boys. No fewer than 86 per cent of female ex-pupils gave estimates that fall within the three middle categories for their co-educational schools, but in sharp contrast as many as 62 per cent thought the discipline too strict in their girls' school if it was attended first, and 54 per cent if it was attended last. If we confine ourselves again to the unfavourable comments for both types of school, we find that many of the women, like the men, expressed themselves strongly about their girls' schools, especially the 'petty irritating rules':[1]

'It was petty being extremely strict. Silence was observed *everywhere*, at *all* times—even at break. You must put your left hand on the banister going up and coming down the stairs; if you walked on the correct side with an armful of books not holding the banisters, then you were sent back in order to come down properly.'

[1] Cf. Collins (1964). Of 478 female student teachers 'a noticeable proportion disliked the atmosphere of girls' schools—authoritarian nature, petty rules, isolation and the teachers' (p. 32).

'The discipline was of the kind that annoyed the pupils because they felt the school would run efficiently if everyone just used their common sense instead of being told what to do in minute detail.'

'There were so many rules not a day went by without us all being punished for breaking one of them.'

'Rules covered four notice boards. Fear was discipline.'

There were 212 comments in this category.

Comments in the same tone about the co-educational schools were not entirely absent, but were few, though some of the women thought the discipline too lax:

'School had absolutely no discipline. I called a teacher an old cow to her face and got away with it.'

'Boys smoked in the classroom. In the lower part of the school the children led some of the teachers a terrible life.'

The last two comments are a jolting reminder that if discipline is too strict pupils suffer, but if it is too lax teachers (as well as pupils) may have to pay a high price. The argument has been stated before that the ameliorating effect on pupils of one sex on the conduct of the other sex makes it less necessary for teachers to impose a severe discipline in co-educational schools, an improvement which is also assisted by the ameliorating effect of masters on mistresses and of mistresses on masters. It is, however, easier for such a discipline to become too lax than too strict, while in the single-sex school the opposite is the case. Yet, in a balanced appraisal of the facts one of the most telling points is that most of the ex-pupils and of the teachers preferred the type of discipline they experienced in their co-educational schools. Over 80 per cent of the ex-pupils gave their estimates for these schools to the middle three categories—'satisfactory', 'a little too strict' and 'a little too lax', with the bulk of them allocated to 'satisfactory'.

In response to ancillary questions the female ex-pupils of the 'Both schools' survey agreed strongly that their single-sex schools made an unnecessary fuss over small details (cf. Figure 17.9), that the staff were more out of touch with adolescents than staff in co-educational schools were, and treated them like children though they felt grown-up.

The difference on the male side was by no means as great, but surprisingly the men also thought that their teachers in boys' schools were more out of touch with adolescents than were those in their co-educational schools.

The topic was extended to an examination of the comparative 'friendliness' and 'helpfulness' of teachers in the two types of school. Overall there was a strong tendency for ex-pupils and pupils to classify teachers as both friendly and helpful, but this is mentioned only to give readers the correct setting, as we are primarily concerned with the differences. The principal one found was the greater emphasis placed by female ex-pupils and 15-year-old girl pupils on the friendliness and helpfulness of teachers in co-educational schools; on the male side this difference is to be seen strongly in the 'Both schools' survey but narrows markedly in

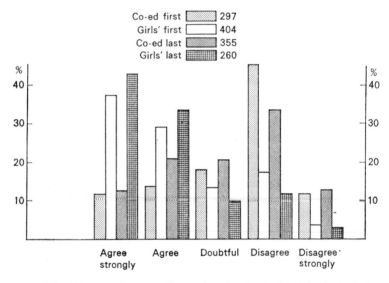

NOTE: The differences between the co-educational and girls' schools, both for 'first' and 'last' schools, are statistically highly significant; chi-square = 126·5 and 122·2.

FIGURE 17.9   *Fuss over details (female ex-pupils): 'Both schools' survey*

the Second College survey and disappears for the sample of present boy pupils aged 11 and 15. Those interested in the comments of the respondents may see a large selection in chapter 5 of volume I; the comments presented here are chosen to illustrate what seems to the writer to be the most important aspect of the differences between girls' and co-educational schools in relation to the present topic, namely that teachers in girls' schools are said to be more aloof from the pupils, or even 'unapproachable', whereas the girls had a distinct liking for the presence of the male teachers in co-educational schools. Female readers who teach in girls' schools, however, should not regard this as a stricture on themselves. Here and there individuals or even schools may escape from this influence to a greater or less degree, but it is necessary for us to concentrate on average tendencies. All the quotations are from female ex-pupils who had attended both a co-educational and a single-sex secondary school.

'There was a near perfect relationship between pupils and staff; this I believe was mainly due to the number of male staff.' (Co-ed school)

'More male teachers tend to be more considerate and friendly than female ones, particularly spinsters. Men are usually more reasonable than women.'

'They were interested and co-operative staff. The women were prevented from being "catty" by the presence of men, and the men were forced to raise their standards because of the women.'

'A far more relaxed atmosphere than in the single-sex school; less tendency to have either favourites or enemies.'

'The "stiff upper lip" was always upheld—no coming down to the pupils' level.' (Girls' school)

'They sort of viewed you from above. What they said went. They didn't listen to your point of view.' (Girls' school)

'Staff considered themselves very much above pupils and made it felt, some went out of their way to be nasty.' (Girls' school)

'Hardly any interest shown at all. We were all numbered.' (Girls' school)

'The teachers in the single-sex school were not as friendly or natural as in the co-educational school.'

These aspects dominated the differences but some ex-pupils, albeit a smaller number, found the teachers at their girls' school more approachable and interested—this was occasionally by contrast with their experience in a very large mixed comprehensive school.

As might be expected from the previous results, when this topic was extended to ascertaining whether any one or more of the teachers had a powerful influence for good, the female ex-pupils once again chose staff from their co-educational school more frequently than from their girls' school. For male ex-pupils the tendency was the same but not conclusively so. For the negative side—'distinctly bad influence'—the preponderant answer for both types of school was 'No', but there tended to be slightly fewer 'Decidedly' and 'Possibly' replies about the co-educational schools, the difference rising to statistical significance for women in the Second College survey and near it in the 'Both schools' survey.

Most of the complaints, from both women and men, were concerned with fear of teachers, and on the female side this fear *motif* is to be found more often in the girls' schools than in the co-educational, the difference appearing to arise from the absence of complaints about women teachers being terrifying, antagonistic, arrogant and domineering in co-educational schools—though there were a few about the men. Some illustrations are given about the girls' schools, but we must remember that although these are severe cases ('Distinctly bad') they are only some 10 per cent of the whole in both surveys of ex-pupils:

'Fear of a particular teacher made me an extremely nervy irritable child.'

'Scripture teacher turned me against religion for years.'

'Frightened to participate in maths—teacher had temper if wrong answer given.'

'A very domineering personality—had to really bow down to her or she made life a misery.'

'Headmistress treated me like a fool—became timid and nervous and scared to go to school.'

'She frightened you out of all natural feelings. She gained results through fear nothing else.'

Now a reminder that male teachers in co-educational schools must be careful not to frighten girls with harsh discipline (though the percentage of 'Distinctly bad' estimates under all categories was only some 6 per cent, and this included a few complaints about *too lax* discipline):

'Headmaster extremely stern and authoritarian.'

'Inferiority complex developed from lack of encouragement and crushing remarks.'

'He was one of the "old school" teachers—unsympathetic, bad-tempered and vicious. I became very antagonistic.' (Am.)

'Intimidated me. Shook my confidence in speaking out in class or any oral work.'

'He nurtured in me an aversion for mathematics by always shouting and being sarcastic.'

We now come to that section of the research which is concerned with academic work. As the full account is contained in the early part of the present volume the summary will be brief.

Co-education is only one variable that affects the comparison of co-educational and single-sex grammar schools in attainment—or preferably, in *progress*; other powerful factors are at work, some commonplace, others comparatively unknown. It is therefore indeed difficult to separate out the effect of co-educational versus single-sex schooling, and in the long string of researchers since 1925 no one has identified *all these extraneous variables* and some have ignored them entirely. Fortunately for this appraisal, however, all of these variables except one and part of another favour the single-sex schools. Their pupils have, on average, an appreciably higher verbal (and non-verbal) intelligence, are of higher social class, probably have better qualified staff (save for the exception mentioned later) and on the female side take the first external examination at a later age and drop more weak subjects. The exceptions acting in the opposite direction have been the greater incidence of premature leaving in co-educational schools—a small difference for girls but larger for boys—and the probably better staffing of co-educational schools as opposed to girls' schools in mathematics and maybe the physical sciences. The premature leaving factor could exert no real effect on the comparison of girls, and for boys it would not be strong enough to out-weigh—or even balance—the more selective entry of the boys' schools. How long the reverse staffing position for mathematics etc has been in existence we do not know—there seem to be no such statistics available either centrally or locally. Moreover it could be argued that girls' schools do not need the same numbers of highly qualified teachers as do co-educational schools because the latter have a considerably higher percentage of their pupils taking mathematics; this question of need, however, is partly in the realm of speculation and there are no facts with which to take it further.

Given sufficient finance and manpower and the *co-operation of all in ensuring scrupulous objectivity in the choice of pupils for the comparative samples*, it would have been possible to have planned a research in which most of the extraneous variables were controlled or allowed for—though the comparative staffing of schools would have been rather intractable to deal with. But the research funds were non-existent. Even if such a research were done today there would be difficulties with comprehensive schools that are not comprehensive schools, comprehensive schools that are half comprehensive and comprehensive schools that are really comprehensive, to say nothing of grammar schools that are bilateral, grammar schools that are grammar schools, and grammar schools that are super-selective. In addition the matching of individuals by socio-economic class might be inadequate, in itself, to control social class influences—regard would need to be taken of the dominant social class *ethos* in opposing schools.

In view of all these difficulties the persistence of a common pattern of results (with one or two minor deviations) throughout almost fifty years of research, conducted in several regions of different types and often with large numbers of pupils and of schools, is quite astonishing. Briefly, although handicapped in a number of ways, boys in co-educational schools did better in the first external examination in five very large surveys and three smaller ones, than boys in boys' schools. One small survey showed a slight difference in the opposite direction; this concerned only nine boys' schools, seven of which had highly selective entries and attracted highly qualified staff. In those surveys which analysed the results subject by subject the superiority of the co-educated boys extended over almost all of them, with French a possible exception. In mathematics their superiority was more marked than in most subjects, yet the boys' schools would almost certainly have the more highly qualified staff (cf. chapter 3). This analysis of research has shown with reasonable definitude that the common belief that boys make better progress in single-sex schools—and even that such schools have a higher attainment level than co-educational ones—is a myth, and it appears probable that the advantage lies with the boys in co-educational schools. One does not of course include in this statement those comprehensive schools (mostly co-educational) that are merely re-named secondary modern schools, or indeed compare single-sex grammar schools with co-educational true comprehensive schools.

That attainment in French is a possible exception to this tendency or that the co-educational lead may be less certain in this subject, is rather curious. A tentative explanation is that in early and middle grammar school years the girls in co-educational schools are so much better than the boys in French that the boys tend not to like exposing their backwardness in oral lessons, and the consequent attitudes tend to persist up to O-level. An examination of the question—whether French or foreign languages are an exception to the general trend, and if so, why—would be an excellent topic for further research.

On the female side the analysis of the general results in all subjects is more complex. One thing, however, emerges clearly, namely that the difference between the two groups of girls is smaller than that between the boys' groups, and in raw scores it is slightly but fairly consistently in favour of girls' schools. Yet in this comparison the co-educated girls are more handicapped in comparison with girls' schools than the co-educated boys are in comparison with boys' schools. This is because two additional extraneous variables 'stack the cards' against them: these are the younger age at which they take the examination and the undeniable fact that in these surveys they are shown to drop fewer of their weak subjects than their counterparts do. To recapitaulate, the girls' schools, like the boys', also have a more selective entry which means the pupils are more intelligent and of higher social class; their pupils are also usually from urban backgrounds while the co-educated pupils are usually from rural backgrounds.

In addition to the above we have to take into consideration that in one major survey (Northern Ireland, 1969) there was a rough equality between the girls' groups, while in a second major survey (that of Gott in Middlesex schools) the co-educated girls had a clear lead, over six years. It is not without interest that in the county concerned the co-educational schools of that time would be nearer to the girls' schools in quality of intake than in most, if not all, the other surveys. Equally interesting is the small lead gained by the girls' schools in the same county in the next five years. This might have been caused by the publication of Gott's results spurring the girls' schools to catch up, or causing them to intensify their policy of weeding out or delaying their weaker candidates. Recently, however, the writer has been informed by a present headmaster, a pupil in Middlesex in the period of Gott's survey, that children who passed the 11-plus examination at that time were allocated to the nearest grammar school, but around the late twenties parents were given choice of schools; this change may have resulted in aspirant middle-class parents pushing their children into single-sex schools (which would be mostly older) and this loss by the co-educational schools of some of their better pupils with a corresponding gain to the single-sex schools may have been responsible—or partly responsible—for the reversal experienced by the opposing girls' groups.

Throughout the eleven years of the Middlesex surveys it is probable that the girls from girls' schools would take the examination at a higher average age and would drop more weak subjects than the girls from the co-educational schools; this is so in all the surveys for which the information is given or can be calculated.

Throughout the surveys another trend stands out with quite surprising consistency—the superiority of the co-educated girls over their 'rivals' in mathematics. This was also found by Cameron (1923) who attributed it to the girls in mixed classes getting educated in mathematical thinking by the work of the boys. The research of Booth (1967) raises considerable doubt that the difference could be explained by the theory that men might teach mathematics better than women do; from his work there even emerged the possibility that women might teach geometry better than men! Such a finding in this difficult field would need to be replicated before it could be accepted as definite. Another possibility is that the co-educational schools had the better qualified mathematics teachers, as demonstrated for recent years in chapter 4, but we do not know whether this staffing difference in the subject extended back to the 1920s. Neither is it by any means certain that it is the cause of the difference in the recent surveys.

A cautious summing up would be that the progress of boys is probably improved by co-education while that of girls is not harmed, *and*

*that the question of comparative progress in academic work should never
again be raised as an obstacle to a policy of co-education.*

The reasons for the good results of the co-educated boys are quite
likely to be several related ones put forward by a number of the questionnaire respondents, both teachers and ex-pupils; namely that the
boys are spurred on by friendly competition with the girls, and some of
the girls' greater industriousness and conscientiousness is communi-
cated to the boys. These forces seem to be stronger than the 'distracting
effect' mentioned by other respondents. Possibly the happier atmosphere of the co-educational schools also helps to improve the work, but
this becomes speculation.

The section on academic work has been about average tendencies, and
there is undoubtedly a large overlap in attainment between single-sex
and co-educational schools, and also between the two types of school in
the rates of progress of pupils of equal relevant qualities. The range of
attainment and the variations in 'teaching efficiency' are great within
each *type* of school. It is also well known that within any individual
school, whatever the type, there will be decided differences in the
efficiency of this teaching in the various subjects of the curriculum.

The finding also needs qualifying in another way. So far we have
really been considering pupils in general and examining large-scale
tendencies, but there may well be a small minority of pupils who because
of their psychological make-up or even because of their upbringing
would work better in a single-sex school and even be happier there. The
question might still arise as to whether this segregation from the other
sex would be wise in the long term, because the pupil would need to
learn, in some way, how to associate naturally with the opposite sex in
later life. These questions have not been examined in the present
research.

Closely related to the topic of attainment is that of interest in academic
work and in particular subjects. This has been covered less exhaustively
than many other aspects in these researches, and suffers from having
been largely confined to the Schools project, with its somewhat limited
number of schools.

From the picture which has evolved so far would we expect pupils'
interest in the subjects of the curriculum to be stronger in the co-
educational or in the single-sex schools? Surely we would opt for the co-
educational on the basis of rather better academic progress (boys', at
least), happier atmosphere and friendlier pupil–teacher relationship, but
the problem is not as simple as that.

In the ensuing discussion the writer is endeavouring, through all the
imperfections of the research and especially of the sample, to discern the
emerging of a pattern of results; if found this would be more reliable, for

many reasons, than the result for any one subject. The chief difficulties have been mentioned before—the small number of school subjects investigated and the nature of the sample of schools; of these the latter is the more important. The number of pupils was sufficient for reliability but the number of schools was small; for some parts of the work there were 14 of each type, 42 in all, but for other parts there were only 12 of each. Although pupils of 15 years of age may have had several teachers of a subject, those of 11 years and some of the 13-year-olds would have had only one. The average or mean level of liking for any one subject at the age of 11 usually depends in these studies on only 14 teachers in each type of school, and this is too small for us to be reasonably sure that it is a representative sample of teachers from each type. Pupils of the age of 13 will have had more teachers—perhaps 26 or so—and this number is much better for the research purposes though it should preferably be larger. We have seen that there is also a known bias in the sample in intelligence, social class and the nature of the drop-outs, all operating against the co-educational schools.

Against this background the findings are naturally tentative, but surprisingly consistent and falling into a logical pattern. When the two types of school are compared the co-educated boys show a stronger interest in arithmetic, mathematics and physics, less interest in French, with equality in English literature. On the female side the co-educated record more interest in French; on the other hand they record less in physics than the girls' schools do in their mainly general science, with again equality in English literature. The opposing groups of girls are also equally interested in arithmetic and mathematics at the age of 13, confirmed by the large check sample without allowance for the higher intelligence and social class levels of the girls from girls' schools. At 15 years of age, however, there are difficulties of interpretation, with the girls' schools having a decidedly higher interest level in both subjects, but again without allowing for the intelligence and social class factors. This difference in interest at age 15 is peculiarly due to pupils of social class 3 only,[1] in both subjects, the difference being reversed in the other social classes except for equality in one case. This causes some uneasiness, but overall it seems probable that the girls' schools would, in this sample, have a rather higher level of interest in these subjects at the age of 15.

If the results are assessed closely they do fall into a pattern, the co-educated boys having an increased interest in mathematical and scientific subjects and the co-educated girls an increased interest on the literary–language side (French). Correspondingly the co-educated boys have a reduced liking on the literary–language side and the co-educated girls similarly in physical science (with a decided question mark about

[1] This was not due to the inclusion of the farmers in class 3.

M S S—K

the comparisons with general science) and in mathematics at the age of 15, though there is the equality at 13 years of age and there is in addition the question of the influence of men teachers of mathematics on the level of interest in girls' schools. This question of accentuated polarization of interest in co-educational schools according to sex and subject is, from the data presented, more clearly resolved on the boys' side than on the girls', but more results are needed from other samples, exploring additional school subjects as well as testing the soundness of the present results.

At first sight one would think that reduced interest would lead to a lower level of attainment, and so it might if other factors were not involved. For example, in a class of both sexes the girls' interest in the physical sciences might be reduced because of their lower level of success compared with the boys; on the other hand the presence of the boys may tend to raise the girls' standard of attainment, and the girls may also learn something from the approach of the boys to the subject. There may be a similar process in mathematics. Of the subjects of the curriculum, mathematics is perhaps the one in which the co-educated girls do best in comparison with the girls in girls' schools. Much depends on the relative strength of the interacting forces in each subject. In French the lower general success level of the co-educated boys in relation to the girls is reinforced by their less competent, less fluent approach to oral work, and the influence of this comparison on the attitude of the boys may be the force making French one of the few subjects in which boys in boys' schools occasionally do slightly better than those in co-educational schools. As a reverse example let us take mathematics and the co-educated boys. The increase in their interest, due to the stronger polarization factor in co-educational schools, may be responsible for their consistently clear superiority in attainment at O-level over boys in boys' schools, in spite of the teachers of mathematics in boys' schools being more highly qualified.

No sooner does one provide evidence to help to solve one problem than others rear their heads. For example, co-educational schools may be a setting more conducive to academic progress up to O-level, but does this influence continue to A-level? This question has been deliberately omitted from the research because some selection was inevitable. If anyone attempts it they will find it more difficult than it looks, not only because of the probably different qualities of pupils entering the sixth forms in the three types of school, but because the qualifications of the teachers increase in importance with the advanced standard of the work.

A second query comes to mind, namely does any distinctive influence last beyond school so that it affects academic progress in the university? The chapter which examines this is the only research which has been done on the topic, so that its results are more tentative than is most of the other research in the book. Here the students from co-educational schools, paired on a large number of variables with students from single-sex schools, had at the end of their first year fewer bad failures in the science faculty, to a degree which was statistically reliable, and there was a small unreliable tendency in the same direction in the arts faculty. Since the students were paired on university entrance standard, the results are a comparison of the academic *progress* of the opposing groups of students rather than a comparison of their university attainment without regard to their standard on entry. A somewhat amusing fact is that the co-educated students admitted to being 'more distracted' by the opposite sex than did those from single-sex schools. The latter liked the co-educational atmosphere of the university and some claimed that it steadied them down and even gave them a drive towards the setting up of a home. The proof of their claim would lie in their superior academic progress, but this does not appear to take place; perhaps the liking for the co-educational nature of the university tended to warp the judgment of students from single-sex schools when assessing the extent to which they were 'distracted'. It could be, of course, that some of them thought that the 'distraction' was more important than their studies, in which case the roles of the opposite sex and of studies would be reversed, the studies becoming the distraction! However, substantiation of the comparative progress finding is needed before any claim can be made. As it depends on only one study made in a complex of variables, of which one or two may be unknown, this is perhaps the least dependable part of the research.

During the last few pages one of the underlying central issues has been whether the interests of boys and girls are sufficiently close for them to be educated together, or more precisely whether classes of mixed sexes enable each sex to be educated to the best advantage. The chapters on comparative academic progress have given one answer, but it is only a partial one—that, judged by the end product, attainment, this progress does not suffer and in the case of the boys is probably improved. Later chapters, on interest in academic work and in various subjects of the curriculum, comparing co-educated pupils with those from single-sex schools, do not indicate that overall the co-educated pupils show less interest than the others. Yet it would be foolish to ignore the important differences in the scholastic interests of the two sexes. The feminine sex tends to prefer the literary and humanistic subjects while the male sex leans towards the mathematical and scientific, but the large area of similarity in their preference should also not be forgotten. In co-educational schools, however, it is not the practice to impose an identical curriculum on the two sexes. Both the difference and the similarity are given attention by means of subject options in middle and senior forms, though the query arises—in single-sex schools also—

as to the desirability of such early options; whether it is wise to make choices then which determine or at least limit the pupil's career. The adequacy or inadequacy of this provision seems to be more a matter of the training of heads and of their educational wisdom, rather than an inevitable concomitant of a co-educational system. Some doubts may arise because of the different subject load of fifth form girls in co-educational schools compared with that of girls in girls' schools, but this again could be decided as a separate issue. It is something which has grown up over many years and it is due for examination. A more important question is that of the selection of topics within each subject of the curriculum. In an earlier chapter, for example, it was found that both boys and girls liked social, political and military history, together with biographies and exploration, while both disliked constitutional history until about the age of 15 or 16. Thus there is a substantial area of similarity between the sexes, marred by the girls' dislike of economic history, though boys also do not like it as much as other aspects until about the age of 14 or 15. Similarly—though it is more peripheral—boys do not like the history of dress as much as girls do. In the same way, though the girls like Scripture better than the boys (with an overlap), yet there is appreciable agreement between the sexes about which parts each likes and each dislikes (Forrester, 1946; Jones, J. A., 1962).

In geography there is again a large area of agreement, but sufficient difference between the sexes for some researchers to advocate separate syllabuses (Bartlett, 1948). This, however, seems to be an extremist viewpoint, entailing separate external examinations for the two sexes, especially as Bartlett finds that 'differences towards the major groups or parts of the subject are not as marked as differences in the attitudes towards the individual topics within these groups', and continues, 'The broad content of the syllabus may be largely similar for both.' Bottoms (1953) analysed five aspects or lines of approach in geography and found a close similarity in order of interest for boys and girls. The researchers (cf. also Swainson, 1939; Long, 1949) seem to agree that both sexes like human, descriptive, practical and field work and 'useful' geography. There is a tendency for them both to dislike physical geography; here liking and disliking depend on the topics chosen but the preferences are similar for the two sexes. Economic geography is the aspect which produces the widest differences between the sexes, 'it being less popular with girls than with boys'.

At this point it is perhaps time to ask some more fundamental questions. Should interest be the sole determinant of the topics chosen? Geography as a subject can scarcely be studied if the economic side is omitted; history also must lose meaning if the economic side is excluded. Neither can the possible enriching of the lessons by the interests and approaches of both sexes be ignored.

On the other hand interest is naturally a desirable element in the lesson, and not only should we cater for differences between the sexes in this respect, but also for differences *between individuals*. Fortunately, the over-emphasis on didactic class teaching is now recognized, and educationists are pioneering changes towards group work and the individual topic. This system provides admirable outlets for individual interests and usually arouses enthusiasm. Organized judiciously, there can be a good compromise between the retention of a subject's central core and enabling individuals—and both sexes—to explore those aspects of the subject which interest them. Thus in satisfying the special interests of individuals, we automatically allow also for any difference in interests between the sexes. Yet the change needs a more widespread awareness on the part of teachers; it also demands an equipment in books, apparatus, specialist rooms and specialist storerooms which has been, and still is, inadequate.

Now it is time to survey in a sentence or two the whole research. Although co-education has been the central theme of these books, the work has included a fairly detailed survey of pupil–teacher relationships and of other aspects of the functioning of secondary schools. The writer therefore hopes that the books may be found useful in a wide area of educational studies in addition to their contribution towards the assessment of co-educational and single-sex schools.

It has been demonstrated that the average co-educational grammar school is a happier community for both staff and pupils than the average single-sex school; it has equally been demonstrated that this happiness is not at the expense of academic progress. The greater happiness is reflected in numerous ways in the interaction between pupils and teachers, boys and girls, masters and mistresses, and these in turn interact among each other, all contributing to the pleasantness of the school. There seems to be little reason why this should not be true for comprehensive and secondary modern as well as for grammar schools. This finding does not mean that all co-educational schools are good and all single-sex schools bad; other powerful influences which shape a school's character were mentioned at the opening of this chapter, such as the personality of the head and of the individual teachers, the social class of the pupils, and the nature of the neighbourhood. The overlap between co-educational and single-sex schools has been a recurring theme of this book, whether the criterion be academic progress or the happiness and well-being of pupils and staff. Yet these researches point unmistakably to co-education as the preferable system.

It has been a long, an arduous, but a fascinating journey. When it began some twenty-six years ago, at the suggestion of Sir Fred Schonell, then Professor of Education at Swansea, the advocacy of co-educational schools was almost heretical in the best circles; even the Ministry of Education pronounced in favour of single-sex secondary schools where these were economically possible (1945). Research on the subject was resented by some. One headmistress wrote to enquire why I was 'flogging a dead horse'! Today the climate of opinion has veered round and it is rapidly becoming accepted policy to make schools co-educational. One by one even the bastions of single-sex education—the public schools—are becoming co-educational or flirting with the concept.

With this quickening change, attention should be given to some problems which will become more acute. It is of the essence of co-education that the two sexes should be deemed equal and treated equally. This entails a balance in the numbers of boys and girls, masters and mistresses, in the school and, as remarked earlier, the re-styling of the senior mistress as headmistress, usually as second and certainly not third in seniority. The training of teachers and of heads should be orientated more towards work in co-educational schools (cf. Breuse, 1970), and new heads should usually have had teaching experience in them.

In this analysis of co-educational and single-sex schooling an effort has been made to include as much of the visible spectrum as possible, given certain limitations of time and resources. Regrettably there are some aspects which are inadequately covered; notably there is a lack of 'objective' evidence on pupils' emotional and social development. What is the relative incidence of juvenile delinquency, of truancy, of school phobia, in these schools, with other relevant variables controlled? Will the present findings on the happiness of marriage be confirmed? Are there other long-term effects? These and other questions must necessarily be left to others. Finally, we must never forget that schools are a part of the society in which they are placed and their success, whether they be co-educational or single-sex, depends upon the well-being of that society. If society fails the schools falter.

Appendix I

The questionnaires[1]

SECOND COLLEGE SURVEY

Research questionnaire I

[Only a few items of this questionnaire are used in this volume and they are given in the relevant chapters.]

'BOTH SCHOOLS' SURVEY

Research questionnaire II

FORM B. *For students who have attended both a co-educational and a single-sex grammar, or comprehensive, or grammar technical school in Britain.*
[For the full preamble and preliminary instructions see volume I or volume II.]

Your co-educational school

Underline the answer which is correct for you.
   8. Do you agree or disagree with the following statements about your co-educational school? *Underline* your answers.
      (1) Good quality of teaching.
         1. Agree strongly/2. Agree/3. Doubtful/4. Disagree/5. Disagree strongly.
      (5) The organized games were enjoyable.
         1. Agree strongly/2. Agree/3. Doubtful/4. Disagree/5. Disagree strongly.
      (12) The intense pressure of work for examinations worried me.
         1. Agree strongly/2. Agree/3. Doubtful/4. Disagree/5. Disagree strongly.

---

[1] Only those parts of the questionnaires are given which have relevance to the material in Part 2; those items dealt with in volumes I and II and referred to in the 'Overview' may be consulted in the appendices to those volumes.

17. Do you consider that the amount of homework to be done in the school was:
    1. Far too much/2. A little too much/3. Just right/4. Rather too little/5. Far too little?
    Comment if you wish ....
    ....

18. Did the pressure of work in this school make you:
    1. Very anxious/2. Anxious/3. A little anxious/4. No effect?
    Comment if you wish ....
    ....

Your single-sex school

[The questions under this heading were exactly the same as for the co-educational school.]

SCHOOLS PROJECT

Age ......   Sex ... Boy/Girl (Please tick)

Name of school .... Date ....

Please answer the following questions according to the instruction given. *Do not* write your name on this sheet. Your answers will be kept strictly private, so please be *completely frank and truthful.* If you are 17 plus commence at Question 6.

Now read the following statements about each subject and *underline* the answer which is true for you. Answer *ALL* questions.

1. Arithmetic.
   1. Like much/2. Like a little/3. Neither like nor dislike/4. Dislike a little/5. Dislike much.
   Comment if you wish ....
   ....

2. Mathematics.
   1. Like much/2. Like a little/3. Neither like nor dislike/4. Dislike a little/5. Dislike much.
   Comment if you wish ....
   ....

3. French (omit if you have never taken it).
   1. Like much/2. Like a little/3. Neither like nor dislike/4. Dislike a little/5. Dislike much.
   Comment if you wish ....
   ....

276

4. English literature.
   1. Like much/2. Like a little/3. Neither like nor dislike/4. Dislike a little/5. Dislike much.
   Comment if you wish ....
   ....

5. Physics (omit only if you have never taken physics).
   1. Like much/2. Like a little/3. Neither like nor dislike/4. Dislike a little/5. Dislike much.
   Comment if you wish ....
   ....

Here is a list of statements about school. Underneath each statement is a list of opinions. *Underline* the opinion with which you agree.
   7. I try my hardest in school work.
      1. Nearly always/2. Often/3. Sometimes/4. Occasionally/5. Rarely.
   8. I do my written homework.
      1. Nearly always/2. Often/3. Sometimes/4. Occasionally/5. Rarely.
   9. I do my learning homework.
      1. Nearly always/2. Often/3. Sometimes/4. Occasionally/5. Rarely.
  10. (1964 only) I do my reading homework.
      1. Nearly always/2. Often/3. Sometimes/4. Occasionally/5. Rarely.
  10. (1966 only) The intense pressure of work at school worries me.
      1. Agree strongly/2. Agree/3. Doubtful/4. Disagree/5. Disagree strongly.
  51. (1966 only) Taking the subjects all together, how much do you *enjoy* your school work?
      1. Enjoy much/2. Enjoy a little/3. Jogging along/4. Dislike a little/5. Dislike much.

FOR GIRLS ONLY

52. Do you like gymnastics at school?
    1. Like much/2. Like a little/3. Undecided/4. Dislike a little/5. Dislike much.
[The format for the choice of reply for the following questions up to Question 88 is the same as for Question 52.]
53. Do you like athletics at school? (Running, high jump, long jump etc).
58. Do you like playing hockey at school?
59. Do you like cooking?
60. Do you like needlework?

FOR BOYS ONLY

86. Do you like playing football (either rugby or soccer) at school?
87. Do you like gymnastics at school?
88. Do you like athletics at school?

[1966 only]

FOR ALL PUPILS

89. Our lessons are made more enjoyable because teachers and pupils
are usually ready to share a joke.
1. Agree strongly/2. Agree/3. Doubtful/4. Disagree/5. Disagree
strongly.
Please comment ....
90. I'm rather afraid to speak out in class.
1. Always afraid/2. Often/3. Sometimes/4. Hardly ever/5. Never.
Please comment ....
91. We have lots of interesting discussions in class.
1. Agree strongly/2. Agree/3. Doubtful/4. Disagree/5. Disagree
strongly.
Please comment ....
95. To what extent do you consider your school keeps a fair balance
between school work and other aspects of school life?
1. Far too much work/2. Rather too much/3. Balanced/4. Rather
too little/5. Much too little.

SCHOOLS PROJECT

'Check' questionnaire

Name of school .... Grammar/High School

[Occupation of Father or Guardian ...... For full instructions see
volume I or II.]

OCCUPATION ....

Please answer the following questions according to the instruction given.
Do not write your name on this sheet. Your answers will be kept strictly
private, so please be *completely frank and truthful*. Read the following
items and underline the answer which is true for you.

1. Arithmetic.
1. Like much/2. Like a little/3. Neither like nor dislike/4. Dislike a
little/5. Dislike much.
My arithmetic teacher this term is a man/woman. (Please underline)

2. Taking the subjects all together, how much do you *enjoy* your school work?
   1. Enjoy much/2. Enjoy a little/3. Jogging along/4. Dislike a little/5. Dislike much.
10. Our lessons are made more enjoyable because teachers and pupils are ready to share a joke.
    1. Agree strongly/2. Agree/3. Doubtful/4. Disagree/5. Disagree strongly.

Appendix 2

Additional tables

TABLE A2.1 *Average 'intelligence' scores*[1]

Schools project, 1964 full sample

| | Girls in: | | | Boys in: | | |
	Co-ed schools	Girls' schools	Differ-ence	Co-ed schools	Boys' schools	Differ-ence
Aged 11+	6·975	7·293	−0·318*	7·093	7·179	−0·086
Aged 15+	7·871	8·121	−0·250*	7·907	7·896	+0·011

[1] Factor B in the High School Personality Questionnaire. It has a maximum score of only 10 and is only useful for the comparison of large groups. No better data were available.

The asterisks indicate significance beyond the 0·05 level.

TABLE A2.2 *Occupational class composition of the project sample*
Schools project, 1964 full sample

		Occupational class of pupils' parents										Totals[1]	
		1		2		3		4		5			
		N	%	N	%	N	%	N	%	N	%	N	%
Girls	Co-ed schools	81	14·5	152	27·1	230	41·1	74	13·2	19	3·4	560	100
	Girls' schools	90	16·1	143	25·5	241	43·0	56	10·0	25	4·5	560	100
Boys	Co-ed schools	70	12·5	130	23·2	274	49·0	55	9·8	27	4·8	560	100
	Boys' schools	74	13·2	164	29·3	249	44·5	47	8·4	20	3·6	560	100

[1] Includes a few unclassifiable.

TABLE A2.3   *Average intelligence scores (HSPQ 'B' factor)*

Schools project, longitudinal sample

	Co-educational schools		Single-sex schools	
	N	Mean	N	Mean
1964				
Boys aged 11+	225	7·24	217	7·23
15+	133	8·14	137	8·19
Girls aged 11+	215	7·11	215	7·28
15+	115	8·24	120	8·27
1966				
Boys aged 13+	225	7·54	217	7·57
17+	133	8·38	137	8·33
Girls aged 13+	215	7·38	215	7·80
17+	115	8·44	120	8·56

NOTE: The co-educated girls have a lower score than those from girls' schools at all four ages; one of these differences (at 15 plus) can obviously be dismissed but that at 13 plus is statistically significant.

TABLE A2.4   *Distribution of intelligence test scores: girls*

Schools project, longitudinal sample

	Age 13 plus		17 plus	
Score (range 0–10)	Co-ed	Girls' schools	Co-ed	Girls' schools
10	5	12	11	20
9	49	55	53	49
8	54	73	32	35
7	47	47	14	11
6	40	15	5	4
5	15	8		1
4	4	3		
3	1	2		
	215	215	115	120

TABLE A2.5 *Occupational class composition of the longitudinal sample*
Schools project

		Occupational class of pupils' parents										Totals[1]	
		1		2		3		4		5			
		N	%	N	%	N	%	N	%	N	%	N	%
Girls aged 11 plus and 13 plus	Co-ed schools	32	14·9	60	27·9	80	37·2	33	15·3	10	4·7	215	100
	Girls' schools	37	17·0	59	27·0	90	41·2	23	10·6	6	2·8	218	100
Girls aged 15 plus and 17 plus	Co-ed schools	24	20·9	37	32·2	39	33·9	12	10·4	3	2·6	115	100
	Girls' schools	28	23·1	33	27·3	41	34·0	9	7·4	9	7·4	121	100
Boys aged 11 plus and 13 plus	Co-ed schools	28	12·4	57	25·2	106	47·0	22	9·7	12	5·3	226	100
	Boys' schools	27	12·3	78	35·5	88	39·9	16	7·3	8	3·6	220	100
Boys aged 15 plus and 17 plus	Co-ed schools	20	14·9	36	26·9	60	44·8	10	7·5	7	5·2	134	100
	Boys' schools	31	22·6	39	28·5	52	37·9	12	8·8	3	2·2	137	100

[1] Includes a few unclassifiables. In the tables in the text the unclassifiables are sometimes omitted.

NOTE: The analysis is based on occupations and follows the classification used in the Early Leaving Report, *viz.* class 1 professional, managerial, executive; class 2 clerical occupations; class 3 skilled occupations; class 4 partly skilled; class 5 unskilled.

TABLE A2.6 *Occupational class composition of the 'Check' sample*

Occupational class of pupils' parents

	I		2		3		4		5		Totals[1]	
	N	%	N	%	N	%	N	%	N	%	N	%
Girls in co-ed schools	88	19·6	95	21·2	184	41·0	51	11·4	22	4·9	449	100
Girls in girls' schools	149	22·1	152	22·6	289	42·9	54	8·0	23	3·4	673	100

NOTE: One school became co-educational and another was discovered to be comprehensive. These together with their 'matched' schools are excluded.
[1] Includes 15 unclassifiable.

TABLE A2.7 *The drop-out problem*

School anxiety test 1964: comparison of mean scores for leavers and the remainder of the sample (age 11 plus—longitudinal sample)

Schools project

	1964 sample		Leavers and absentees		Remainder 1964 sample	
Girls						
co-educated	236	12·52	25	11·2	211	12·45
from girls' schools	238	12·61	21	14·3	217	12·43
Boys						
co-educated	235	11·10	13	9·8	222	11·17
from boys' schools	238	11·73	20	12·55	218	11·65

TABLE A2.8 *Percentages of pupils having marks of 300 and over, and percentages having marks of less than 100: N. Ireland Senior Leaving Certificate, 1957 (Sutherland)*

Subjects	Number % having marks of 300 and over			
	Co-ed boys	Boys in boys' schools	Co-ed girls	Girls in girls' schools
English lang.	1·48	1·76	1·50	1·88
English lit.	1·36	1·62	4·14	3·86
Latin	7·22	2·56	7·53	4·00
French	2·23	2·47	3·86	3·48
History	1·87	0·00	1·97	1·17
Trad. maths	10·53	5·26	6·61	8·26
Alt. maths	34·33	17·74	17·51	14·14
Geography	1·37	0·60	0·69	1·61
Physics	6·71	6·88	8·11	5·09
Chemistry	8·59	4·32	6·20	10·00

	Number % having marks of less than 100			
English lang.	0·56	0·50	0·00	0·00
English lit.	3·50	3·78	3·22	0·72
Latin	7·22	19·66	2·15	0·27
French	11·36	11·78	7·26	3·73
History	5·02	8·88	11·84	8·59
Trad. maths	8·42	17·54	9·92	9·92
Alt. maths	0·92	4·89	5·00	2·62
Geography	0·68	2·38	4·12	2·90
Physics	0·58	4·20	2·70	0·00
Chemistry	0·00	6·15	0·00	2·22

TABLE A2.9 *Social class of examination candidates (Sutherland): Protestant schools in Northern Ireland*

	Social class								
	Farmers	a	b	c	d	e	f	g	Unclassified
Boys (seg.)	31	55	56	44	54	31	46	23	57
(co-ed)	76	49	32	41	78	42	69	40	112
Girls (seg.)	46	61	57	47	56	30	37	24	68
(co-ed)	95	41	31	48	59	35	42	39	77

Appendix 2

TABLE A2.10 *Northern Ireland Ordinary level results[1]* (*1968*)

Schools:	Boys Co-ed Vol.	Boys Co-ed County	Boys Single-sex Vol.	Girls Co-ed Vol.	Girls Co-ed County	Girls Single-sex Vol.	Girls Single-sex County
Qualified pupils							
Subjects attempted by examinees 1						1	1
2						1	
3	1					1	1
4							
5	2	1	1			3	5
6	8	5	19	6	4	34	9
7	26	57	201	23	89	191	55
8	151	123	402	154	134	375	101
9	165	66	394	117	79	211	81
10	30	18	39	11	15	48	29
11	2	13			4		
Subjects passed by examinees 0	4	2	10	1		3	3
1	9	7	19	5	2	6	7
2	7	14	36	9	12	20	4
3	19	16	54	14	20	42	16
4	14	11	79	18	23	78	16
5	30	24	105	28	30	96	27
6	45	34	139	38	50	118	42
7	66	60	199	52	65	163	54
8	95	65	219	78	74	183	53
9	81	31	182	61	40	124	40
10	13	10	14	7	6	32	20
11	2	9			3		
Non-examinees Early leavers, 1963–4						2	
1964–5	2	1	11	2	4	23	3
1965–6	6	9	44	6	19	35	5
1966–7	1	4	6	1		3	4
Still at G.S.	11	10	29	3	4	45	5
Transferred G.S.	16	14	36	9	10	39	16
Transferred T.S.	2	12	23	9	20	51	8
Transferred S.S.		4	28	2	5	17	5
Unknown	5	5	50	11	7	18	3
Deceased		1	2	1			2
Totals	**428**	**343**	**1285**	**355**	**394**	**1098**	**333**

[1] By permission of N. Ireland Council for Educational Research (Report of the Review Procedure Panel, follow-up study, February 1969).

TABLE A2.11   *Pressure of work for examinations worrying (males)*

'*Both schools*' *survey*

| | Replies from ex-pupils about 'first' schools | | | | Replies from ex-pupils about 'last' schools | | | |
| | Co-ed schools | | Boys' schools | | Co-ed schools | | Boys' schools | |
	N	%	N	%	N	%	N	%
Agree strongly	5	6·0	13	10·9	9	8·7	7	9·9
Agree	17	20·5	34	28·6	31	29·8	25	35·2
Doubtful	15	18·1	23	19·3	25	24·0	16	22·6
Disagree	30	36·1	38	32·0	27	26·0	17	23·9
Disagree strongly	16	19·3	11	9·2	12	11·5	6	8·4
Totals	83	100	119	100	104	100	71	100

NOTE: The difference between co-educated boys and those from boys' schools is a little short of statistical significance, but that for senior pupils, though smaller, is in the same direction.

TABLE A2.12   *Pressure of work made me anxious (males)*

'*Both schools*' *survey*

| | Replies from ex-pupils about 'first' schools | | | | Replies from ex-pupils about 'last' schools | | | |
| | Co-ed schools | | Boys' schools | | Co-ed schools | | Boys' schools | |
	N	%	N	%	N	%	N	%
Very anxious	4	4·8	10	8·4	5	4·8	4	5·7
Anxious	6	7·2	28	23·5	16	15·4	17	24·3
A little anxious	34	41·0	33	27·7	49	47·1	27	38·6
No effect	39	47·0	48	40·4	34	32·7	22	31·4
Totals	83	100	119	100	104	100	70	100

NOTE: The difference between the co-educated juniors and those from boys' schools is statistically significant almost at the 0·01 level.

Appendix 2

TABLE A2.13   *Pressure of work made me anxious (females)*

'Both schools' survey

| | Replies from ex-pupils from 'first' schools | | | | Replies from ex-pupils from 'last' schools | | | |
| | Co-ed schools | | Girls' schools | | Co-ed schools | | Girls' schools | |
	N	%	N	%	N	%	N	%
Very anxious	2	0·7	36	9·0	7	2·0	24	9·3
Anxious	39	13·1	83	20·7	57	16·0	63	24·3
A little anxious	144	48·3	144	35·9	186	52·2	106	40·9
No effect	113	37·9	138	34·4	106	29·8	66	25·5
Totals	298	100	401	100	356	100	259	100

NOTE: The difference between co-educational and girls' schools is statistically highly significant both for 'first' and for 'last' schools.

TABLE A2.14 *Free responses on anxiety about work (females, 'first' schools)*

'Both schools' survey

Estimate	Comment	Co-ed schools	Girls' schools
Very anxious	standard very high, large amount homework		2
	high standard demanded—otherwise a failure		1
	pressure re examinations	1	
	exams excessive pressure, terrified, threats		6
	staff inaccessible, attitude one teacher		2
	only clever girls counted		1
	not used to atmosphere		1
	nervous—illness resulted; cried frequently		3
	nervous illness—pressure of work and presence of boys	1	
Anxious	general, not specific	2	3
	standard very high, large amount homework	4	3
	work and exams all-important, competitive tense atmosphere	2	9
	examination time mostly	3	1
	afraid speak if doubtful, teacher unhelpful		3
	staff belittle chances pass exams		1
	didn't want let teacher down		1
	particularly some subjects	5	1
	weak subjects, lost confidence	1	3
	the place terrified me, always anxious		3
	larger school than used to		1
	rivalry between sexes	1	
	partly parents' ambition	2	
	others	2	2

TABLE A2.14—*contd*

Estimate	Comment	Co-ed schools	Girls' schools
A little anxious	general, not specific	6	5
	school high level, staff never satisfied		4
	homework, neglect of, too late	6	1
	examinations only or particularly	26	14
	at times	4	
	harsh punishments about work	1	3
	impatient teachers, inadequate teaching		2
	wanted high stream, keep up	14	9
	certain subjects only	7	
	boys so good, especially science	2	
	ability poor, felt inferior	2	
	worrying disposition, unsure	4	3
	overawed by large school	1	
	parents' ambition	1	
	enough, necessary	4	1
	but exciting not worrying	1	
	more pressure than co-ed		2
	but less than co-ed		1
	others	2	3
No effect	general, not specific	2	6
	little or no pressure, especially lower forms steady rate	19	11
	work too little, low standard	2	2
	enjoyed work and good marks	2	1
	pressures do not worry	3	
	only 'exam nerves'	2	1
	competition worried		1
	determined pass O-levels		1
	better here than any school	1	
	not conscientious	4	2
	others	2	

TABLE A2.15   *The intense pressure of work at school worries me*

Schools project (girls)

| | Replies from girls aged 13 plus | | | | Replies from girls aged 17 plus | | | |
| | Co-ed schools | | Girls' schools | | Co-ed schools | | Girls' schools | |
	N	%	N	%	N	%	N	%
Agree strongly	13	6·0	22	10·3	10	8·7	10	8·3
Agree	71	33·1	46	21·5	41	35·7	55	45·9
Doubtful	56	26·0	76	35·5	19	16·5	16	13·3
Disagree	63	29·3	53	24·8	38	33·0	35	29·2
Disagree strongly	12	5·6	17	7·9	7	6·1	4	3·3
Totals	215	100	214	100	115	100	120	100

NOTE: See text for comment on statistical significance.

TABLE A2.16   *Afraid to speak out in class: free responses of boys (13 plus)*

Schools project

Always + often + sometimes	Co-ed schools	Single-sex schools
Afraid to be wrong, look foolish, laughed at	35	41
embarrassed, lack confidence, shy, hate it	24	31
forget what I'm saying, lost for words	3	2
out of my depth	1	
dislike being disagreed with	2	1
not good speaker	1	2
stammer	3	
depends on teacher	7	9
teacher finds fault, sarcastic, annoyed		3
teacher not helpful	1	
depends on subject (+ teacher?)	6	6
not enough practice	1	3
when speaking French	1	
depends what one has to say	1	
don't know anybody	1	
about personal things		1
others, general	13	10
Totals	100	109

TABLE A2.17 *Afraid to speak out in class: free responses of boys (17 plus)*

Schools project

Always + often + sometimes	Co-ed schools	Single-sex schools
afraid to be wrong, look foolish, laughed at	28	30
embarrassed, lack confidence, hate it	6	3
nothing to say	1	
own views uncertain	1	
views different	1	
introvert	1	
stutter	2	1
opportunity rare		1
depends on teacher	1	4
teacher unhelpful	1	3
depends on subject (+ teacher?)	1	5
depends on mood		1
too much trouble		1
depends who in class	1	
others	2	2
Totals	46	51

TABLE A2.18 *Liking for arithmetic: 15 plus girls by social class*

Schools project, 1964 full sample

	Co-educated				Girls' schools			
Social class:	1 & 2	3	4 & 5	Total[1]	1 & 2	3	4 & 5	Total
Like much	30	13	8	51	21	32	6	59
Like a little	38	21	11	71	42	40	12	95
Neither like nor dislike	25	22	14	61	18	21	12	51
Dislike a little	12	34	8	54	19	17	13	49
Dislike much	16	23	4	43	13	10	3	26
Totals	121	113	45	280	113	120	46	280
Weighted means	3·45	2·71	3·22	3·12	3·31	3·56	3·11	3·40

[1] Includes a few unclassifiables.

TABLE A2.19 *Playing-fields provision*[1]

'*Both schools*' survey

Replies to 'Were the playing-fields around (or adjacent to) the school?'	Replies from male ex-pupils				Replies from female ex-pupils			
	Co-ed schools		Boys' schools		Co-ed schools		Girls' schools	
	N	%	N	%	N	%	N	%
Yes	129	66·2	114	62·6	482	73·8	481	72·4
No	40	20·5	51	28·0	99	15·2	113	17·0
Part	26	13·3	17	9·4	54	8·3	52	7·9
No replies					18	2·7	18	2·7
Totals	195	100	182	100	653	100	664	100

[1] The estimates are not one estimate per ex-pupil but one estimate by each ex-pupil for each of the two or three schools attended. A number of pupils would have attended some of the schools, and the exact number of schools is unknown but it must have been several hundreds.

TABLE A2.20 *The organized games were enjoyable*

'*Both schools*' survey (*men*)

	Replies about 'first' schools attended				Replies about 'last' schools attended			
	Co-ed schools		Boys' schools		Co-ed schools		Boys' schools	
	N	%	N	%	N	%	N	%
Agree strongly	28	33·7	27	22·8	27	26·0	20	28·2
Agree	30	36·2	51	43·3	44	42·3	21	29·6
Doubtful	12	14·5	19	16·1	20	19·2	17	23·9
Disagree	8	9·6	10	8·5	11	10·6	9	12·7
Disagree strongly	5	6·0	11	9·3	2	1·9	4	5·6
Totals	83	100	118	100	104	100	71	100

TABLE A2.21 *Girls' attitude to hockey*

Schools project

| | Replies from 15 plus girls (1964) | | | | Replies from 17 plus girls (1966) | | | |
| | Co-ed schools | | Girls' schools | | Co-ed schools | | Girls' schools | |
	N	%	N	%	N	%	N	%
Like much	54	47·3	35	32·3	43	37·7	29	26·9
Like a little	23	20·2	31	28·7	28	24·6	28	25·9
Undecided	3	2·6	2	1·9	1	0·9	8	7·4
Dislike a little	19	16·7	18	16·7	14	12·3	15	13·9
Dislike much	15	13·2	22	20·4	28	24·5	28	25·9
Totals	114	100	108	100	114	100	108	100

TABLE A2.22 *Girls' hockey: change of attitude*

Schools project, 15 plus and 17 plus girls

	Co-ed schools	Girls' schools
Attitude improved	14	9
Attitude same	66	67
Attitude declined	32	32

TABLE A2.23 *The organized games were enjoyable*

'Both schools' survey (women)

| | Replies about 'first' schools attended | | | | Replies about 'last' schools attended | | | |
| | Co-ed schools | | Girls' schools | | Co-ed schools | | Girls' schools | |
	N	%	N	%	N	%	N	%
Agree strongly	63	21·2	53	13·1	61	17·2	41	15·9
Agree	138	46·5	179	44·2	151	42·7	102	39·7
Doubtful	57	19·2	83	20·5	86	24·3	62	24·1
Disagree	33	11·1	71	17·5	35	9·9	39	15·2
Disagree strongly	6	2·0	19	4·7	21	5·9	13	5·1
Totals	297	100	405	100	354	100	257	100

Appendix 3

The Douglas National Sample: A fundamental fallacy[1]

This criticism deliberately begins with an acknowledgment of the good work done by Douglas and Ross with their national sample of children. The section which is criticized[2] is only a small part of the whole, but the criticism is important because, first, it pinpoints a fault in procedure and interpretation which could occur again in the same or in other important surveys, and second, because the misleading conclusions are being quoted and might lead to wrong decisions in national educational policy.

Douglas and Ross followed up a national sample of children from birth until they went to secondary schools and took the General Certificate of Education at Ordinary level, or left school beforehand. They then compared the academic level in arithmetic and English at 11 plus of those at co-educational schools with those at single-sex schools, and by testing again at 15 plus claimed to be assessing the academic 'advantages' and 'disadvantages' of co-educational and single-sex schooling. The present writer insists that this procedure is quite invalid because it produces two grossly unequal samples, biased heavily in social class and in IQ in favour of the single-sex schools. The writer's reasons for stating this are given below, and because of this invalidity the findings of Douglas and Ross are not presented. As, however, their findings are in part contradictory to the general trends of research it is the writer's duty to the public to give in detail the reasons for this rejection.

Before doing this, however, mention is made of two points raised by Douglas. He tries to explain the discrepancy between his own findings and those of other research studies by contrasting his own 'national sample' with 'the few local studies'. This is thoroughly misleading, because there are no less than seven other studies which refute his findings, and they are all regional rather than local, three of them with thousands of pupils and hundreds of schools and the remaining four can without exaggeration be termed large-scale. From 1923 to 1969 they produce, over almost 50 years, the same type of findings. In contrast to the reliability given by the large numbers in these researches the

---

[1] Much of this appendix was published in *Bulletin Br. Psychol. Soc.*, 23 (1970), 4, 223–5.
[2] Chapter 10 in *All Our Future* (1968) by J. W. B. Douglas *et al.*, published also, with small changes in *Where*, 25 (1966).

Douglas national sample had only 269 pupils in mixed grammar schools, of which (because more girls are selected than boys) there would only be at best some 120 boys. When this is divided unequally into middle and working class (because the middle class are less well represented in co-educational grammar schools in the sample than in single-sex schools) the middle class group is probably only about fifty in size, and badly biased for social class and intelligence in addition. This seems to be a very dubious foundation on which to pronounce national findings about the relative efficacy of co-educational and single-sex schooling. Readers of this book will also be aware of other variables handicapping the co-educational schools which are not allowed for in the Douglas and Ross findings even though one or two are mentioned earlier in the chapter. The above account gives the reader a general picture, but some more technical detail follows.

At the outset the sample is probably impeccably selected, but later the children underwent a second selection—not controlled by Douglas and Ross—to determine whether they went to a grammar school or not. The researchers themselves divided the sample once again into those who attended (a) co-educational schools and (b) single-sex schools, and compared their progress by giving tests of reading and arithmetic at 11 and 15 years of age. They then asked whether the 'disadvantages' of co-education for the boys are outweighed by the 'advantages' for the girls. This is where the fallacy lies. Whereas it would have been reasonably valid to have compared the attainment level of the two (or four) groups of children without attributing any causal effect to the type of schooling, it is certainly not valid to do otherwise.

The reason for this is that in practice different criteria are used for selection for co-educational grammar schools compared with those used for single-sex grammar schools, producing from the national sample two selected samples which are unequal in intelligence and in social class—two qualities rather important not only for attainment on entry at 11 but also for quality of progress at school (which the researchers tested and commented on). The same argument applies to the contrasted secondary modern groups.

There are a number of reasons for the differences in selection criteria, stemming mostly from the situation of many co-educational secondary schools in less populous areas, whereas the single-sex schools are more frequently in the cities and large towns—and especially at the period of the survey. Possibly because of depopulation the rural co-educational grammar schools accept an appreciably higher proportion of the 11 plus age group than the city single-sex schools do (markedly so in Wales where the intake rises to 40 per cent or even higher in some counties, compared with 13 per cent for SE England where the schools were mostly single-sex). The children in single-sex grammar schools will therefore tend to be higher in intelligence and also in social class (for the latter cf. Sutherland's survey). By an interesting phenomenon the higher the cut-off line for grammar school selection the higher is the mean intelligence level not only of the grammar pupils but also that of the secondary modern pupils—and similarly for social class.

Douglas and Ross try to equate the two types of school for social class effects by dividing their samples into 'middle' and 'manual working class', but this represents equality in name only as the single-sex schools would be expected to have a greater proportion of class 1 (or higher middle) under the heading 'middle',[1] while the co-educated would similarly have a greater proportion of classes 4 and 5 (as against 3) under 'manual working class'. This danger in coarse grouping is ignored in many researches.

Again, for many purposes the sample included all the relevant children of agricultural workers, but only one-quarter of all other manual workers. If this still holds good for the above section of the work it would bias the sample against co-educational schools because the full quota of their least promising children academically would be included, but only one-quarter for single-sex schools. The argument holds even if one compares only the 'manual working class' category for the two types of school, because within this category the urban single-sex schools would have a representative sample (if we ignore the selection criterion), but the co-educational schools sample would be overweighted at the bottom end.

In short, the further a national sample gets from its starting point the more it is subjected to new forms of 'selection' and to attenuation, and the possibility for valid judgments about cause and effect is steadily diminished.

In view of the above remarks it should be noted that the large-scale surveys of Tyson, Clark, Gott, Walton and Sutherland reach a remarkable consensus in their comparisons of attainment in co-educational and single-sex grammar schools, but the findings of Douglas and Ross are discrepant from these and lack a logical pattern internally. This consensus is that in state grammar schools co-educated boys reach a rather higher standard of attainment in most subjects at O-level than do boys in single-sex state grammar schools, while the co-educated girls reach a slightly lower standard (in a majority of subjects) than their opposite numbers, the difference between the girls' groups being not as large as

[1] Douglas in *All Our Future*, p. 68, actually gives data on this—whereas just over half the manual working class in the sample were at co-educational schools, these schools included only two-fifths of the lower middle class and only one-quarter of the upper middle class. The single-sex and co-educational sub-samples are therefore so unequal that the concept of using them to compare the part played by the two types of school in securing academic progress is not really tenable.

that between the boys'. This however is only the raw difference, before taking into account variables such as social class, percentage of intake to the 11 plus population, age at taking the examination (girls), and the dropping of weak subjects (girls), all of which handicap the co-educational grammar schools in the comparison. If these are allowed for, the co-educational grammar schools are shown in an even more favourable light.

Though the necessity for brevity in this analysis has led to some over-simplification, the provision of further detail would not change the conclusions.

Annotated bibliography

This bibliography includes mainly books which make a research contribution to the subject of co-education in secondary schools or add to our knowledge of the topic in other ways.

The voluminous research on psychological sex differences is excluded unless the work is directly concerned with co-education. As the historical and comparative sides of the topic were not part of the writer's research plan these are only thinly covered. Articles which merely reiterate arguments for or against co-education are omitted except for a few pioneer versions. Comments are necessarily brief. Asterisked books are those mentioned in the text of the present volume.

Bibliographical

BREUSE, E. (1970), *La Coéducation dans les écoles mixtes*, Paris. The references are mostly French and for the most part are useful discussions of the topic without adding much to our knowledge, though a few others present research findings.

DALE, R. R. (1969, 1971), *Mixed or single-sex school?* vols I, II, Routledge & Kegan Paul, London. Most references in vols I and II are now included in Grandpré, and in the present volume, in which the notes are intended to aid researchers.

EDWARDS, R. (c.1971), 'Co-education. An annotated, partial bibliography', McGill University, Toronto (mim.). Coverage slight but notes detailed, mainly historical and general.

GRANDPRÉ, MARCEL DE (1970), *La Coéducation dans les écoles officielles et les écoles catholiques de 45 pays*, Montreal. An inclusive, thorough and scholarly bibliography. International in character, its usefulness is increased by a discerning commentary in chapter 6, though the final conclusion ignores the weight of evidence for western civilizations. It is of interest that the survey was aided by L'Office International de l'Enseignement Catholique.

General

ACADÉMIE DE GRENOBLE, FRANCE (1970), 'Journées académiques des surveillants généraux'. *Rapport de la Commission No. 4: Les Problèmes de la mixité* (mim.).

ACADÉMIE D'AIX-EN-PROVENCE, FRANCE (1970), *Rapport de la Commission No. 5: La Psychologie de l'adolescent et la mixité* (mim.). Illustrates the ferment in France on this problem.

*ADAMS, JOHN (1924), *Educational Movements and Methods*, London, Chapter 1, Sir. B. Gott, 'Co-educational and dual schools'. Examination results in Middlesex schools. 'The results of the Matriculation and General Schools examination of London University shows (for Middlesex schools) fairly uniformly, year after year, that girls do very much better in mixed schools than they do in girls' schools and that boys do equally well and often better in mixed schools.'

ALLENDY, R. and LOBSTEIN, A. (1948), *Sex problems in school* (tr. E. Larsen), London. Chapter on co-education; of pupils in one co-educational school all except one boy and two girls content to stay co-educated.

ALVA PLASENCIA, J. L. (1961), *Cinco anos de coeducacion*, Lima.

ANASTASI, A. (1958), *Differential Psychology*, New York. Chapter 14, important for sex differences. Good bibliography.

ARNOLD, DR THOMAS (1878), *Selected sermons preached at Rugby College*, London, vol. II, No. 7. Homosexuality in the single-sex Public Schools.

ASP, E. (1964), *Teachers' conception of a mixed class as an educational environment*, report from the Institute of Education, No. 6, University of Turku, Finland.

ASSOCIATION OF HEADMISTRESSES (1935), *Report of a Conference at the Haberdashers Hall*, London. Mainly arguments against co-education, in address by Dr Brock. Intellectual differences between the sexes, and girls of that age need the guidance of women.

ASSOCIATION OF HEADMISTRESSES (1968), *Sauce for the Goose? The education of girls*, London.

*ATHERTON, B. F. (1971), 'The relative merits of co-educational and single-sex schools with special reference to the happiness of marriage of former pupils', M.Sc. thesis, University College of Swansea. Breaks new ground. Large-scale statistical. Results favour co-education.

AUSTRALIAN COUNCIL FOR EDUCATIONAL RESEARCH (1948), *Opinions of Victorian Teachers on Co-education*, Bulletin No. 11, Melbourne. In Gallup Poll of parents in 1947 a small majority of parents favoured co-education, and in 1945–6 teachers by questionnaire gave a large majority in favour. Also Bulletin No. 32, 1954, Melbourne.

BADLEY, J. H. (1914), *Co-education in Practice*, Cambridge and London. Experience of a headmaster.

BADLEY, J. H. (1920), *Co-education and its part in a complete education*, Cambridge.

BADLEY, J. H. (1923), *Bedales: A Pioneer School*, London.

BARR, F. (1959), 'Urban and rural differences in ability and attainment', *Educ. Research*, 1, 2, London. Summary of research; implications for co-education.

*BARTLETT, D. B. (1948), 'The attitudes of boys and girls to the content and methods of teaching geography in grammar schools', M.A. thesis, London. Large scale. Need for differentiation between sexes in method and content, but wide individual differences should be catered for. Sex differences in attitude to the major sections of the subject not so marked as differences in attitudes to individual topics. The broad content may be similar for both sexes.

BASTIN, G., (1966), 'Enquête sur l'école mixte', *Enfance*, 4–5, pp. 25–43, Paris. Useful study within one school. Girls especially favour co-education.

BASTIN, G. (1968), 'Introduction à un dialogue sur la coéducation', *Bulletin d'Information No. 2*, Ministère de l'éducation nationale, Bruxelles.

BEAUMONT, G. P. (1957), 'A study in the construction and application of a scale measuring the attitude of adolescents towards the use of force', M.A. thesis, London (summary *Br. J. Educ. Psychol.*, June 1959). Useful idea but underestimates importance of social class. Only one school of each type. Pupil sample very small.

BENDER, M. R. (1962), 'Do prospective teachers desire a co-educational environment in the secondary schools in which they wish to teach?', MS (study at St Paul's College, Cheltenham). Of 241 students 63 per cent preferred to teach in a co-educational school and 17 per cent in a single-sex school. Only 32 per cent were co-educated.

BERGE, A. (1966), 'Mixité et co-éducation', *Cahiers Pédagogiques*, 59, Percipient analysis of interaction of the sexes in co-educational schools.

BIBBY, CYRIL (1946), *Sex Education*, London. Much on advantages of co-education, e.g. pp. 91, 106, 112, 115.

*BLACKWELL, A. M. (1950–6), *List of Researches in Education and Educational Psychology* (and Supplements), NFER, London.

BOARD OF EDUCATION (1923), *Report of the Consultative Committee on the Differentiation of the Curriculum*, London. Still a valuable résumé of arguments and of facts. Concludes differentiation (by sex) neither 'practical nor desirable' (p. 105). See Appendix 3.

BOARD OF EDUCATION: Consultative Committee (1926), *Report on the education of the adolescent* (Hadow Report), London. Brief pronouncement against co-education as a policy (p. 91).

*BOOTH, J. W. (1967), 'An examination of the hypothesis that the sex of the teacher is a source of variance in the O-Level NUJMB mathematics results of pupils in certain co-educational grammar schools', M.A. thesis, University College of Swansea. Large sample of pupils. The female teachers had better results than the men in geometry; awaits replication.

*BOTTOMS, S. H. (1953), 'An investigation into the attitude of grammar school children towards the study of physical geography', M.Ed. thesis, Leeds. Valuable analysis of this topic for the researcher in co-education. In co-educational schools no difference between the sexes in liking. Bibliography.

Annotated bibliography

*BREUSE, E. (1970), *La Coéducation dans les écoles mixtes*, Paris. Valuable appraisal of the special needs of co-educational schools, special pedagogy, training of teachers. 'La mixité' must be real and not a pretence. Also questionnaire to 71 teachers who had taught in both co-educational and single-sex schools; the results favoured co-education. Reports other useful enquiries. Statistics of co-education in France, p. 65. Good historical, recent comparative and analytical aspects.

BROWNE, M. (1918), *Dream of youth*, London. Defence of public schools, but unconscious plea for co-education in chapter on morality.

BRUNSCHWIG, O. G. (1964), 'L'éducation mixte', *Pédagogie*, September. Co-education inevitable—shortage of male teachers etc; also desirable. Practical problems and advice. (*Inspectrice générale de l'Ed. Nat.*)

BUBER, M. (1937), *I and Thou* (tr. R. Gregor Smith), Edinburgh. Social education. 'Children are being educated the whole day long, by all those, both contemporary and older, whom they meet.' '. . . our education consists of contacts with things and persons, but contacts with persons are the most significant, for persons grow above all through personal relations.'

BULLOCK, R. (1967), 'The co-educational boarding schools', *Where*, 33, p. 9 *seq.*, September.

BURKS, A. W. (1966), 'Gains in social adjustment of co-educational classes and segregated classes in physical education', University of Arkansas, Diss. Abstracts 27, 3.

BURNESS, G. F. (1912), *La Coéducation dans les écoles secondaires*, Lille. Head of West Ham Municipal Secondary School. Compares examination results of his boys and girls. Discusses problems of teaching mixed classes, organization etc.

*BURT, C. (1921), *Mental and Scholastic Tests*, London. Useful early comparison of the abilities of boys and girls with a note on the possible modification of differences between them in co-educational schools.

BURY, J. H. (1941), 'The development of co-education in English secondary schools', M.A. thesis, Reading. Some good chapters, especially on the history of co-education. Good bibliography.

*CAIRNS, T. (1953), 'Interest in history shown by secondary school pupils with special reference to the aims of history teaching', M.A. thesis, King's College, Newcastle. Useful attempt to ascertain the relative appeal of different aspects of history to the two sexes in school.

CALO, GIOVANNI (1914), *Il problema della co-educazione*, Milan. Early Italian interest.

*CAMERON, A. E. (1923), 'A comparative study of the mathematical abilities of girls and boys in secondary schools', M.A. thesis, London (summary *Br. J. Psychol.*, 16, part 1, 1925). By a headmistress of a girls' grammar school. A useful study, using special tests, but some uneven features in co-educational versus single-sex school sampling, favouring the single-sex schools. Results are in favour of co-educated girls as opposed to girls from girls' schools.

302

CAMPBELL, DUDLEY (1874), *Mixed Education of Boys and Girls in England and America* (pamphlet), London. Far-sighted pioneer.

CAMPBELL, E. H. (1939), 'The social-sex development of children', *Genetic Psychol. Monograph*, 21.

*CAMPBELL, R. J. (1969), 'Co-education: attitudes and self-concepts of girls at three schools', *Br. J. Educ. Psychol*, 39, 1, p. 87, February (based on M.Sc. thesis, Bradford, 1968). Research study.

*CAMPBELL, W. J. (1952), 'The influence of home environment on the educational progress of selective secondary school children', *Br. J. Educ. Psychol.*, 22, 2. Indirect concern only.

CAPRIO, F. S. (1959), *Female Homosexuality*, London (p. 268). 'The separation of the sexes is the surest method of confirming homosexual tendencies in young people if they have any predisposition of that sort.'

*CENTRAL ADVISORY COUNCIL FOR EDUCATION (ENGLAND) (1954), *Early Leaving report*, London.

CENTRAL ADVISORY COUNCIL FOR EDUCATION (ENGLAND) (1959), *Fifteen to Eighteen* (Crowther Report) pp. 253-4. London. Proportions of pupils in science sixth forms in co-educational schools.

CHAMP, J. (1948), 'The attitude of women towards teaching as a career', M.A. thesis, London. Quotes survey among sixth form pupils. But no allowance for boarding and social class variables. p. 149: case study of woman with 'strong dislike of working in an entirely feminine community'. Champ says typifies large number of young teachers.

CHMARA, MARIE S. (1959), 'Personal and social adjustment in co-educational and separate Catholic secondary schools', thesis, Wayne State University, Detroit. Reports no significant effect on personal adjustment. Pupils in single-sex schools reported greater satisfaction with school. (Last finding is contrary to findings of other researchers.) [Is this an unconscious bias due to the traditional opposition of the Roman Catholic church to co-education?] Chmara states herself that generalization of these findings is dangerous as there were only three schools (one of each type). The mixed school was staffed by nuns; it was also parochial while the others were not.

CHRISTIAN AUXILIARY MOVEMENT, 'The attitude of sixth form pupils to science and religion', in Champ, J. (1948). Questionnaires completed by pupils of sixty-four schools. Co-educational and single-sex schools compared, but no mention of social or boarding differences in their pupil entries.

*CLARK, G. (1937), 'Co-education', M.A. thesis, Liverpool. A percipient analysis of the work and principles of the mixed school. Valuable discussion of the replies of 72 heads of co-educational schools to a questionnaire. Ninety per cent of them had also taught in boys' schools. Pupil leadership by personality and suitability, not sex. Heads report sexual difficulties of adolescence decreased by co-education. Single-sex schools build up a 'sex potential'. Good historical section. Comparative attainment co-educational and single-sex schools (large-scale).

COLLINS, M. (1964), *Women graduates and the teaching profession*, Manchester, pp. 29, 33. Sound large-scale enquiry. Some useful findings relating to co-education.

COMAS, M. (1931), *La coeducacion de los sexos*, Madrid.

COMBER, C. L. (1938), 'The scientific interests of boys and girls in relation to the teaching of sciences', M.A. thesis, London. Most girls interested in biological science and most boys prefer physical sciences.

COMMISSION ON EDUCATION IN NEW ZEALAND (1962), *Report*, Wellington. p. 223: 'The matter is of much less ultimate importance than would sometimes appear from the debate upon it.' It therefore makes no recommendation.

COURTOIS, C. (1967), *Coéducation et mixité*, Paris.

*CROFTS, J. M. and JONES, D. C. (1928), *Secondary School Examination Statistics*, London. In spite of its date, invaluable for comparison of the attainment of boys and girls.

CROWTHER REPORT, *see* Central Advisory Council for Education (England) (1959).

CURRIE, K. (1962), 'A study of the English comprehensive school system with particular reference to the educational, social and cultural effects of the single-sex and co-educational type of school', Ph.D. thesis, London. Useful ideas and procedures for future research. But the inclusion of comprehensive, secondary grammar and secondary modern schools as well as co-educational and single-sex makes the study too wide. There seem to have been too few schools of each type. How were pupils matched? Was social class controlled sufficiently? Why did only one school assist in the test administration?

CURRY, W. B. (1947), *Education for Sanity*, London. Gives his experience at Dartington Hall school as talks between the headmaster and a visitor. Strongly for co-education.

CURTIS, E. (1906), *An Uppingham for boys and girls*, Oxford.

*DAINES, J. W. (1949), 'A psychological study of the attitude of adolescents to religion and religious instruction', Ph.D. thesis, London.

DALE, R. R. Most of the contributions to journals under this name are incorporated in chapters of the three volumes but are listed because they often include additional material.

(1949), 'Co-education: an enquiry', *Times Educational Supplement*, 28 August 1948. Reprinted in *Childhood and Youth*, January.

(1949), 'Co-education and the modern age', Assistant Masters Association, September.

(1955), 'Co-education: The verdict of experience', *Br. J. Educ. Psychol.*, November.

(1962), 'Co-education: A critical analysis of research on the effects of co-education on academic attainment in grammar schools—I', *Educational Research*, June.

(1962), 'Co-education: A critical analysis of research on comparative attainment in mathematics in single-sex and co-educational grammar schools—II', *Educational Research*, November.

(1964), 'Co-education: Comparative attainment in English in single-sex and co-educational grammar schools respectively—III', *Educational Research*, June.

(1965), 'Research on co-education', *New Education*, April.

(1965), 'Co-education: The verdict of experience—II: a qualitative approach', *Br. J. Educ. Psychol.*, June.

(1965), 'Teachers of mathematics in Northern Ireland grammar schools', *Northern Teacher*, October.

(1966), 'A comparison of the academic qualifications of teachers of mathematics in single-sex and co-educational grammar schools respectively, in three contrasted areas', *Educational Review*, February.

(1966), 'The happiness of pupils in co-educational and single-sex grammar schools: a comparative assessment', *Br. J. Educ. Psychol.*, February.

(1966), 'A study of the comparative popularity of organized physical activities among girls in girls' grammar schools and girls in co-educational grammar schools respectively', *Research Papers*, Carnegie College of Education, April.

(1966), 'A study of the comparative popularity of organized physical activities among boys in boys' grammar schools and boys in co-educational grammar schools respectively', *Research Papers*, Carnegie College of Education, April.

(1966), 'Are children happy at co-educational schools?', *Where*, 28, October.

(1966), 'Pupil–teacher relationships in single-sex and co-educational grammar schools: a comparative assessment', *Br. J. Educ. Psychol.*, November.

(1967), 'A study of the comparative popularity of cookery and needlework among girls in girls' grammar schools and girls in co-educational grammar schools respectively', *University College of Swansea Faculty of Education Journal*.

(1967), 'Teachers who have had a good influence', *Education for Teaching*, February.

(1967), 'A tentative comparison between co-educational and single-sex schooling as possible minor influences on the desire for marriage', *Br. J. Educ. Psychol.*, February.

(1967), 'Attainment in co-educational secondary schools: a reply', *Educational Research*, June.

(1967), 'Co-ed or single-sex. An answer to Douglas and Ross', *Where*, 31, May.

(1967), 'Teachers who have had a bad influence', *Education for Teaching*, Autumn.

(1967), 'The comparative incidence of the premature retirement of women teachers from girls' and mixed secondary schools', *Br. J. Educ. Psychol.*, November.

(1968), 'Co-education', in *Educational Research in Britain*, ed. H. J. Butcher, London.

(1968), 'Co-education and women's attitudes to men in work and social life', *Occupational Psychology*, 42.

(1968), 'How are girls affected by co-education? Are they happier?', *Where*, Supplement 16, October.

*(1969), *Mixed or single-sex school?* vol. I, London. A research study in pupil–teacher relationships.

(1969), 'Anxiety about school among first-year grammar school pupils', *Br. J. Educ. Psychol.*, February.

(1969), 'Co-education in secondary schools', *Trends in Education*, April.

(1969), 'Education of girls: a fundamental question', *Higher Education Journal*, Summer.

(1969), 'Co-education and men's attitudes to women in work and social life', *Occupational Psychology*, 43.

(1970), 'The Douglas national sample: a fundamental fallacy', *Bulletin Br. Psychol. Soc.*, 23.

*(1971), *Mixed or single-sex school?* vol. II: *Some social aspects*, London.

(1972), critical notice on 'Attainment in co-educational and segregated schools' by O. K. Kyostio (*Scandinavian J. of Educ. Research*, 14, 1970) in *Scandinavian J. of Educ. Research*, pp. 38–9. The notice tries to correct a misleading impression in Kyostio's summary.

*DALE, R. R. and GRIFFITH, S. (1965), *Downstream: Failure in the grammar school*, London. Indirect value only.

*DALE, R. R. and JONES, I. (1957), 'The interest shown by boys and girls in the principal aspects of history in grammar schools', *Educational Review*, November.

*DALE, R. R. and JONES, J. A. (1964), 'An investigation into the comparative response of boys and girls to Scripture as a school subject in certain co-educational grammar schools in South Wales', *Br. J. Educ. Psychol.*, June.

DALE, R. R. and MILLER, P. MCC. (1972), 'A semantic differential comparison of certain attitudes of university students from co-educational and single-sex schools towards their schools', *Br. J. Educ. Psychol.*, February.

DALE, R. R. and MILLER, P. MCC. (1972), 'Attitudes of co-educated and single-sex educated students towards the opposite sex', *Irish J. of Educ.*, 6, 1, Summer.

*DALE, R. R. and MILLER, P. MCC. (1972), 'The urban or rural background of first-year university students in relation to their academic performance', *Br. J. Educ. Psychol.*, June.

DALE, R. R. and MILLER, P. MCC (1972), 'The academic progress of university students from co-educational and single-sex schools', *Br. J. Educ. Psychol.*, November. *See also*, Miller and Dale.

DANE, CLEMENCE [Winifred Ashton] (1917), *Regiment of Women*, London.

DAVIES, W. E. (1950), 'A study of the attitudes of secondary school teachers towards co-education, differentiation of curriculum and sex teaching', Ph.D. thesis, London. Duplicates the writer's findings on teacher preference, but some reservations about percentage of completed forms. The weight of secondary school teacher opinion is opposed to the essential differentiation of the curriculum on the grounds of sex. There is a wide overlap between the sexes in ranges of attainment, interest or distaste.

DEBESSE, M. (1966), 'La contribution de la recherche aux changements dans l'éducation des adolescents', *Paedagogica Europaea*, 2, pp. 203–25.

DEMANT, H. (1955), *Koedukation oder getrennte Erziehung?*, Frankfurt am Main.

*DEPARTMENT OF EDUCATION AND SCIENCE (1967), Annual Report, London.

DOCUMENTATION (LA) FRANÇAISE (1954), *Articles et Documents*, Nos 142, 145, Paris. Co-education in the Soviet Union.

DOUGLAS, J. W. B. and ROSS, J. M. (1966), 'Single-sex or co-ed? The academic consequences', *Where*, 25, May (but see reply by Dale in *Where*, 31, May 1967).

*DOUGLAS, J. W. B. and ROSS, J. M. (1968), *All Our Future*, London. A valuable book for many purposes, but in the small section relating to co-education the sample is not valid for assessing the *rate of progress* of pupils in co-educational and single-sex schools.

EARLY LEAVING REPORT, *see* Central Advisory Council for Education.

EELLS, W. C. (1951), 'Co-education in Japan', *School and Society*, 74, 183–5, September, New York.

ELMGREN, JOHN (1952), A report on the research work of the 1946 School Commission, 1948: 27, tr. from Swedish, Stockholm.

*ENTWISTLE, N. (1971), 'Have we got more able science students than we think?', *New Academic*, No. 1, 6 May. (Also mimeographed report, Dept. Educ. Research, University of Lancaster, December 1970.)

ERASMUS, *see* Woodward (1904).

*EVANS, H. G. (1961), 'An examination of the causes of premature and early leaving in a selected grammar school of South Wales', M.A. thesis, University College of Swansea. Indirect concern.

FEATHER, N. T. (1972), 'Value similarity and school adjustment', *Australian Journal of Psychology*, 24, 2. An important addition to research. Based on a very large sample from 19 secondary schools. Reported satisfaction with people in class was greater for co-educated students than for those in single-sex schools. Co-educational schools 'obviously fill an important need in later adolescence in providing affiliative contacts involving both sexes'. These schools reported greater satisfaction with the typical teacher and yielded higher ratings on happiness with school. Method is sound and comment percipient.

*FIELD, R. (1935), 'An inquiry into the relative achievement of boys and girls at a first S.C. examination', M.A. thesis, Birmingham. Too few schools for reliability on co-education and not well matched, but some useful points raised. Chapter 2 useful on sex differences research up to 1935. Best subject for co-educated girls was mathematics.

FISHER, J. K. and WAETJEN, W. (1966), 'An investigation of the relationship between the separation by sex for eighth-grade boys and girls and English achievement and self-concept', *J. Educ. Res.*, 59, 9, Madison.

*FLOUD, J. and HALSEY, A. H. (1951), 'Homes and Schools: social determinants of educability', *Educ. Research*, pp. 83–8. Useful study, only indirectly related to the co-education problem.

*FORRESTER, J. F. (1946), 'A study of the attitudes of adolescents to their own intellectual, social and spiritual development', Ph.D. thesis, London.

FRANCE (1970), see Académie de Grenoble and Académie d'Aix-en-Provence.

*FRISON, B. (1959), *Co-education in Catholic Schools*, Rome. Reluctant acceptance of co education as sometimes necessary, emphasizing moral dangers and favouring 'Dual schools'.

*FULLER, ELIZABETH (1946), 'The use of measures of ability and general adjustment in the pre-service selection of Nursery School—Kindergarten—Primary Teachers', *J. Educ. Psychol.*, 37, 6, September.

*FURNEAUX, W. D. (1961), *The Chosen Few*, Oxford, pp. 80–1. Incidental finding on incidence of high neuroticism among male university entrants from co-educational schools. (Possibly due to social class factors or relative IQs; needs separate enquiry.)

GIMSON, B. L. (Bedales) (1927), *Problems in Co-education*, New Education Fellowship pamphlet, London.

GITS, A. (1945), *Parent, Priest and Teacher*, Catholic Truth Society, London. Discussion only—opposition.

*GLASS, D. V. (1954), *Social Mobility in Great Britain*, London.

*GLASSEY, W. (1945), 'The attitude of grammar school pupils and their parents to education, religion, and sport', *Br. J. Educ. Psychol.*, vol. 15, 2, June.

*GLOUCESTERSHIRE EDUCATION COMMITTEE (1971), 'Report of Science Advisory Group' (mim.).

GOODSELL, W. (1923), *The Education of Women*, New York, pp. 122–38.

GORDON, IRA (1965), *Human Development*, Glenview, Illinois. Useful summary on sex differences in abilities, interests etc.

GOTT, SIR B. [1907, 1912], *Higher education in the administrative county of Middlesex*, 2 parts (report), London.

*GOTT, SIR B. (Director of Education for Middlesex), see Howard (1928).

*GOTT, SIR B., see Adams (1924).

GRANDPRÉ, M. DE (1968), *Notes à l'Unesco pour son étude comparée sur l'enseignement mixte*, Brussels.

GRANT, C. and HODGSON, N. (1913), *Case for Co-education*, London. Experience of head of co-educational school who was educated in a public school. Examines arguments of opposition. Refutes Hall.

*GRIFFITH, STEPHEN (1958), 'An examination of the causes of deterioration in academic performance among pupils in a secondary school', M.Sc. thesis, University College of Swansea. Indirect value only.

HADOW REPORT, *see* Board of Education.

HALL, S. G. (1904), *Adolescence* (vol. 2), New York. Psychologist against identity of education for the sexes; against over-pressure of girls.

HALL, STANLEY [GRANVILLE, S.] (1911), *Educational Problems*, 2 vols, New York and London. Section against co-education, vol. 2, ch. 17.

HARE, R. J. (1969), 'A survey of research into co-education in England and Wales', B.Ed. thesis, St Luke's College, Exeter. Small scale but useful survey into school preference.

*HASHIM, A. (1948), 'A study of the attitudes of secondary school pupils towards certain school subjects', M.A. thesis, London. Good coverage of historical aspect.

HAWTREY, MABEL (1896), *The Co-education of the Sexes* (pamphlet), London. Arguments against.

*HEISE, D. R. (1969), 'Some methodological issues in semantic differential research', *Psychological Bulletin*, 72, 406–22.

HERBERT, DENNIS (1950), *Co-education*, London.

*HIGGS, ESTHER (1897), 'Woman, the individual' (lecture to Fowler Institute), London.

HOLMES, F. N. (1949), 'Co-education in the grammar school', Dip. Ed. thesis, University of Cambridge, Junior researcher.

*HOUSLOP, H. L. and WEEKS, E. J. (1948), 'The interests of school children', *School Science Review*, June.

*HOWARD, B. A. (1928), *The Mixed School*, London. By the headmaster of a co-educational school. A discussion of the arguments for and against co-education. Contains Gott's comparative table for the examination results of single-sex and co-educational schools in Middlesex (p. 158). Useful discussions of sex differences and the problems of co-educational schools.

HUSEN, TORSTEN (ed.) (1967), *International study of achievement in Mathematics*, New York. Finds sex differences widest in countries where boys and girls separately taught.

HUXLEY, JULIAN (1944), *On living in a revolution*, London, esp. pp. 188–92. 'The central problem of education can no longer be regarded as an intellectual one; it is a deep emotional one, and consists in the adjustment of conflict and the abolition of repression.'

INCORPORATED ASSOCIATION OF ASSISTANT MASTERS (1938), pamphlet on co-education, London.

309

INCORPORATED ASSOCIATION OF HEADMASTERS (1940), *Report of the mixed schools committee*, London. The case for co-education in secondary schools. P. 2. Useful on the developing attitude of the sexes to each other.

INGLIS, A. J. (1922), *Principles of Secondary Education*, London. Section on co-education. Discussion only.

JENKINSON, A. J. (1940), *What do boys and girls read?*, London. Similarity of interests, boys and girls. *See* Whitehead.

*JOHNSTON, L., see *Times Educational Supplement*, 1971.

*JONES, C. V. (1962), 'A case study enquiry into the causes of gross discrepancy between the performance of pupils in the 11 + examination and their performance at the end of the first year in a selected grammar school in South Wales', M.Sc. thesis, University College of Swansea. Indirect value only.

*JONES, I. (1955), 'An investigation into the response of boys and girls' respectively, towards the content of the history syllabus in grammar schools', M.A. thesis, University College of Swansea.

*JONES, J. A. (1962), 'An investigation into the comparative response of boys and girls to Scripture as a school subject in certain co-educational grammar schools in industrial South Wales', M.A. thesis, University College of Swansea.

JONES, W. E. (1933), 'Difference in geographical work of boys and girls, *Geography*, March (summary of M.A. thesis, London, 1933). Compares examination marks of 22,000 condidates for 1930—boys in co-educational schools better than those in boys' schools and the reverse for girls, but like many of these early studies of attainment and of interest, assumes wrongly that the quality of intake is equal for the opposing types of school.

*JORDAN, D. (1937), 'The attitude of central school pupils to certain school subjects and the correlation between attitude and attainment', M.A. thesis, London (also *Br. J. Educ. Psychol.*, February 1941).

*KING, W. H. (1949), 'A critical analysis of the results of a School Certificate examination', Ph.D. thesis, London.

KING, W. H. (1966), 'Comparative attainment in mathematics in single-sex and co-educational secondary schools', *Educ. Research*, 8, 2. *See also* Dale's analysis in *Educ. Research*, 9, 3, 1967.

*KING, R., see *Times Educational Supplement*, 1971.

KNIGHT, FRANCIS A. (1908), *History of Sidcot School*, London.

*KNIGHT, F. B. (1922), *Qualities related to success in teaching*, Teachers College, Columbia University, New York.

KYOSTIO, O. K. (1970), 'Attainment in co-educational and segregated schools. An enquiry into the prediction of secondary school final success', *Scandinavian J. of Educ. Research*, 14. Attainment research, but see critical notice on this by Dale, *Scand. J. Educ. Res.*, 1972, pp. 38–9.

*LAMBERT, C. (1944), 'A study of interest in school subjects among secondary school pupils at different ages', M.A. thesis, London.

LAMBERT, R. (with Spencer Millham) (1968), *The Hothouse Society*, London. Boys' boarding schools and unpleasant attitude to sex. See especially p. 72.

*LAWTON, J. (1939), 'A study of factors useful in choosing candidates for the teaching profession', *Br. J. Educ. Psychol.*, 9, 131–44.

*LEE, DORIS M. (1955), 'A study of specific ability and attainment in mathematics', *Br. J. Educ. Psychol.*, 25, 3, 178–89. Statistical study examining the influence of age, among other things.

*LEWIS, E. O. (1913), 'Popular and unpopular school subjects', *J. Exper. Ped.*, June.

*LILLIS, M. A. (1965), 'An investigation and comparison of the academic achievements of boys and girls at the tenth and eleventh grade levels in three types of schools, single-sex, co-educational, co-institutional', Ph.D. thesis, Fordham University, New York. An inconclusive result. The groups compared were too small.

LLOYD, A. (1936), 'The years between. An enquiry into the bases of co-education for adolescents and some account of its practice', M.A. thesis, Birmingham. Includes enquiry to 20 heads.

*LONG, J. L. A. (1949), 'An investigation into the relationship between interest in and knowledge of school geography, by means of a series of attitude tests', M.A. thesis, London. Large scale 12–16. Boys and girls find the same aspects interesting, but may be differences in intensity which would make separate syllabus and approach for each sex desirable. Sexes unanimous about what is uninteresting. But pupils' interests etc should not be the sole influence.

LOTZ, H. R. (1952), 'The relation between the emotional and social adjustments of individuals and their attendance at co-educational and single-sex high schools', Ph.D. thesis, School of Education, New York University. Useful pioneer study. Written tests. Findings strongly favour co-education, but used sample of only three schools. Co-educated students more mature understanding and grasp of life situations. Co-education has a significant relationship to the emotional and social adjustment of the female adolescent. Co-educated men are better adjusted.

LOW, BARBARA (1928), *The Unconscious in Action*, London. Arguments for co-education.

LYTTLETON, REV. E. (1900), *The training of the young in the laws of sex*, London. Head of Eton. 'The temptations of school life, especially those due to the separation of the sexes, are such as to test the weak points in any boy's armour' (p. 9).

*MCCRACKEN, D. (1969), *University student performance*, British Student Health Association, University of Leeds. Valuable for other purposes, but in comparing co-educated students with those from single-sex schools no attempt is made to equate on entry standard.

MCNEILLE, F. M. (1959), 'The future of girls' grammar schools', *Educ. Review*, 11, 3, June. Effects of new policy of appointing male teachers to girls' grammar schools.

311

*MACPHERSON, J. (1958), *Eleven Year Olds Grow Up*, Scottish Council for Research in Education, London. p. 151: 'High scores more likely to come from cities than are the low scores.'

MacRAE, D. G. (1951), 'Some attitudes of university entrants to their school experience', *Higher Education Journal*, 8, 1, Spring. Free essay by school leavers. Seventeen per cent of day pupils included favourable mention of co-education; none against.

*MATHEWS, M. E. (1925), 'The advantages and disadvantages of co-education', M.A. thesis, Birmingham. Compares attainment of the two sexes within two grammar schools. Useful. Sex differences in attitude to literature.

MAZZEO, A. (1962), *La coeducazione*, Urbino.

MICHAEL, W. B. *et al.* (1951), 'Survey of student–teacher relationship', *J. Educ. Res.*, May. Majority of girls willing to undergo strict discipline and lengthy assignments to get high marks; boys unwilling to do so.

MILES, M. (1971), article in *Business and Professional Woman* (special issue), London. Head of a London girls' school states a case for co-education.

MILHAM, S. *et al.* (1971), 'Co-education in Approved Schools', parts 1 and 2. *Child in Care*, March and April, Westbury. Breaks new ground. Quotes statistics on polarization of attitude in single-sex boarding schools. Artificial view of opposite sex.

MILLER, DEREK (1969), *The Age Between*, London. Clearly written. Favours co-education, includes comments on research and adds some small-scale but important clinical evidence. Ch. 5 on co-education.

*MILLER, P. MCC. (forthcoming), 'A note on sex differences on the semantic differential', *Br. J. Soc. Clin. Psychol.*

*MILLER, P. MCC. and DALE, R. R. (1972), 'The academic progress of male and female first-year university students compared', *Research in Education*, 8, November.

*MILLER, P. MCC. and DALE, R. R. (1973), 'A semantic differential study of certain attitudes towards university', *Educ. Review*, 25, 2, February.

MINISTRY OF EDUCATION (1943), *Sex education in schools and youth organizations*, London. 'For real sympathy and understanding between the sexes, children of both sexes should have opportunities for growing up and mixing together.'

MINISTRY OF EDUCATION (1945), *Handbook of Suggestions*, London. p.43 f. Practical suggestions how sex differences in interests might be catered for in the classroom, by group work, private study, etc. Pronounced changes of tone since 1932 edition.

MINISTRY OF EDUCATION (1945), *The Nation's Schools*, pamphlet No. 1, London. Brief passage opposing co-education in secondary schools. Withdrawn on instructions of the Minister and 'fuller' statement promised —this was pamphlet No. 9 (1947) which withdrew the opposition.

MINISTRY OF EDUCATION (1947), Central Advisory Council for Education, *School and Life*, London.

MINISTRY OF EDUCATION (1954), *Early Leaving*, Report of the Central Advisory Council for Education (England), London, Table 7, pp. 77 etc. Invaluable for educational statistics related to social class, but only indirectly related to co-education.

MIRZA, N. K. (1931), 'Co-education with special reference to the adolescent', M.A. thesis, Leeds. Pp. 79–80: Includes letter from Dr Geheeb describing work at Odenwaldschule. Useful historical chapter. Surveys the advantages and disadvantages.

MORETON, F. E. (1944), 'Attitudes to religion among adolescents and adults', *Br. J. Educ. Psychol.*, 14.

MORETON, F. E. (1946), 'Attitudes of teachers and pupils towards co-education', *Br. J. Educ. Psychol.*, 16, 2, (summarizes Ph.D. thesis, London, 1939). Preceded the writer's large-scale survey of teacher preference etc. Unfortunately had only about 17(?) per cent of questionnaires returned. Results very favourable to co-education. Made a start on assessing the contribution of co-educational boarding schools.

MORRIS, J. (1929), 'The position and teaching of science in co-educational schools, M.A. thesis, Liverpool. Argues for co-educational schools but differential curriculum. But both sexes have good influence on other in class. Best boys invariably ahead of best girls.

MOSELY COMMISSION (1904), Reports of, London, pp. 13, 113, 143, 166, 267, 319. Co-education in USA as seen by British commission.

NATIONAL COUNCIL OF VOLUNTARY CHILD CARE ORGANISATIONS (1951), symposium 'Boys and Girls Together', *Child Care Quarterly Review*, vol. 5, No. 1, London. Advocates mixed children's homes, hostels and schools.

NATIONAL UNION OF TEACHERS (1952), *Report of Committee on the curriculum of the secondary school*, London. Important research appendix on the opinions of nearly 3,000 teachers on co-education and on the differentiation of the curriculum for boys and girls.

NEW EDUCATION FELLOWSHIP (1927), 'Freedom through co-education', report on group meetings on *problems* of co-education at Locarno World Conference on New Education, August 1927: contribution from Paul Geheeb. *New Era*, October 1927.

NEWMAN, F. B. (1946), 'The Adolescent in Social Groups', *Applied Psychol. Monographs*, Stanford University, California, pp. 9–15.

NEWSOM, SIR JOHN H. (1948), *The Education of Girls*, London. Suggests modified curriculum for girls, mainly on vocational grounds—training for work in home.

NEW ZEALAND (1962), *see* Commission on Education in New Zealand.

NICHOLLS, A. (1967), 'The opinions on co-education of a group of secondary modern children in the Manchester area, their teachers and their parents', *Br. J. Educ. Psychol.*, 37, 3. Useful summary of M.Ed. thesis, Manchester (1961). Parts good, parts need careful appraisal. Small samples. Parents' sample heavily biased—majority from single-sex schools, and similarly for pupils. Social class not sufficiently stressed as intervening variable. Some interesting findings independent of this bias. Teachers strongly prefer co-education—these findings resemble those of Dale and Davies.

*NORTHERN IRELAND COUNCIL FOR EDUCATIONAL RESEARCH (1969), *Report of the Review Procedure Panel*. A follow-up study of pupils accepted and rejected under the Review Procedure (mim.). Valuable statistical study of examination results from co-educational and single-sex schools, dependable and well handled. Protestant and Catholic school results are combined and the latter, which are single-sex, tend to have lower class pupils; but the Protestant single-sex schools have higher social class pupils than the co-educational schools.

OESER, O. and EMERY, F. (1958), *Information, Decision and Action*, Melbourne. Rate of absorption of the teacher's standards is greater when the sex of the teacher and child is the same. Awaits confirmation.

*OKSANEN, KAINO (1919), *Yhteiskasvatuksesta I*, Helsinki. An old study, not allowing for handicaps of co-educational schools in type of entry etc, found that although the co-educated boys had generally lower standards than boys in boys' schools they excelled over all groups in mathematics.

OLLERENSHAW, K. (1961), *Education for girls*, London, pp. 60–7 (182–9). Arguments against co-education.

ORRING, J. (1962), *Comprehensive school and continuation schools in Sweden*, Stockholm.

*OSGOOD, C. E., SUCI, G. J. and TANNENBAUM, P. H. (1957), *The Measurement of Meaning*, Urbana, Illinois.

PATTERSON, A. C. (1950), 'The effects of pupil migrancy on ability and achievement in rural and burgh schools', *Br. J. Educ. Psychol.*, 20, 3, November.

PAULSTON, R. G. (1968), *Educational change in Sweden*, New York. Detailed account of change to co-education in statute and practice.

PAYNTER, R. H. (1966), 'An investigation of the effects of eighth-grade sex-segregation on pupil academic achievement, self-concept, and social relationships', thesis, University of Tennessee (Ann Arbor, University microfilms). No difference on academic changes, measures, self-concept and social relations. Balanced samples, but segregated *for part of each day only*.

PEKIN, L. B. (pseudonym for Snell) (1939), *Co-education*, London. Fairly full statement of the case for co-education based on experience as headmaster.

PEKIN, L. B. (pseudonym for Snell) (1934), *Progressive schools*, London. Written from practical experience. States the arguments for co-education and against the single-sex boarding school.

314

PESTALOZZA, HANNA VON (1923), *Der Streit um die Koedukation in Deutschland*, Sachsen.

*PIDGEON, D. A. (1967), *Achievement in Mathematics*, NFER, Slough. Valuable book in general but could be misleading on the comparative academic *progress* of pupils in co-educational and single-sex schools unless Pidgeon's warning is observed. *Attitude to school* better in his co-educational schools.

PIRET, R. (1965), *Psychologie différentielle des sexes*, Paris. Females solve problems better when in a group of both sexes rather than in a group by themselves (p. 55).

*PIUS XI (Pope) (1929), *Divini illius Magistri* (Encyclical; *Acta Apostolicae Sedis*, 22, 49–56, 1930). Enshrines officially the former condemnation of co-education by the RC church.

POIRSON, S. (1911), *La Coéducation*, Paris. Well-written early book advocating co-education. Includes percipient views of heads of well-known co-educational secondary schools in Europe and the United States.

*PRITCHARD, R. A. (1935), 'The relative popularity of secondary school subjects at various ages', *Br. J. Educ. Psychol.*, 5, pp. 157, 229 (M.A. thesis, Birmingham, 1928). Large scale, 12 to 16 years. Compares boys', girls' and co-educational schools.

PUBLIC SCHOOLS COMMISSION (1968), *Report of, Part 1*, London, paras. 19 and 148. Advised changes towards co-education.

*QUINTILIAN, *Institutiones Oratoriae*.

RALLISON, R. (1939), 'The scientific interests of senior school children', *Br. J. Educ. Psychol.*, 9, pp. 117–29.

RALLISON, R. (1943), 'The interests of senior school children in non-scientific subjects', *Br. J. Educ. Psychol.*, 13, 1.

RAMUND, B. (n.d.), 'Kommunala flickskolan och praktisk realskola', (mim.), Department of Education, Uppsala University (c.1959).

REED, B. H. (ed.) (1950), *Eighty Thousand Adolescents*, London. Section comparing mixed with single-sex youth clubs.

REEVES, MARJORIE E. (1946), *Growing up in Modern Society*, London. Quotes Martin Buber, *I and Thou* (tr. R. Gregor Smith), 1937.

ROFÉ, J. A. D. (1959), 'Co-education in the grammar school', M.A. thesis, Birmingham. Mainly a history of co-education—in England, the USA and Russia—but other aspects are examined.

ROMAN, F. W. (1930), *The New Education in Europe*, 2nd ed., London. Survey of practices—includes enthusiastic account of co-educational schools in Hamburg etc.

*ROWLAND, BASIL (1955), 'An enquiry into the standards of behaviour of boys and girls towards each other with special reference to three Surrey grammar schools', M.A. thesis, London. Interesting pioneer work (but tester known in co-educational school and not in the two single-sex schools).

Annotated bibliography

RUEGG, P. C. (1953), 'Investigation into the meaning of co-education as shown by a study of two classes of children in secondary modern schools', M.A. thesis, London. 'Co-educated girls markedly more concerned with love and marriage than girls in girls' schools.' (But very few schools.)

RUSSELL, BERTRAND (1926), *On Education*, London. He and his wife ran Beacon Hill, a co-educational school, for some years.

SADLER, MICHAEL E. (Admin. County of Essex: Education Committee) (1900), 'In what sense ought schools to prepare boys and girls for Life?' (lecture to Ruskin Society of Birmingham, 1899), Bournville. *See also* Board of Education.

SADLER, MICHAEL E. (1906), *Report on Secondary and Higher Education in Essex*, Chelmsford. 'The result of my inquiry has been to make me much more conscious of the benefits and practical advantages of co-education than I was before.' Influenced Gott.

*SCOTT, W. J. (1947), *Reading, film and radio tastes of high school boys and girls*, New Zealand Council for Educational Research.

*SECRÉTARIAT GÉNÉRAL DE L'ENSEIGNEMENT CATHOLIQUE FRANÇAIS (1966), note du 'Sur la Mixité dans les Écoles', June. Useful, succinct and percipient advice on co-educational schooling.

SELIGMAN, E. (ed.) (1950), 'Co-education' in *Encyclopaedia of the social sciences*, New York, vol. 3, pp. 614–17.

SERMUL, M. J. (1961), 'The effects of co-education on attitudes of male college students', *J. Educ. Sociol.*, 35, New York, September.

*SHAKESPEARE, J. J. (1936), 'An enquiry into the relative popularity of school subjects in elementary schools', *Br. J. Educ. Psychol.*, 6. Based on M.A. thesis (Birmingham, 1934). Thesis useful. Article has serious mistakes.

*SHANNON, J. (1941), 'Elements of excellence in teaching', *Educational Administration and Supervision*, 27.

SHEARS, L. W. (1953), 'The dynamics of leadership in adolescent school groups', *Br. J. Psychol.*, 44, 3, August. Two co-educational schools (mixed group); sex of leader is specific to the occasion.

*SIMPSON, JAMES (1844), 'Report of Lecture delivered to the Working Class of Edinburgh on Joint Education of the Sexes', *Edinburgh Weekly Chronicle*, 9 March. Refreshing early statement advocating co-education, based on his experience in school.

*SIXTH FORM OPINION, 2, March 1968. Useful as supplementary survey of opinion on co-education among secondary school pupils.

SMITH, A. (n.d.), *Some Ideals in Education and an attempt to carry them out*, London (c.1930). Head's account of the Arundale Theosophical School at Letchworth.

SMITH, ANNA T. (1903), 'Co-education in the schools and colleges of U.S.', *Report of U.S. Commission of Education*.

316

*SMYTH, A. M. (1946), 'An investigation into the interests of children in school geography; special reference to girls 11 to 16', M.A. thesis, London. In relation to other subjects. Sample of *teachers small*.

SOCIETY FOR CULTURAL RELATIONS WITH USSR (1947), report of conference in London with Russian delegation, in *Childhood and Youth*, I, I. Soviet preference in 1947 for single-sex schools.

STATON, T. F. (1963), *Dynamics of Adolescent Adjustment*, New York. P. 289: 'Failure to achieve successful adolescent heterosexual adjustment, . . . necessarily fixates emotional development at an immature level.'

*STEVENS, F. (1962), *The Living Tradition*, London. Interesting— includes a comparison of 7 boys', 7 girls' and 5 co-educational schools. But these samples are too unequal, e.g. the single-sex includes two direct grant schools, and the percentage of pupils neither of whose parents attended a grammar school was 57 for co-educational, 34 for boys' and 32 for girls' schools.

STEVENSON, R. L. (1881), *Virginibus Puerisque*, London. 'But', he observes sarcastically, 'it is the object of a liberal education not only to obscure the knowledge of one sex from the other, but to magnify the natural differences between the two. . . . So when I see a raw youth and a green girl fluted and fiddled in a dancing measure into that most serious contact, and setting out upon life's journey with ideas so monstrously divergent, I am not surprised that some make shipwreck, but that any come to port.'

STEWART, W. A. C. (1947), 'A critical estimate of the educational theory and practice of the Society of Friends as seen in their schools in England', Ph.D. thesis, London (published in *Quakers and Education*, London, 1953). Valuable study. Some of these boarding schools are co-educational.

STEWART, W. A. C. (1967–8), *The Educational Innovators*, 2 vols, London (particularly vol. 2, *The Progressive Schools in 1881–1967*).

STROOBANT, R. Large-scale statistical study in progress in Sydney, with co-education as part issue. Interesting comparisons on corporal punishment are to hand but await confirmation.

*SUTHERLAND, M. (1961), 'Co-education and school attainment', *Br. J. Educ. Psychol.*, 31, 2. Valuable statistical review with qualifications as in text.

*SWAINSON, B. M. (1939), 'An enquiry into the likes and dislikes of elementary school children in geography', *Geography*, 24, June. Large-scale, ages 7 to 13. Reported increase of 'dislike' in both sexes in mixed classes.

SWEDEN (1923), *Report of the Commission of 1919*, Stockholm. Also decision of the Swedish Parliament in 1927 on adopting the report. Tr. in Clark, 1937.

SWEDEN (1947), *Flickskolan, 1940* (report) in *Års Skolutrednings Betankanden Och Utredningar*, Statens Offentliga Utredningar, Ecklesiastikdepartementet, Stockholm.

SWEDEN (1961), 'Report of the 1957 school commission', *Grundskolan* (mim.) (ch. 31, *Flickskolan*), Stockholm, esp. pp. 528 *seq.* Girls' schools to be opened to boys.

SWEDEN, *see* Ramund (n.d.).

THOMPSON, R. H. T. (1957), 'Co-education: A survey of parental opinion', *Austral. J. Psychol.*, 9, 1, pp. 58–68, Melbourne.

*TIMES EDUCATIONAL SUPPLEMENT, Letters: 6 January 1950 (Head's opinions—writer's interpretation dubious); 25 August 1950 (Russia); 14 November 1969 (worst features of a girls' grammar school); 10 September 1971, 15 October 1971 (boy/girl polarization in choice of A-level subjects); reports: 20 January 1950 (statistical enquiry, interpretation dubious); 25 July 1958 (co-education banned in Spain); 8 August 1969 (breaking subject-sex barrier).

TRUSCOT, B. (1945), *Redbrick and these Vital Days*, London. Sexual perversion at boys' boarding schools, p. 164.

TYSON, G. (1928), 'Some apparent effects of co-education suggested by a statistical investigation of examination results', M.Ed. thesis, Manchester.

UNESCO (1968), *Questionnaire sur l'enseignement mixte*, Paris.

UNESCO (1970), *Étude sur l'enseignement mixte*, United Nations (E/LN. 6/537 and Add. 1), New York.

UNITED STATES BUREAU OF EDUCATION (1883), 'Co-education of the sexes in the public schools of the U.S.', *Circulars of Information*, 2, Washington. Analysis of facts and opinions about co-education from 360 towns and cities of U.S. Strongly favours co-education.

UNITED STATES BUREAU OF EDUCATION (1894), *Report of the Commissioner of Education 1891–2*, pt 1, Washington.

*UNITED STATES BUREAU OF EDUCATION (1906), *Report of the Commissioner of Education*, Washington. Principals of high schools who had been connected with segregated private schools reported atmosphere in co-educational schools decidedly purer—decidedly against idea that co-education would undermine morality in American life.

UNITED STATES BUREAU OF EDUCATION, *Report of the Commissioner of Education for 1900/1901*. Co-education of the sexes. Vol. 2, Washington.

*UPRICHARD, ELIZABETH M. (1947), 'The relationship between interest, aptitude and achievement as shown by an enquiry into curricula in four secondary modern schools', Ph.D. thesis, London.

USSR, *see* Society for cultural relations with USSR.

VALENTINE, C. W. (1965), *Psychology and its bearing on Education*, London, pp. 114, 553. Reports several small-scale enquiries on school preference, homosexuality, schoolgirl crushes, school 'flirting'. Results strongly favour co-education.

VERNET, J. (1969), 'A review of statistics and statistical studies relating to co-education' (mim.), Philips Exeter Academy, U.S. Move towards co-education in private schools in USA.

318

*VERNON, P. E. (1959), 'Educational abilities of training college students', *Br. J. Educ. Psychol.*, 9.

WAETJEN, W. B. and GRAMBS, J. (1966), 'Being equally different', *National Elementary School Principal Journal*, 46, November. Need to recognize differences between the sexes in our teaching in co-educational schools.

WALL, W. D. (1952), *Education and Mental Health*, London. Modern brief statement of arguments, pp. 205–8.

WALTON, H. M. (c.1935), 'Report to Middlesex Education Committee, unpublished typescript. A useful comparison of the examination results of single-sex and co-educational schools in Middlesex, following Gott's survey. No further information obtainable from Middlesex.

WASHBURNE, C. (1926), *New Schools in the Old World*, New York. Favourable to co-education.

WAUGH, ALEC (1917), *The Loom of Youth*, London. Sexual perversion in boys' boarding schools.

*WAWRZYNIAK, KURT (1959), 'Grunfragen der Koeducation', *Zeitschr. Schule u. Psych., Beih.*, 9. Sample of 800 pupils. Though the co-educated pupils were inferior in verbal ability they were superior in mathematical and technical thinking.

WHIPPLE, A. H. (1939), *Education up to 15 years*, London, pp. 34–7. An administrator. Restates the arguments against co-education.

WHITEHEAD, F. (1956), 'The attitude of grammar school pupils towards some novels commonly read in school', *Br. J. Educ. Psychol.*, 26, 104–11. In only one (*Pride and Prejudice*) of eleven novels was there a significant sex difference in attitude. Supported by Jenkinson (1940) and opposed by Scott (1947).

WISENTHAL, M. (1964), 'A study of attitudes, reinforcement and attainment in the Junior schools', Ph.D. thesis, London. Interesting thesis. Purports to show girls in girls' junior schools receive more positive reinforcement (correct answers) and less negative reinforcement (i.e. pupils giving incorrect answers). On the boys' side those in boys' schools 'do not appear to profit academically'. Finding should not be quoted without careful study and reflection of the effect of the rather higher intelligence of the girls in girls' schools, nor do we know the proportion of lessons, according to subject, seen in each type of school. The latter could be crucial.

WOBER, M. (1971), *English Girls' Boarding Schools*, London, pp. 64–5: deprivation effect in girls' boarding schools. P. 65: 'We are cut off and suffer because of it. But we are *never* allowed any dances or social occasions or boys. . . . '

WOLLSTONECRAFT, MARY (1792), *Vindication of the Rights of Women*, vol. 1 (only), London. Pioneer. W. E. Gladstone pencilled in his copy, 'Though I know not what to say of the scheme of educating boys and girls together, yet on the whole I think this is the [best] chapter in the book and many hints in it worth consideration.'

WOODS, ALICE (ed.) (1903), *Co-education*, London. Introd. by M. E. Sadler. Essays by different hands.

WOODS, ALICE (ed.) (1914), *Advance in Co-education*, London. Includes important evidence from a psychoanalyst.

WOODS, ALICE (1935), 'Theory of co-education', *Quarterly Review*, 265, October, pp. 199–208.

WOODWARD, W. H. (1904), *Desiderius Erasmus concerning the aim and method of Education*, Cambridge. Historical interest.

WOODY, T. (1929), *A History of Women's Education in the United States*, 2 vols, New York, vol. 2, ch. 5. Standard work, though repetitive.

WRIGHT, D. and COX, E. (1967), 'Religious belief and co-education in a sample of sixth-form boys and girls', *Br. J. Soc. Clin. Psychol.*, 6, 1, London. Large sample of sixth formers. Questionnaire supervised by schools staff. Found co-educated girls and co-educated boys studying science were less religiously minded than pupils in single-sex schools. Staff supervision could be a hidden variable because of the difference in discipline between school types.

ZAZZO, R. (1964), 'La coéducation', *L'École des Parents*, 4, April, Paris. Spread of co-education in France. Parents in favour.

ZIEGLER, M. E. (1958), 'A comparative study of the problems, personality adjustment, and values of Catholic adolescent girls attending two types of secondary schools', Ph.D. thesis, Fordham University, New York, 1958.

Index

Interests—*contd.*
  duals, 273; and intelligence, 110;
  polarization of, 49, **150–1**, 153,
  154–69, 269–70, 271; sex differences: 108, 109, **146–69,** (history) **191–9,** (scripture) **200–9,**
  232, 246, **271–3**; sex interaction,
  178, 198; *see also* Attitudes;
  separate subjects
International Project for the
  Evaluation of Educational
  Achievement, 57
Introversion, *see* Extraversion

JOHNSTON, L., 168
Joie de vivre, 231, 259
Joke, sharing, 132, **133–4,** 139, 141–
  4 *passim*, 279
JONES, D. C., 35
JONES, I., **191–9**
JONES, J. A., **200–9,** 272
JONES, V., 26
JORDAN, D., 191

KING, R., and polarization of sexes,
  168
KING, W. H., xiv, 8, **15–17,** 35, **54–5,**
  84–5, 92
KNIGHT, F. B., 64

Laboratory facilities, 99
LAMBERT, C., 191
Lancashire, 5
'Last' schools: compared with
  'First', 233; definition of, 106;
  more popular, 112; results sepa-
  rated, 112; type of, 112; *see also*
  Estimates (*passim*)
Latin: attainment, comparative, 6, 7,
  9, **16, 18–20,** 21, **28,** 58, 158, **285**;
  and deteriorators, 146; dislike of,
  146; percentage taking, 20; and
  test stress, 80; for university, 89
LAWTON, J., 63
Lecture theatre: 'activity' of, **216–**
  18; 'evaluation' of, **216–18**;
  'potency' of, **216–18, 220**
LEE, D. M., 23, 59

'Levels' of performance, *see* Ad-
  vanced Level
Leverhulme Trust, xiv
LEWIS, E. O., 200
Likert, 201
LILLIS, M. A., 58
Literary subjects, *see* Subjects,
  literary
Load (academic), *see* Subjects
London University, General School
  Examinations, **11–12, 12–14, 15–**
  17, 54, **84–5**
LONG, J. L., interest and usefulness,
  169, 272
Longitudinal sample, **127–8,** 147,
  148, 151–2, 154–65, 176, **182,**
  189; composition of, 107

MCCRACKEN, D., 94
MCPHERSON, J., 7
Maladjustment, 3
Marking, and sheltered norm,
  144–5
Marriage, happiness of, **222, 255–6,**
  274
Masculine, dislike of, 159
Matched pairs, *see* Sample
Mathematics: attainment, comparative, 6–9, 15, 16, **18–20,** 21,
  24–5, 27, **28,** 34–6, **39, 44,** 45,
  47, 49, 50, **51–61, 58,** 81, 146,
  158, 266–7, 269–70, **285**; attainment, sex differences, **53,** 60,
  151; attitude to, **146–53,** 167,
  270, 271; attitude of girls, 54, 60,
  147, 162, 269; boys' schools
  best staffed, 29, 65–75 *passim*,
  81, 140, 152, 270; choice by
  girls, 168; and deteriorators,
  146; examinations, comparative
  entry, 65, 67–8, 81; fear of
  teachers, **78–82,** 118, **264**; free
  responses, **76, 78–9, 114–17, 153**;
  girls better in mixed groups, 51;
  girls less confident, 81, 146;
  girls not taking, 53, 54–6, 65–75
  passim, 81; influence of boys on
  girls, **51,** 60, 62, 231–2, **267**;